# I Freed Myself

## *African American Self-Emancipation in the Civil War Era*

For a century and a half, Abraham Lincoln's signing of the Emancipation Proclamation has been the dominant narrative of African American freedom in the Civil War era. However, David Williams suggests that this portrayal marginalizes the role that African American slaves played in freeing themselves. At the Civil War's outset, Lincoln made clear his intent was to save the Union rather than free slaves – despite his personal distaste for slavery, he claimed no authority to interfere with the institution. By the second year of the war, though, when the Union army was in desperate need of black support, former slaves who escaped to Union lines struck a bargain: they would fight for the Union only if they were granted their freedom. Williams importantly demonstrates that freedom was not simply the absence of slavery but rather a dynamic process enacted by self-emancipated African American refugees, which compelled Lincoln to modify his war aims and place black freedom at the center of his wartime policies.

David Williams is professor of history at Valdosta State University in Georgia, where he specializes in the Civil War era and the antebellum South. He is the author of ten books, including *Bitterly Divided: The South's Inner Civil War* and *A People's History of the Civil War*.

# I Freed Myself

## African American Self-Emancipation in the Civil War Era

**DAVID WILLIAMS**

*Valdosta State University*

CAMBRIDGE
UNIVERSITY PRESS

# CAMBRIDGE
UNIVERSITY PRESS

32 Avenue of the Americas, New York, NY 10013–2473, USA

Cambridge University Press is part of the University of Cambridge.

It furthers the University's mission by disseminating knowledge in the pursuit of education, learning, and research at the highest international levels of excellence.

www.cambridge.org
Information on this title: www.cambridge.org/9781107602496

First published 2014

Printed in the United States of America

*A catalog record for this publication is available from the British Library.*

*Library of Congress Cataloging in Publication Data*
Williams, David, 1959–
I freed myself : African American self-emancipation in the Civil War era / David Williams, Valdosta State University, Georgia.
pages cm
ISBN 978-1-107-01649-1 (hardback)
1. United States – History – Civil War, 1861–1865 – African Americans.
2. United States – History – Civil War, 1861–1865 – Participation, African American. 3. Slaves – Emancipation – United States. 4. African Americans – History – 19th century. 5. African American soldiers – History – 19th century. 6. Lincoln, Abraham, 1809–1865 – Views on slavery. I. Title.
E540.N3W55 2014
973.7′415–dc23        2013044583

ISBN 978-1-107-01649-1 Hardback
ISBN 978-1-107-60249-6 Paperback

*For Duncan Winslow*
*and so many others,*
*who suffered so much,*
*and struggled so long,*
*in so many ways,*
*to free themselves.*

If there is no struggle there is no progress. . . . This struggle may be a moral one, or it may be a physical one, and it may be both moral and physical, but it must be a struggle. Power concedes nothing without a demand. It never did and it never will.

– *Frederick Douglass*

# Contents

# Illustrations

# Acknowledgments

No work of scholarship is a singular effort. Never has that been more true than in this case. Those who contributed in some way to my efforts over the years are far too numerous to list and I thank them all, but a few deserve special recognition for their support of this project.

At Cambridge University Press, Deborah Gershenowitz, senior editor, and Dana Bricken, editorial assistant, offered especially helpful advice and encouragement, as did Eric Crahan, former senior editor. Others associated with the Press who contributed mightily to the project include Sumitha Nithyanandan, Kristine Tobin, Annie Woy, and Shari Chappell.

Also much appreciated is the input of scholars and friends, among them Paul D. Escott of Wake Forest University; Lee W. Formwalt, former director of the Organization of American Historians; Victoria E. Bynum, professor emeritus at Texas State University; Mark D. Hersey of Mississippi State University; Jennifer Hildebrand of the State University of New York at Fredonia; David Carlson of Troy State University; Dixie Ray Haggard of Valdosta State University; and Christopher C. Meyers of Valdosta State University.

A good deal of logistical support came at Valdosta State University, especially from Denise Montgomery, Ramona Ice, Meghan Donathan, and David Funk of Interlibrary Loan; Alan Bernstein, university librarian and dean of the Master of Library and Information Science Program; Deborah Davis and Stacey Wright of Archives and Special Collections; and Rex Devane of the Media Center. Further direct support in the way of both time and funding came with help from Paul Riggs, head of the Department of History; Jay Rickman, chair of the department's scheduling committee; Connie Richards, dean of the College of Arts and Sciences; Alfred Fuciarelli, former assistant vice president for research and dean of the Graduate School;

James LaPlant, assistant vice president for research and dean of the Graduate School; and the VSU Graduate Faculty Scholarship Fund.

A very special thanks goes to Leonard L. Winslow, who graciously provided a photograph of his great-grandfather, Duncan Winslow, along with other information and documents dealing with the family's "American journey," as Leonard so aptly put it.

Finally, I would like to extend my most affectionate gratitude to my wife, Teresa Crisp Williams, who read early versions of the manuscript and has been a constant pillar of support throughout.

# Introduction

## *Following the Footsteps of the Slaves*

### THEY ARE FREEING THEMSELVES

Duncan Winslow escaped from slavery in Tennessee during the Civil War and eventually joined the Union army. April of 1864 found him along the Mississippi River with the Sixth U.S. Heavy Artillery defending Fort Pillow, Tennessee, from attack by General Nathan Bedford Forrest and his Confederate cavalry. Outnumbered nearly four to one, the defenders were quickly overwhelmed. As rebel troops overran the fort, Winslow and his comrades threw down their arms and tried to surrender, but Forrest's men took few prisoners. In what came to be known as the Fort Pillow Massacre, Confederates slaughtered nearly 300 of their captives, most of them former slaves. To rebel officers' shouts of "Kill the God damned nigger," Winslow was shot in his arm and thigh. In the confusion, he managed to escape by crawling among logs and brush, hiding there until the enemy moved on. When darkness fell, Winslow made his way down to the riverbank and boarded a federal gunboat.

After his release from a military hospital in Mound City, Illinois, Winslow settled on a farm three miles west of town, where he raised garden vegetables and sold them house to house. One day a candidate for local office asked Winslow for his support in an upcoming election. As if to seal the deal, the candidate remarked, "Don't forget. We freed you people." In response, Winslow raised his wounded arm and said, "See this? Looks to me like I freed myself."[1]

---

[1] Testimony of Duncan Harding [Winslow], U.S. House of Representatives, *Fort Pillow Massacre*, Thirty-Eighth Congress, First Session, Report no. 65 (1864), 15–16; Rollins Winslow, "Duncan (Hardin) Winslow," in *Pulaski County, Illinois, 1819–1987*

FIGURE I.I. "I freed myself" – Duncan Winslow. Winslow is seen here in a postwar photo wearing a Masonic stole and gauntlets. His cap signifies membership in the Grand Army of the Republic, a fraternal organization of Union veterans founded just after the war. Photo courtesy of Leonard L. Winslow.

Generations of Americans have grown up believing that Abraham Lincoln freed the slaves with a stroke of his pen by signing the Emancipation Proclamation. Lost in this simple portrayal is the role that African Americans such as Duncan Winslow played in forcing the issue. At the war's outset, knowing that most white northerners were hardly abolitionists, Lincoln made clear that his intent was to save the Union, not to free the slaves.

(Paducah, Ky.: Turner Publishing, 1987), 355–56. *Fort Pillow Massacre* identifies Winslow as "Duncan Harding," using the surname of his former owner. It was only after the war that he adopted the surname "Winslow" from a prominent abolitionist family. Winslow's grandson, Rollins Winslow, gives the spelling of the former surname as "Hardin."

The sort of demeaning presumptiveness that Winslow suffered continues to this day. When Darren Foreman, a black city employee in Fort Worth, Texas, directed a white worker to perform a task, the man balked and shot back, "We freed y'all." It was but one example of repeated abuse from white coworkers and supervisors that finally compelled Foreman to file suit against the city. See Scott Gordon, "Fort Worth Employee Claims Racial Discrimination in Law Suit," *NBC 5 Dallas-Fort Worth*, June 4, 2013 (www.nbcdfw.com).

Although Lincoln personally disliked slavery, he claimed no authority to interfere with the institution. On the contrary, he promised to enforce all laws upholding slavery, including the Fugitive Slave Act. Desperate to appease slaveholders, Lincoln even supported a thirteenth amendment to the Constitution, the Corwin Amendment, which would have guaranteed slavery forever. Said Lincoln of the amendment in his first inaugural address, "I have no objection to its being made express and irrevocable."[2]

Nevertheless, enslaved men and women escaped to Union lines by the tens of thousands and could not or would not be forced back into slavery. The actions of those many self-emancipated refugees eventually compelled Lincoln and Congress to modify their war aims and formulate a policy that reflected a slave-initiated reality.[3] To say, as the government at first did,

[2] Roy P. Basler, Marion Dolores Pratt, and Lloyd A. Dunlap, eds., *The Collected Works of Abraham Lincoln* (New Brunswick, N.J.: Rutgers University Press, 1953–55), 4: 270. The amendment, authored by Thomas Corwin, a Republican congressman from Ohio, passed Congress and was sent to the states for ratification shortly before Lincoln took office. It read: "No amendment shall be made to the Constitution which will authorize or give to Congress the power to abolish or interfere, within any State, with the domestic institutions thereof, including that of persons held to labor or service by the laws of said State." The phrases "domestic institutions" and "persons held to labor or service" were direct references to slavery and slaves. See *Congressional Globe*, Thirty-Sixth Congress, Second Session (1861), 1284.

[3] Although many modern historians eschew the phrase, and some are openly critical of it, "self-emancipation" was commonly used before the war, falling out of favor in the postwar era as whites increasingly claimed credit for ending slavery. William Lloyd Garrison referred to Frederick Douglass as "self-emancipated" in his foreword to Douglass's first book, *Narrative of the Life of Frederick Douglass* (Boston: Anti-Slavery Office, 1845), v. For other examples see *An Exposition of Difficulties in West Brookfield, Connected with Anti-Slavery Operations* (West Brookfield, Mass.: Anti-Slavery Society, 1844), 15; Rev. Almon Underwood, *A Discourse on the Death of the Late Rev. C. T. Torrey, a Martyr to Human Rights* (Newark, N.J.: Small and Ackerman, 1846), 9; Rev. William H. Marsh, *God's Law Supreme. A Sermon Aiming to Point Out the Duty of a Christian People in Relation to the Fugitive Slave Law* (Worcester, Mass: Henry J. Howland, 1850), 19; *The Thirteenth Annual Report of the American and Foreign Anti-Slavery Society* (New York: American and Foreign Anti-Slavery Society, 1853), 113; *Speech of Hon. Horace Mann, of Massachusetts, on the Institution of Slavery* (Washington, D.C.: Buell and Blanchard, 1852), 22; Josephine Brown, *Biography of an American Bondman, by His Daughter* (Boston: R. F. Wallcut, 1856), 50; Osborne P. Anderson, *A Voice from Harper's Ferry* (Boston: author, 1861), 21; Rev. William H. Boole, *Antidote to Rev. H. J. Van Dyke's Pro-Slavery Discourse* (New York: Edmund Jones and Co., 1861), 8.

Some modern historians who emphasize black self-agency employ the phrase "self-emancipation," or some variation of it, quite unreservedly, especially when referring to fugitives. They include Graham Russell Hodges, *David Ruggles: A Black Abolitionist and the Underground Railroad in New York City* (Chapel Hill: University of North Carolina Press, 2010), 4; Glenn David Brasher, *The Peninsula Campaign and the Necessity of Emancipation: African Americans and the Fight for Freedom* (Chapel Hill: University of

that escapees within Union lines technically remained slaves was problematic. If escapees were neither free nor actually held in slavery, then what was their legal status? The label "contraband" imposed upon them in 1861 satisfied few and settled nothing. Lincoln and Congress wrestled with the issue of refugee status for more than a year before finally deciding with the Second Confiscation Act, then the Emancipation Proclamation, that the refugees had been right all along. They had effectively freed themselves.[4] Lincoln practically admitted as much. Writing of slavery's demise in April 1864, he stressed, "I claim not to have controlled events, but confess plainly that events have controlled me."[5]

North Carolina Press, 2012), 79; Anthony B. Mitchell, "Self-Emancipation and Slavery: An Examination of the African American's Quest for Literacy and Freedom," *Journal of Pan African Studies* 12 (July 2008): 78; Guyora Binder, "Did the Slaves Author the Thirteenth Amendment? An Essay in Redemptive History," *Yale Journal of Law and the Humanities* 5 (1993): 473–74; David Williams and Teresa Crisp Williams, "'Yes, We All Shall Be Free': African Americans Make the Civil War a Struggle for Freedom," in Dixie Ray Haggard, ed., *African Americans in the Nineteenth Century: People and Perspectives* (Santa Barbara, Calif.: ABC-CLIO, 2010), 84.

[4]  The best collection of documents in print dealing with black refugees and their impact on slavery's demise is Ira Berlin et al., eds., *Freedom: A Documentary History of Emancipation, 1861–1867*, series 1, vol. 1, *The Destruction of Slavery* (Cambridge: Cambridge University Press, 1985), hereafter cited as *Destruction of Slavery*. This volume was published as part of the now six-volume *Freedom* series, compiled by the Freedmen and Southern Society Project headquartered at the University of Maryland. Students of the Civil War era owe a tremendous debt to the project's many editors, associates, and assistants, especially Ira Berlin, the project's founder and lead editor of *Freedom*'s first four volumes. These scholars combed through a maze of documents at the National Archives to bring us a collection that has helped transform our understanding of the emancipation process and its aftermath.

[5]  Lincoln to Albert G. Hodges, April 4, 1864, in Basler et al., *Collected Works of Abraham Lincoln*, 7: 282. Among the best edited collections highlighting Lincoln's views on blacks, slavery, and their relation to the war are Henry Louis Gates Jr. and Donald Yacovone, eds., *Lincoln on Race and Slavery* (Princeton, N.J.: Princeton University Press, 2009), and Michael P. Johnson, ed., *Abraham Lincoln, Slavery, and the Civil War: Selected Writings and Speeches* (Boston: Bedford/St. Martin's, 2001).

A number of books on Lincoln have appeared in recent years, mostly prosaic celebratory biographies timed to coincide with Lincoln's 200th birthday and the Civil War's sesquicentennial. Happily, a few are more insightful and enlightening. Those that best deal with Lincoln and race are Paul D. Escott, *What Shall We Do with the Negro?: Lincoln, White Racism, and Civil War America* (Charlottesville: University of Virginia Press, 2009), and Eric Foner, *The Fiery Trial: Abraham Lincoln and American Slavery* (New York: W. W. Norton, 2010). Whereas Foner leans toward emphasizing Lincoln's moral growth, Escott reminds us of the limits of that growth. Brian R. Dirck, in *Abraham Lincoln and White America* (Lawrence: University Press of Kansas, 2012), addresses those limitations in terms of what it meant to be white in nineteenth-century America. Most critical of Lincoln is Lerone Bennett, who views Lincoln as an unrepentant white supremacist for whom the Emancipation Proclamation was a tactical step on the way toward his preferred solution of colonizing blacks out of the country. See Lerone Bennett Jr., *Forced into Glory: Abraham Lincoln's White Dream* (Chicago: Johnson Publishing Company, 2000), 9–10.

Others knew that as well. Union General John Logan, speaking to a crowd of potential recruits, echoed Lincoln's assertion that saving the Union, not ending slavery, was the war's prime objective. "Yet," he acknowledged, "the negroes are getting free pretty fast. It is not done by the army, but they are freeing themselves; and if this war continues long, not a slave will be left in the whole South."[6] Years after the war, the formerly enslaved Betty Guwn told how her husband "ran away early and helped Grant to take Fort [Donelson]. He said he would free himself, which he did."[7]

Roughly 200,000 blacks, most of them refugees from slavery, served in the Union armed forces. Hundreds of thousands more were employed as laborers.[8] Without their efforts, and those of increasingly resistant slaves, the Union would likely not have survived. Freedom was what they struggled for, but that freedom is often viewed as dependent on,

---

[6] Thomas M. Stevenson, *History of the 78th Regiment Ohio Veteran Volunteer Infantry* (Zanesville, Ohio: Hugh Dunne, 1865), 186.

[7] Guwn is referring to Fort Donelson in Tennessee, which fell to Union forces under Ulysses S. Grant on February 16, 1862. See Betty Guwn, *Indiana Narratives*, 99, in *Slave Narratives: A Folk History of Slavery in the United States from Interviews with Former Slaves*, Manuscript Division, Library of Congress, Washington, D.C. The *Slave Narratives* collection is available online at the website *Born in Slavery: Slave Narratives from the Federal Writers' Project, 1936–1938*. Interviews are collected into numbered volumes by state. In this book, I cite the interviews by state, with narrators' names appearing first. A more complete collection, which includes interviews from additional sources, is published as George P. Rawick et al., comp., *The American Slave: A Composite Autobiography*, series 1 and 2, and supplement, series 1 (Westport, Conn.: Greenwood Press, 1972 and 1977).

Interviewers with the Federal Writers' Project and others who quoted former slaves, nearly all of them white, often attempted to preserve dialect and pronunciation in written form. The results were at best mixed, often misleading, at worst demeaning, even racist. Of course, the interviews were products of their time, reflecting nearly as much about the interviewers as the narrators. When quoting from the *Narratives* and other sources for which former slaves were interviewed, I have frequently taken the liberty of changing spelling and punctuation, but never the words or their meaning, to improve flow and clarity.

[8] Blacks in the Union army totaled almost 179,000. Figures for those in the Union navy, according to Howard University's Black Sailors Project, show that approximately 18,000 served, although some sources give higher estimates. At least eleven black women passed themselves off as men and served in the Union navy. Three are known to have served in the Union army, although there were probably more. See John David Smith, ed., *Black Soldiers in Blue: African American Troops in the Civil War Era* (Chapel Hill: University of North Carolina Press, 2002), xiii; Barbara Brooks Tomblin, *Bluejackets and Contrabands: African Americans and the Union Navy* (Lexington: University Press of Kentucky, 2009), 188; DeAnne Blanton and Lauren M. Cook, *They Fought Like Demons: Women Soldiers in the American Civil War* (Baton Rouge: Louisiana State University Press, 2002), 6.

Historian W. E. B. Du Bois estimated the number of black military laborers at about 300,000. See W. E. B. Du Bois, *Black Reconstruction: An Essay toward a History of the Part which Black Folk Played in the Attempt to Reconstruct Democracy in America, 1860–1880* (New York: Harcourt, Brace, and Co., 1935), 716.

almost a by-product of, a war to preserve the Union. Considering the invaluable contributions of black folk toward Union victory, one could as easily say the opposite – that preserving the Union was dependent on ending slavery.

For most northerners who backed the war, it remained primarily – and for many exclusively – a war to save the Union. Slavery was almost beside the point. "If I could save the Union without freeing *any* slave," Lincoln wrote in August 1862, "I would do it, and if I could save it by freeing *all* the slaves I would do it; and if I could save it by freeing some and leaving others alone I would also do that. What I do about slavery, and the colored race, I do because I believe it helps to save the Union."[9]

Lincoln meant what he said. Of course he felt that slavery was wrong, knew it was a source of conflict, and wished it to end sooner or later. But, like most whites who thought slavery wrong, he was deeply conflicted regarding when, how, and to what extent. He led no drumbeat for abolition. He could hardly have been elected had he done so. The Union was Lincoln's priority, and he frequently said so in public and private. When Lincoln moved against slavery, he did so cautiously, even reluctantly, fearing that it might do more harm than good to the Union war effort. But by the summer of 1862, although still hesitant, he came to see that the issues of Union and slavery could not be separated. Blacks would not allow it. Every refugee who entered federal camps, by the act of escape and refusal to be reenslaved, issued a personal statement that slavery was over. Arriving in such numbers that they could hardly be ignored, the government had little choice but to recognize their claim to freedom. Thus it was, as W. E. B. Du Bois observed, that "with perplexed and laggard steps, the United States Government followed the footsteps of the black slave."[10]

---

[9] Lincoln to Horace Greeley, August 22, 1862, in Basler et al., *Collected Works of Abraham Lincoln*, 5: 388.

[10] Du Bois, *Black Reconstruction*, 81. Among the first works to stress African American roles in bringing on freedom, notably by black authors, were William Wells Brown, *The Negro in the American Rebellion* (Boston: Lee and Shepard, 1867); George Washington Williams, *A History of the Negro Troops in the War of the Rebellion* (New York: Harper and Brothers, 1888); and Joseph T. Wilson, *The Black Phalanx* (Hartford, Conn.: American Publishing, 1890). In the early twentieth century, Du Bois led the call for more attention to black roles in the emancipation process. His *Black Reconstruction* became a springboard for later research. Other Du Bois contemporaries who shed new light on black resistance during the Civil War era include Harvey Wish, "Slave Disloyalty under the Confederacy," *Journal of Negro History* 23 (1938): 435–50; Raymond A Bauer and Alice H. Bauer, "Day to Day Resistance to Slavery," *Journal of Negro History* 27

By the war's second year, the government badly needed black support. White recruits were difficult to come by. Lincoln and Congress had at first refused to enlist black volunteers, but the war was not going well for Union armies, and there was no end in sight. They now wanted blacks to fight, and they knew that blacks would fight only for liberty. That was the price of their service, a service that Lincoln knew was indispensable to the Union's survival. "Any different policy in regard to the colored man," Lincoln wrote in 1864, "deprives us of his help, and this is more than we can bear. . . . This is not a question of sentiment or taste, but one of physical force which may be measured and estimated as horse-power and Steam-power are measured and estimated. Keep it and you can save the Union.

(1942): 388–419; Bell Irvin Wiley, *Southern Negroes, 1861–1865* (New Haven, Conn.: Yale University Press, 1938); Herbert Aptheker, *American Negro Slave Revolts* (New York: Columbia University Press, 1943); Benjamin Quarles, *The Negro in the Civil War* (Boston: Little, Brown, and Co., 1953).

In more recent years, Professor Ira Berlin has stressed that "no one was more responsible for smashing the shackles of slavery than the slaves." See Berlin, "Who Freed the Slaves? Emancipation and Its Meaning," in David W. Blight and Brooks D. Simpson, eds., *Union and Emancipation: Essays on Politics and Race in the Civil War Era* (Kent, Ohio: Kent State University Press, 1997), 111. Other modern works that draw attention to black self-agency during the Civil War era include Eugene Genovese, *Roll, Jordan, Roll: The World the Slaves Made* (New York: Vintage, 1976); John Hope Franklin and Loren Schweninger, *Runaway Slaves: Rebels on the Plantation* (New York: Oxford University Press, 1999); Larry Eugene Rivers, *Rebels and Runaways: Slave Resistance in Nineteenth-Century Florida* (Champaign: University of Illinois Press, 2012); John Ashworth, *Slavery, Capitalism, and Politics in the Antebellum Republic*, 2 vols. (Cambridge: Cambridge University Press, 1995 and 2007); Stephanie M. H. Camp, *Closer to Freedom: Enslaved Women and Everyday Resistance in the Plantation South* (Chapel Hill: University of North Carolina Press, 2004); David Williams, *Bitterly Divided: The South's Inner Civil War* (New York: New Press, 2008); William W. Freehling, *The South vs. the South: How Anti-Confederate Southerners Shaped the Course of the Civil War* (New York: Oxford University Press, 2001); Armstead L. Robinson, *Bitter Fruits of Bondage: The Demise of Slavery and the Collapse of the Confederacy, 1861–1865* (Charlottesville: University of Virginia Press, 2005); Richard M. Reid, *Freedom for Themselves: North Carolina's Black Soldiers in the Civil War Era* (Chapel Hill: University of North Carolina Press, 2008); John Cimprich, *Slavery's End in Tennessee, 1861–1865* (Tuscaloosa: University of Alabama Press, 1985); Leon F. Litwack, *Been in the Storm So Long: The Aftermath of Slavery* (New York: Alfred A. Knopf, 1979); Heather Andrea Williams, *Self-Taught: African American Education in Slavery and Freedom* (Chapel Hill: University of North Carolina Press, 2005); Steven Hahn, *A Nation under Our Feet: Black Political Struggles in the Rural South from Slavery to the Great Migration* (Cambridge: Harvard University Press, 2003); Stephanie McCurry, *Confederate Reckoning: Power and Politics in the Civil War South* (Cambridge: Harvard University Press, 2010). Both McCurry and Hahn view the Civil War, with considerable justification I think, as "among other things, a massive slave rebellion" (McCurry, *Confederate Reckoning*, 259). See also Hahn's essay, "Did We Miss the Greatest Slave Rebellion in Modern History?" in Steven Hahn, *The Political Worlds of Slavery and Freedom* (Cambridge: Harvard University Press, 2009), 55–114.

Throw it away, and the Union goes with it."[11] Lincoln finally came to realize, although he did not always make it so clear, that the Union was as dependent on freedom as the other way around.

Blacks had known that from the start. They publicly and repeatedly stressed that Lincoln's initial notion of preserving the Union without reference to slavery was self-defeating. Slavery and slave resistance had brought on the war. There could be no Union victory without slavery's defeat. With a foresight born of experience, Frederick Douglass warned in May 1861 that the war against secession "bound up the fate of the Republic and that of the slave in the same bundle."

Any attempt now to separate the freedom of the slave from the victory of the Government over slaveholding rebels and traitors; any attempt to secure peace to the whites while leaving the blacks in chains; any attempt to heal the wounds of the Republic, while the deadly virus of slavery is left to poison the blood, will be labor lost.[12]

Less than a year later, with the war going badly for Lincoln, Harriet Tubman made much the same point in her own direct way. "They may send the flower of their young men down South. . . . They may send them one year, two years, three years, till they are tired of sending, or till they use up all the young men. All no use! God's ahead of Master Lincoln. God won't let Master Lincoln beat the South till he do the right thing." Decades after the war, former slave Marshall Mack remembered that the war's tide began to turn only after Lincoln committed the Union to emancipation. The Confederacy was whipping the Union "two battles to one," he said.

---

[11] Lincoln to Isaac M. Schermerhorn, September 12, 1864, in Basler et al., *Collected Works of Abraham Lincoln*, 8: 1–2. Some of the best works on blacks in the Union military include Keith P. Wilson, *Campfires of Freedom: The Camp Life of Black Soldiers during the Civil War* (Kent, Ohio: Kent State University Press, 2002); Joseph T. Glatthaar, *Forged in Battle: The Civil War Alliance of Black Soldiers and White Officers* (New York: Free Press, 1990); Tomblin, *Bluejackets and Contrabands*; Dudley Taylor Cornish, *The Sable Arm: Black Troops in the Union Army, 1861–1865* (1956; reprint, Lawrence: University Press of Kansas, 1987). The best collection of documents in print dealing with blacks in the Union military is Ira Berlin, Joseph P. Reidy, and Leslie S. Rowland, eds., *Freedom: A Documentary History of Emancipation, 1861–1867*, series 2, *The Black Military Experience* (Cambridge: Cambridge University Press, 1982), hereafter cited as *Black Military Experience*.

[12] *Douglass' Monthly* (Rochester, N.Y.), May 1861. For a fine collection of Douglass's most important works see Philip S. Foner, ed., *The Life and Writings of Frederick Douglass*, 4 vols. (New York: International Publishers, 1950–1955).

"Then Grant whipped Lee two battles to one 'cause he had Negroes in the Union Army."[13]

Northern blacks volunteered for the army early on and sometimes served despite Lincoln's refusal to accept them. Nicholas Biddle, a former slave, went to war with Pennsylvania's Washington Artillerists in May 1861 and became perhaps the first man wounded in the conflict.[14] When the army officially allowed blacks to enlist, they came forward by the tens of thousands. On the civilian side, northern blacks organized to aid southern refugees. Others went south to render assistance. Many became politically involved, demanding not only freedom for slaves but equal rights for themselves.

Blacks in the South contributed mightily to the freedom war as well. They helped refugees, black and white, escape to federal lines. They helped Confederate deserters make their way back home. And they served as spies, guides, and informants to Union forces. As one escaped Union prisoner of war later wrote, "They were always ready to help anybody opposed to the Rebels. Union refugees, Confederate deserters, escaped prisoners – all received from them the same prompt and invariable kindness."[15]

Slave resistance took many forms during the war. In what W. E. B. Du Bois called a "general strike" against the Confederacy, southern blacks staged work slow-downs, refused instruction, resisted punishment, demanded pay for their work, gathered freely, traveled at will, and took freedom for themselves in various other ways long before the Union army arrived. In doing so, they forced the Confederacy to divert tens of thousands of men who might otherwise have been put on the front lines, engaging them in a vain effort to maintain control.[16]

Enslaved blacks also struck out violently against slaveholders and local authorities, sometimes cooperating with anti-Confederate whites in the effort. Two slaves in Dale County, Alabama, helped John Ward, leader of a local deserter gang, kill their owner in his bed. In the spring of 1862, authorities arrested three white citizens of Calhoun County, Georgia, for

---

[13] Tubman quoted in Lydia Maria Child to John G. Whittier, January 21, 1862, *Letters of Lydia Maria Child* (Boston: Houghton, Mifflin, and Co., 1883), 161; Marshall Mack, *Oklahoma Narratives*, 213.

[14] Francis B. Wallace, *Memorial of the Patriotism of Schuylkill County, in the American Slaveholder's Rebellion* (Pottsville, Pa.: Bannan, 1865), 77–78; Heber S. Thompson, *The First Defenders* (n.p., 1910), 14.

[15] Albert D. Richardson, *The Secret Service, the Field, the Dungeon, and the Escape* (Hartford, Conn.: American Publishing Co., 1866), 445.

[16] Du Bois, *Black Reconstruction*, 57; Sally E. Hadden, *Slave Patrols: Law and Violence in Virginia and the Carolinas* (Cambridge: Harvard University Press, 2001), 177.

supplying area slaves with firearms in preparation for a rebellion. Two years later, slaves in nearby Brooks County conspired with a local white man, John Vickery, to take the county and hold it for the Union.[17]

A STORY TOO LONG IN THE SHADOWS

Although the Union, to a large extent, owed its survival to blacks both on and off the battlefield, white America quickly forgot black contributions in the postwar years. It became the martyred Lincoln, and by extension magnanimous white northerners, who had removed the nation's stain of slavery and granted an unearned freedom to the slaves. In his 1928 biography of Ulysses S. Grant, W. E. Woodward expressed white America's prevailing view that "negroes are the only people in the history of the world, so far as I know, that ever became free without any effort of their own. . . . They twanged banjos around the railroad stations, sang melodious spirituals, and believed that some Yankee would soon come along and give each of them forty acres of land and a mule."[18]

Sadly, the public's general view of blacks during the Civil War has changed little despite decades of scholarly attention. Pop culture media has been far more influential. The 1939 film *Gone with the Wind*, which shapes public views of the war to this day, presents blacks as hardly fit for anything but slavery and perfectly content to remain enslaved. Even the 1989 film *Glory*, which focuses on the white Colonel Robert Gould Shaw and an assortment of fictional black characters, portrays enslaved people of the southeastern lowcountry as hapless "ragamuffins" who simply waited to be freed.[19]

---

[17] Fred S. Watson, *Winds of Sorrow: Hardships of the Civil War, Early Crimes and Hangings, and War Casualties of the Wiregrass Area* (Dothan, Ala.: Hopkins Printing, 1986), 13–14; *Augusta (Ga.) Constitutionalist*, June 14, 1862, and August 26, 1864; *Macon (Ga.) Daily Telegraph*, August 26, 1864. See also Christopher C. Meyers, "'The Wretch Vickery' and the Brooks County Civil War Slave Conspiracy," *Journal of Southwest Georgia History* 12 (1997): 27–38.

[18] W. E. Woodward, *Meet General Grant* (Garden City, N.Y.: Garden City Publishing, 1928), 372. In *Black Reconstruction*, W. E. B. Du Bois pointed to Woodward's comment as an example of the deliberate falsehoods perpetrated by most historians with regard to blacks and the Civil War. "The North went to war without the slightest idea of freeing the slave," Du Bois reminded his readers. "They attacked slavery only in order to win the war," and that with the aid of half a million black servicemen and laborers without whose help "the war against the South could not have been won" (Du Bois, *Black Reconstruction*, 716).

[19] Shaw is the only nonfictional member of the Fifty-Fourth Massachusetts Regiment portrayed in *Glory*. Other real-life members of the Fifty-Fourth included Henry Lewis

More recently, Steven Spielberg's 2012 film *Lincoln* has done perhaps the most damage in robbing blacks of their slavery-ending role in the popular mind. With help from historical advisors Doris Kearns Goodwin and Harold Holzer, Spielberg, America's greatest myth-maker, takes Lincoln, America's most mythical figure, and simply perpetuates the image of Lincoln as the Great Emancipator handing freedom to slaves as a gift. Nowhere does Spielberg credit blacks with having much to do with ending slavery. For Spielberg and his associates, it is as if the past few decades of scholarship on blacks in the Civil War era never happened.[20]

When, on occasion, the public does become briefly aware that black freedom was hard-earned, it seems to come as a revelation. As recently as 2012, an article appeared in a Lancaster, Pennsylvania, news outlet entitled "Black Role in Civil War Among the Best Kept Secrets." An editorial in Virginia's *Roanoke Times* wrote of the "untold" part that blacks played in the state's Civil War history. "Theirs is a story that has too long been in

Douglass and Charles Remond Douglass, both sons of Frederick Douglass, and William Carney, who won the Congressional Medal of Honor for his valor during the assault on Fort Wagner. For some reason, the film's producers chose to ignore Carney, the Douglass brothers, and others whose inclusion could have added more depth and authenticity. Professor Wayne K. Durrill, in "The Struggle for Black Freedom before Emancipation," *OAH Magazine of History* 8 (Fall 1993): 7–10, discusses a few examples of the many ways in which lowcountry slaves carved out freedom for themselves. For a view of what the freedom war meant to one former slave and how he and others responded see David S. Cecelski, *The Fire of Freedom: Abraham Galloway and the Slaves' Civil War* (Chapel Hill: University of North Carolina Press, 2012).

[20] Spielberg has his defenders, foremost among them advisors Harold Holzer and Doris Kearns Goodwin. Holzer, a senior administrator at New York's Metropolitan Museum of Art and a prolific Lincoln author, leaves little doubt where he stands on the question of who freed the slaves in his book *Lincoln: How Abraham Lincoln Ended Slavery in America: A Companion Book for Young Readers to the Steven Spielberg Film LINCOLN* (New York: Newmarket Press, 2012). Doris Kearns Goodwin, author of *Team of Rivals: The Political Genius of Abraham Lincoln* (New York: Simon and Schuster, 2005), upon which the Spielberg film was loosely based, issued a new release of her book (Simon and Schuster, 2012) as a tie-in to the film. Goodwin heaped lavish praise on Spielberg's *Lincoln* in a series of interviews coinciding with the film's release, at one point calling it "a dream come true." See *Charlie Rose*, November 7, 2012; *Examiner.com*, November 10, 2012; *Biography.com*, November 16, 2012; *USA Today*, December 3, 2012.

Other historians have taken Spielberg to task for downplaying the role of blacks in bringing on freedom. Kate Masur of Northwestern University notes that Spielberg leaves one with the impression that blacks "offered little of substance to their own liberation" (*New York Times*, November 12, 2012). Eric Foner of Columbia University calls Spielberg's film "a severely truncated view.... Slavery died on the ground, not just in the White House and the House of Representatives" (*New York Times*, November 26, 2012).

the shadows."²¹ It is to me astounding, and more than a little depressing, that we must use words such as "secrets," "untold," and "shadows" to describe modern America's public awareness when it comes to the role of blacks in gaining freedom.

In our history textbooks, the active and essential part blacks played, which should be a central focus, still tends to be mentioned only in passing, treated as secondary, or ignored completely. In a survey of major high school and college texts, one finds scant explanation of how a Union war moved toward being a freedom war as well, and little sense that blacks were involved in the movement at all.²² The effect of that omission is predictable. I recently asked my incoming freshmen to compose a brief essay on their impressions of how slavery ended. Fewer than 10 percent credited blacks in any way with contributing to the process. Most were sure that Lincoln, nearly single-handedly and of his own volition, had freed the slaves.²³

That mis-impression is so widely ingrained as almost to be a presumption that every U.S. citizen, or anyone hoping to become one, ought to affirm it. A sample question from the current Immigration and Naturalization Service (INS) citizenship test asks "What was *one* important thing that Abraham Lincoln did?" Among three acceptable answers is "Freed the slaves."²⁴

---

²¹ *Lancaster (Penn.) Online*, an edition of the *Intelligencer Journal/Lancaster New Era/ Sunday News*, March 2, 2012; "Untold Stories of the Civil War," *Roanoke (Va.) Times*, October 28, 2010.

²² See for example Alan Brinkley, *American History: Connecting with the Past*, fourteenth ed. (New York: McGraw Hill, 2012); James West Davidson et al., *US: A Narrative History*, second ed. (New York: McGraw Hill, 2012); Mark C. Carnes and John A. Garraty, *The American Nation: A History of the United States*, fourteenth ed. (Boston: Prentice Hall, 2012). Although all mention that slaves fled to Union lines, not one makes any connection between those fugitives and pressures for emancipation. In these and other texts I surveyed, I found only two that made the connection. Eric Foner, *Give Me Liberty: An American History*, third ed., vol. 1 (New York: W. W. Norton, 2011), notes that as "blacks began to escape to Union lines, the policy of ignoring slavery unraveled.... slaves themselves took actions that helped propel a reluctant white America down the road to emancipation" (548–49). Jennifer D. Keene, Saul Cornell, and Edward T. O'Donnell, *Visions of America: A History of the United States*, second ed., combined volume (Boston: Pearson Education, 2013), also make the connection, noting that a "wave of self-emancipation ... forced the Lincoln administration to formulate wartime policies regarding slavery, a process that ultimately led to emancipation" (385).

²³ The exercise, conducted in my U.S. History to 1865 survey courses on the first day of class each semester during the 2010–13 academic years, involved six sections of roughly forty students each. More than a third of the students were African American.

²⁴ The other two acceptable answers are "Saved (or preserved) the Union" and "Led the United States during the Civil War" (http://usgovinfo.about.com/library/blinstst_new.htm).

A word of warning to potential new citizens who may know that the answer is more complex. This is not an essay question. The INS is not looking for a debate. Simply answer as expected. Do not try to educate the INS.

Inadequate as our schools have been at emphasizing black self-agency during the Civil War, fairly well-educated Americans do tend to have some sense that Lincoln's Great Emancipator image has shortcomings. In 2005, then-Senator Barack Obama wrote in a *Time Magazine* editorial that although he admired Lincoln's "moral compass," he could not "swallow whole the view of Lincoln as the Great Emancipator."[25] Not surprisingly, Obama was lambasted in the blogosphere. He had his defenders, to be sure, but they were largely drowned out by people who accused Obama of everything from being uneducated to un-American. Surely some of the criticism was politically motivated, but much of it was born of pure ignorance.

Among scholars of the Civil War era as well, the Great Emancipator icon has lost some of its luster in recent years. Still, the image has its champions, although some tend to come to its defense from nontraditional angles. Gary Gallagher readily acknowledges in his recent book *The Union War* that Lincoln's Great Emancipator star does not shine as brightly among scholars as it once did. He stresses the fairly obvious point that for war-supporting white northerners, including Lincoln, preserving the Union, not ending slavery, was the prime objective. At the same time, he short-changes black contributions to the freedom side of the war, giving credit for black liberation mainly to the Union military, specifically the *white* Union military. "Without the United States Army," says Gallagher, "none of the other actors could have succeeded." Gallagher might have added, as Lincoln himself recognized, that the army succeeded only with the help of many hundreds of thousands of blacks – North and South, soldier and civilian. But Gallagher does the opposite, narrowly arguing that blacks featured in none of the war's "biggest battles," that they were relegated to "supporting tasks," and that they performed no "decisive service." In a series of speculative scenarios, he even imagines that "the United States might have achieved victory with slavery intact and no African American units in its armies." Such speculation is astonishing in light of Lincoln's early – and failed – efforts to do precisely that. The supporting tasks and nondecisive service Gallagher dismisses would have diverted hundreds of thousands of whites had blacks not been there to fill

[25] Barack Obama, "What I See in Lincoln's Eyes," *Time Magazine*, July 4, 2005.

those roles. Black efforts were far broader in scope and more significant in impact than Gallagher appears to recognize.[26]

Gallagher is particularly critical of Professor Steven Hahn's view, outlined in *The Political Worlds of Slavery and Freedom*, that the Civil War involved a "massive rebellion of southern slaves." Gallagher complains that "Hahn relies on an expansive definition of 'rebellion,' finessing the fact that approximately 3 million slaves remained under Confederate control at the time of Appomattox." One might as easily argue that Gallagher relies on an expansive definition of "control," ignoring the internal resistance and liberties taken by so many blacks whose enslavement was little more than "presumptive," as Hahn puts it, long before Appomattox.[27]

Implicit in Gallagher's argument is that Lincoln, as the Union army's commander-in-chief, largely retains his popular title of Great Emancipator even if emancipation was not his prime motive. This sort of sideways approach to preserving the Great Emancipator image is hardly uncommon. Some take an even more direct route. Historian James McPherson, a leading defender of the image, argues in *Drawn with the Sword: Reflections on the American Civil War* that without Lincoln there would have been no war and, hence, no opportunity for freedom. With regard to emancipation, it was Lincoln's determination to maintain the Union – it was the war itself – that was "the essential condition, the one thing without which it would not have happened." Without Lincoln, there would have been no Emancipation Proclamation and no Thirteenth Amendment. Therefore, says McPherson, "Lincoln freed the slaves."[28]

---

[26] Gary W. Gallagher, *The Union War* (Cambridge: Harvard University Press, 2011), 88, 92, 149–50.

[27] Hahn, *Political Worlds of Slavery and Freedom*, 58; Gallagher, *Union War*, 149; Hahn, *A Nation under Our Feet*, 83.

[28] James M. McPherson, *Drawn with the Sword: Reflections on the American Civil War* (New York: Oxford University Press, 1996), 196, 207. Early in his career, McPherson tended to be more critical of Lincoln's conservative approach to, and limited concept of, emancipation. More recently he has become, as Professor Edna Greene Medford puts it, "one of the chief proponents of the 'Great Emancipator' view." In his brief 2009 Lincoln biography, McPherson reaffirms his impression of Lincoln as the indispensable gift-giver of freedom. See James M. McPherson, *The Struggle for Equality: Abolitionists and the Negro in the Civil War and Reconstruction* (Princeton, N.J.: Princeton University Press, 1964); Edna Greene Medford, "Imagined Promises, Bitter Realities: African Americans and the Meaning of the Emancipation Proclamation," in Harold Holzer, Edna Greene Medford, and Frank J. Williams, *The Emancipation Proclamation: Three Views* (Baton Rouge: Louisiana State University Press, 2006), 141 n. 3; James M. McPherson, *Lincoln* (New York: Oxford University Press, 2009).

Arguments such as those of Gallagher, McPherson, and others have some validity as far as they go. To my knowledge, no reputable scholar denies that Lincoln and the Union military played a significant part in the emancipation process. But following their lines of reasoning more deeply, we cannot help but see the efforts of black folk at their core.

Lincoln's insistence on the Union's survival was a reaction to the South's secession, a movement engineered by slaveholders who feared not only Lincoln but, more immediately, their own slaves. Controlling slaves had been increasingly difficult for years. It could only be more difficult, perhaps impossible, with slaves believing that Lincoln's election meant their freedom. How could they believe otherwise? Although Lincoln was no threat to slavery where it existed, and said so often during the 1860 presidential campaign, fire-eating secessionists railed against him as a radical abolitionist with a secret agenda to foment slave rebellion. Such overheated rhetoric was intended to stir up support for secession among southern whites, but southern blacks heard the message too. Resistance and rumors of resistance pervaded the South that year and drove slaveholder fears to a fever pitch. Most significantly, underlying their fear was the certain knowledge that slaves wanted freedom. It was that certainty, born of many decades of slave resistance, that led to secession, war, and slavery's downfall.[29]

Slaveholders' doubts about their ability to maintain slavery indefinitely had a long history. The need to justify slavery had for decades occupied their brightest minds. The need to keep southern whites, three-quarters of whom owned no slaves, supporting slavery made fomenting fear of blacks a political priority. Most threatening to slaveholders were the slaves themselves. Blacks had never submitted to slavery willingly or completely. They did little more than what they had to do and took liberties where they could. They resisted in so many ways that the slaveholders' need to exercise control was constant and all-consuming. Had blacks been content to remain enslaved, slaveholders would have had no cause for alarm. Nor would abolitionist arguments have inspired such panic among them. As it was, slaveholder fears of threats to slavery, as much from within as from without, led them to insist on guarantees for slavery's future and the means

---

[29] For discussions of slave resistance in the summer and fall of 1860 see Aptheker, *Slave Revolts*, 354–57; David Williams, "The 'Faithful Slave' Is About Played Out: Civil War Slave Resistance in the Lower Chattahoochee Valley," *Alabama Review: A Quarterly Journal of Alabama History* 52 (1999): 87–90; William W. White, "The Texas Slave Insurrection of 1860," *Southwestern Historical Quarterly* 52 (1949): 259–85; Donald E. Reynolds, *Texas Terror: The Slave Insurrection Panic of 1860 and the Secession of the Lower South* (Baton Rouge: Louisiana State University Press, 2007).

to control that future. And that fear led them to secede when those guarantees and their means of control seemed at risk. There was, as historian John Ashworth reminds us, a direct causal link between the slaves' desire for freedom and slaveholder politics. "Behind every event in the history of the sectional controversy," Ashworth points out, "lurked the consequences of black resistance to slavery."[30]

That resistance was not confined to the South. Escaping slaves saw to that. By the tens of thousands they headed north, undermining northern efforts to keep the slave's war south of the Mason-Dixon Line. In so doing, as historian Scott Hancock stresses, black folk "maintained an unrelenting pressure on the sectional fault lines of identity, law, and space." That pressure expanded those fault lines and increasingly drew northerners into the conflict. Time and again, northern failures to keep blacks and slavery locked in the South put them at odds with slaveholders' expansionist demands. Hancock concludes, and rightly so, that "not simply slavery, but slaves – black people! – caused the Civil War."[31]

It was, then, at the heart of it all, the unrelenting resistance to slavery among slaves themselves that was the essential condition, the one thing without which the sectional crisis, secession, the Civil War, the Emancipation Proclamation, and the Thirteenth Amendment would not have happened.

Of course, it did not happen overnight. For more than two centuries before the Civil War, millions of African Americans lived in bondage all their lives. But it was a resisted bondage, an ongoing struggle, that would eventually reach its consummation. Some whites recognized that early on. "Freedom must be as dear to them as to us," wrote settlers at Darien, Georgia, in 1739 as they petitioned the colony's trustees to maintain their ban on slavery. One passage was especially prophetic. "It is shocking to human Nature, that any Race of Mankind and their Posterity should be sentence'd to perpetual Slavery; nor in Justice can we think otherwise of it, than that they are thrown amongst us to be our Scourge one Day or other for our Sins." In June 1863, black Union soldiers, many of them formerly enslaved along the Georgia-Carolina coast, ransacked Darien and set the town afire.[32]

---

[30] Ashworth, *Slavery, Capitalism, and Politics*, 1: 6. Much the same theme runs throughout William Link, *Roots of Secession: Slavery and Politics in Antebellum Virginia* (Chapel Hill: University of North Carolina Press, 2003).

[31] Scott Hancock, "Crossing Freedom's Fault Line: The Underground Railroad and Recentering African Americans in Civil War Causality," *Civil War History* 59 (2013): 205.

[32] Darien Antislavery Petition, in Christopher C. Meyers, ed., *Empire State of the South: Georgia History in Documents and Essays* (Macon, Ga.: Mercer University Press, 2008), 111–12.

The internal pressures against slavery – rebellion, resistance, escape – were always there and became ever greater as slavery spread. Slaveholders clamped down with more slave codes, more slave patrols, and increasingly brutal control. But the more they tried to tighten their grip on slaves, the more slaves slipped through their fingers. By the late 1850s, there were perhaps 50,000 escapes annually, temporary and permanent.[33] Such resistance fueled a desperation reflected in slaveholder politics and the secession crisis. The resulting freedom war was neither an isolated event nor an endpoint in itself. It was part of a massive black resistance movement that had been going on for generations, finally becoming so intense that whites could not help but be drawn into it whether they wanted to or not.

Even so, both sides, Union and Confederate, insisted in the war's early months that the conflict was a white man's war. But blacks knew it was theirs and quickly took ownership of it. They struggled for freedom not only as a political right but also seized what liberties they could for themselves, individually and collectively. Blacks knew that freedom was not a single thing, granted from on high by an act of Congress, a presidential proclamation, or even a Constitutional amendment. Nor was freedom simply the absence of slavery. Black northerners of the antebellum era repeatedly testified to that. Segregated, disenfranchised, discriminated against, and denied opportunity, "northern freedom" was, as one disgusted man put it, "nothing but a nickname for northern slavery."[34] For northern blacks, the freedom war was as much a struggle against prejudice as a struggle against slavery.

In the experience of black Americans, freedom was little more than a set of possibilities surrounding a space that had to be carved out and occupied. They had been carving out those spaces for more than two centuries, ever since they were brought to the continent as forced labor. The boundaries of those spaces were rarely obvious, so there was always poking and prodding to discover their edges and push them a little further. Setbacks there were, and plenty of them. Long after emancipation, the struggle for freedom went on. That continual pressure from black folk had always been, and would continue to be, the driving force behind their expanding freedoms.

---

[33] John Hope Franklin and Loren Schweninger, "The Quest for Freedom: Runaway Slaves and the Plantation South," in Gabor Boritt and Scott Hancock, eds., *Slavery, Resistance, Freedom* (New York: Oxford University Press, 2007), 37–38.

[34] *Colored American* (New York), June 1, 1839.

# I

# "Yes, We All Shall Be Free"

## Pressing the Nation Toward Freedom

"I can just barely remember my mother." That was what Tom Robinson, born into slavery on a North Carolina plantation, told an interviewer for the 1930s Federal Writers Project. He was only ten when sold away from his mother shortly before the Civil War began.

But I do remember how she used to take us children and kneel down in front of the fireplace and pray. She'd pray that the time would come when everybody could worship the Lord under their own vine and fig tree – all of them free. It's come to me lots of times since. There she was a'praying, and on other plantations women was a'praying. All over the country the same prayer was being prayed.[1]

Secession and war served only to make such prayers more expectant and intense. Despite efforts to conceal the war's implications from them, slaves had many ways of learning about what its outcome could mean for them. Years after the war, Hattie Nettles of Opelika, Alabama, remembered climbing a fence as a young girl to watch Confederate soldiers pass by. She did not know where they were going at first, but it was not long before she found out. Mary Gladdy, a Georgia freedwoman, recalled "the whisperings among the slaves – their talking of the possibility of freedom."[2]

---

[1] Tom Robinson, *Arkansas Narratives*, part 6, 64. At age eighty-eight, a favorite pastime for Robinson was visiting an elementary school for black youth near his home in Hot Springs. "Almost every day I comes up to sit here and watch the children. It does me good to see 'em. Makes me feel good all over to think about all the fine chance they has to get a good education" (68).

[2] Hattie Anne Nettles, *Alabama Narratives*, 297; Mary Gladdy, *Georgia Narratives*, part 2, 17.

Throughout the war, slaves met in secret to hold prayer meetings for freedom. According to Mary Gladdy, those on her plantation gathered in their cabins two or three nights a week. They placed large pots against the doors to keep their voices muffled. "Then," she said, "the slaves would sing, pray, and relate experiences all night long. Their great, soul-hungering desire was freedom." Those few slaves who could read kept up with events through pilfered newspapers and spread the word to their neighbors. Young Ella Hawkins of Georgia heard the older slaves whispering among themselves, "Us is gonna be free! Jes as sho's anything. God has heard our prayers; us is gonna be free!" When a white minister preached that slavery was ordained by God and prayed aloud for Him to drive the Yankees back, Georgia slave Ella Hawkins prayed silently to herself, "Oh, Lord, please send the Yankees on."[3]

In her reminiscences of the war years, Susie King Taylor wrote vividly of the excitement among her Savannah neighbors. "Oh, how those people prayed for freedom! I remember, one night, my grandmother went out into the suburbs of the city to a church meeting, and they were fervently singing this old hymn."[4]

> Yes, we all shall be free,
> Yes, we all shall be free,
> Yes, we all shall be free,
> When the Lord shall appear.

Pray they did, but enslaved southerners were not simply waiting for either the Lord or the Yankees to give them freedom. They were taking it for

[3] Mary Gladdy, *Georgia Narratives*, part 2, 26–27; Ella Hawkins, in Rawick et al., *The American Slave*, supplement, series 1, vol. 3, *Georgia Narratives*, part 1, 315. Enslaved people of the late antebellum period built multiplantation communities that would keep them connected well into the war years and beyond. See Anthony E. Kaye, *Joining Places: Slave Neighborhoods in the Old South* (Chapel Hill: University of North Carolina Press, 2009). For special treatment of community and resistance in upland regions see Wilma A. Dunaway, *Slavery in the American Mountain South* (Cambridge: Cambridge University Press, 2003), 198–240.

[4] Susie King Taylor, *Reminiscences of My Life in Camp* (1902; reprint, with new introduction by Catherine Clinton, Athens: University of Georgia Press, 2006), 8. Two excellent treatments of slave religion and its significance before and during the war are Albert J. Raboteau, *Slave Religion: The "Invisible Institution" in the Antebellum South* (New York: Oxford University Press, 2004), and Daniel L. Fountain, *Slavery, Civil War, and Salvation: African American Slaves and Christianity, 1830–1870* (Baton Rouge: Louisiana State University Press, 2011). For a fascinating look at the survival of African folkways in spirituality among the enslaved see Jennifer Hildebrand, "'Dere Were No Place for Him in Heaven, an' He Were Not Desired in Hell': Igbo Cultural Beliefs in African American Folk Expression," *Journal of African American History* 91 (2006): 127–52.

themselves. Although Lincoln is often credited with having "freed the slaves," his Emancipation Proclamation did little more than recognize a state of affairs that blacks had already created with what W. E. B. Du Bois later called their "general strike" against the Confederacy. Lincoln's document, as Professor Ira Berlin points out, "heralded not the dawn of universal liberty but the compromised and piecemeal arrival of an undefined freedom. Indeed, the Proclamation's flat prose, ridiculed by the late Richard Hofstadter as having 'all the moral grandeur of a bill of lading,' suggests that the true authorship of African American freedom lies elsewhere – not at the top of American society but at its base."[5]

Georgia slaveholder Laura Comer illustrated Berlin's point when she wrote in August 1862 that "the servants are so indolent and obstinate it is a *trial* to have anything to do with them." Slaves resisted their plight by increasingly feigning ignorance or illness, sabotaging plantation equipment, and traveling freely in defiance of the law. A Confederate officer in Charleston complained that "gangs of negroes" who should have been at work on fortifications were "idle" on city streets. One disturbed white woman on a Georgia rail line was astonished to see "crowds of slaves in gayest attire" getting on and off the trains "at every country stopping place."[6]

As for forced labor, what work slaves did was done with measured effort. Some refused to work at all. A Georgia plantation mistress wrote of one of her slaves, "Nancy has been very impertinent. . . . She said she would not be hired out by the month, neither would she go out to get work." Another mistress wrote to her husband, "We are doing as best we know, or as good as we can get the Servants to do; they learn to feel very independent." Kate Stone of Louisiana had similar problems with her slaves. According to her journal entry of June 1861, "The house servants have been giving a lot of trouble lately – lazy and disobedient. . . . The excitement in the air has infected them."[7]

---

[5] Du Bois, *Black Reconstruction*, 57; Berlin, "Who Freed the Slaves?," 109–10. Berlin's quoted reference is from Richard Hofstadter, *The American Political Tradition and the Men Who Made It* (New York: Vintage, 1948), 132.

[6] Laura Beecher Comer Diary, August 16, 1862, Laura Beecher Comer Papers, Southern Historical Collection, University of North Carolina at Chapel Hill; *Correspondence Relating to Fortification of Morris Island and Operations of Engineers, Charleston, S.C., 1863* (New York: John J. Caulon, 1878), 27; Catherine C. Hopley, *Life in the South; From the Commencement of the War* (London: Chapman and Hall, 1863), 2: 336.

[7] Mary Ann Harden to son, September 27, 1863, and Sally Jackson to Ashbury Jackson, August 23, 1862, Edward Harden Papers, Duke University Library, in T. Conn Bryan, *Confederate Georgia* (Athens: University of Georgia Press, 1953), 125; John Q. Anderson,

Such observations hardly squared with the "faithful slave" image, although slaveholders continued to press it publicly. But what they would not say in public, they had to admit among themselves. So pervasive and open was slave resistance that many slaveholders seemed resigned to it. A Texas woman admitted that it was useless to try to coerce her slaves, "so I shall say nothing and if they stop working entirely I will try to feel thankful if they let me alone." In South Carolina, a plantation mistress wrote to her mother early in the war that slaves knew the crisis provided opportunities for them that "must be taken advantage of. ... Times and slaves have changed." Catherine Edmondston wrote from her North Carolina plantation, "As to the idea of a *faithful servant, it is all a fiction.*"[8]

## SLAVERY WITHOUT SUBMISSION

The "faithful slave" notion had been a delusion from the start. Certainly the slaves knew it. And, as their actions made clear, slaveholders knew it too. Despite their claims to the contrary, the "wise master," as historian Kenneth Stampp put it,

did not take seriously the belief that Negroes were natural-born slaves. He knew better. He knew that Negroes freshly imported from Africa had to be broken into bondage; that each succeeding generation had to be carefully trained. This was no easy task, for the bondsman rarely submitted willingly. Moreover, he rarely submitted completely. In most cases there was no end to the need for control – at least not until old age reduced the slave to a condition of helplessness.[9]

Control of elderly slaves was hardly a concern in any case. Few lived to see old age.

ed., *Brokenburn: The Journal of Kate Stone, 1861–1868* (Baton Rouge: Louisiana State University Press, 1955), 33.

[8] Lizzie S. Neblett to William H. Neblett, August 13, 1863, in Erika L. Murr, ed., *A Rebel Wife in Texas: The Diary and Letters of Elizabeth Scott Neblett, 1852–1864* (Baton Rouge: Louisiana State University Press, 2001), 135; Mary Elliott Johnstone to Mamma [Mrs. William Elliot], [December?] 15 [1861?], Elliot and Gonzales Family Papers, Southern Historical Collection, University of North Carolina at Chapel Hill; Beth G. Crabtree and James W. Patton, eds., *Journal of a Secesh Lady: The Diary of Catherine Anne Devereaux Edmondston, 1860–1866* (Raleigh: North Carolina Division of Archives and History, 1979), 463.

[9] Kenneth M. Stampp, *The Peculiar Institution: Slavery in the Ante-Bellum South* (New York: Vintage Books, 1956), 144. For a comprehensive study of resistance in the colonial and antebellum periods see Walter C. Rucker, *The River Flows On: Black Resistance, Culture, and Identity Formation in Early America* (Baton Rouge: Louisiana State University Press, 2007). See also Alan Taylor, *The Internal Enemy: Slavery and War in Virginia, 1772–1832* (New York: W. W. Norton, 2013).

FIGURE 1.1. Harriet Tubman and the many enslaved people she led out of bondage made clear not only that slavery would be resisted but also that the slaves' struggle would not be confined to the South. They kept mounting tension on the line between slavery and freedom and increasingly drew reluctant northerners into the conflict. Time and time again, northern failures to keep blacks and slavery locked in the South put them at odds with slaveholders' expansionist demands. Photo courtesy of the Library of Congress.

Slave resistance took many forms, the most celebrated of which were various escape routes popularly called the Underground Railroad. Its earliest reference remains unclear. One tradition tells of an escaping Kentucky slave named Tice Davids who disappeared in southern Ohio almost within sight of his pursuing owner. The slaveholder quipped that Davids must have found an underground railroad. Another source relates the torture in Washington of a young refugee named Jim, who, after having his fingers pressed in a blacksmith's vise, confessed that he was in the capital city looking for a railroad that "went underground all the way to Boston."[10]

[10] William H. Siebert, *The Underground Railroad From Slavery to Freedom* (New York: Macmillan, 1898), 45; Eber M. Pettit, *Sketches in the History of the Underground R.R.* (Fredonia, N.Y.: W. McKinstry and Son, 1879), 35–36; *Tocsin of Liberty* in *New York*

Whatever the case, by the early 1840s, nearly every escaping slave was said to be traveling via the Underground Railroad.

Harriet Tubman, the most famous of the railroad's "conductors," led hundreds of escapees to freedom. Rewards offered for her capture totaled as much as $40,000 but she was never caught. Neither was Arnold Gragston, an enslaved Kentuckian who ferried hundreds of fellow slaves across the Ohio River before making his own escape. Mary Stark, a black woman in Chesterfield County, Virginia, gave shelter to escaping slaves. So did Peter, a "tall, black African" in Petersburg, who, when his home was searched for refugees, proclaimed that he "would harbor as many negroes as he d—d well pleased." A local court sentenced him to twenty lashes. Jacob Dill, a Richmond slave, was also whipped for sheltering refugees. Thanks to these men and women, and many others like them, perhaps 100,000 enslaved people escaped north in the first half of the nineteenth century.[11]

Not all escape routes ran northward. Spanish Florida was a haven for refugees in the Deep South until it became a U.S. territory in 1821. In the Southwest, Mexico was attractive for those escaping bondage. "In Mexico you could be free," recalled former slave Ben Kinchlow. "They didn't care what color you was, black, white, yellow or blue."[12]

Regardless of distance or direction, escaping slavery was dangerous work. Slavecatchers and bloodhounds were hot on the heels of nearly every escapee. Captured refugees could have toes or even half a foot cut off to discourage further escapes. Death could also result. One slave was whipped so badly after a failed attempt that he died three days later.[13]

Fear of bloodhounds, capture, and death weighed heavily on Henry Bibb before he fled Kentucky for freedom in Detroit. But the heaviest burden on his heart was his "strong attachments to friends and family." For most enslaved people, the greatest deterrent to escape was the near certainty that they would never see loved ones again. Henry had planned to buy his wife out of slavery, but his former owner sold her away before Henry could raise the money. Most slaves did not want to take such a

---

*Spectator*, September 28, 1842; *Boston Emancipator and Free American*, April 20 and May 11, 1843.

[11] Catherine Clinton, *Harriet Tubman: The Road to Freedom* (Boston: Little, Brown, and Co., 2004), 142; Arnold Gragston, *Florida Narratives*, 146–54; Link, *Roots of Secession*, 104–05; J. F. H. Claiborne, *Life and Correspondence of John A. Quitman* (New York: Harper and Brothers, 1860), 2: 28; Siebert, *Underground Railroad*, 341, 346. Siebert estimates that at least 40,000 refugees passed through Ohio alone between 1830 and 1860.

[12] Ben Kinchlow, *Texas Narratives*, part 2, 265.

[13] Caroline Holland, *Alabama Narratives*, 186.

risk. "My pappy tried to get away," recalled Mary Ella Grandberry, whose family was held in Alabama, "but he couldn't see how to take all us children with him, so he had to stay with us."[14]

Those torn between the burdens of slavery and the love of family often resorted to local escapes. "Sometimes slaves run away and hid out in caves," remembered Georgia freedman Benny Dillard. Other slaves "would slip 'em something to eat at night." Enslaved Georgian Willis Earle ran off to the woods and dug a cave where he spent fifteen years. Some escapees lived in small isolated groups and raided farms and plantations for hogs, chickens, corn, and vegetables. Others set up camp deep in the woods, swamps, and mountains, living off the land. It was not unheard of for these refugees, commonly referred to as *maroons*, to have communities with dozens of members. A few, such as those in the Great Dismal Swamp on the North Carolina–Virginia border and those in the Florida Everglades, numbered in the hundreds. Some communities lasted for generations.[15]

Local escapes were more often temporary affairs lasting days or weeks. It was not unusual for slaves to absent themselves overnight, especially on weekends, to visit friends or family, to attend dances or prayer meetings, or simply to get some rest. Such absenteeism carried risks, most notably from slave patrols. Slaves caught without a written pass from their owner could be severely whipped by the "paddyrollers," as the slaves called them. "But us was young and spry," recalled Virginia freedwoman Sis Shackelford, "an' could outrun 'em."[16]

Whipping and other physical abuse was often a reason for temporary escapes. "If they were treated too cruelly," Virginia Shepard recalled, "our folks would always run away and hide in the woods." Delicia Patterson told of running off after being mistreated by her owner. "He sent everybody he thought knew where I was after me, and told them to tell me if I would only come on back home, no one would ever bother me anymore. ... So I went back home ... and no one ever bothered me any more." Such bargaining was not uncommon. After being sold to a slave trader, Fannie Berry's father fled to the woods rather than be parted from

[14] Henry Bibb, *Narrative of the Life and Adventures of Henry Bibb* (New York: the author, 1849), 47; Mary Ella Grandberry, *Alabama Narratives*, 161.

[15] Benny Dillard, *Georgia Narratives*, part 1, 292; Tom Hawkins, *Georgia Narratives*, part 2, 131; Charles Crawley, *Virginia Narratives*, 8; Julia Brown, *Georgia Narratives*, part 1, 147.

[16] Sarah Wells, *Arkansas Narratives*, part 7, 90; Sis Shackelford, in Charles L. Perdue Jr., Thomas E. Barden, and Robert K. Phillips, eds., *Weevils in the Wheat: Interviews with Virginia Ex-Slaves* (Charlottesville: University Press of Virginia, 1976), 253.

his wife and three children, who lived on a neighboring plantation. A year later, his wife's owner finally purchased the absent man, probably at a discount, and he soon showed up at his new owner's place. Other reasons that slaves might escape temporarily included bargaining for better food, clothing, working conditions, housing, or visiting rights.[17]

Slaves who bargained in such ways walked a fine line. Punishments for unsuccessful attempts, or for any other conduct the owner disliked, could be severe. Owners and overseers frequently administered beatings to slaves in the "Buck" or "Rolling Jim" positions. In each case the slave was stripped naked and bound tight. One former slave remembered the Buck as "making the Negro squat, running a stout stick under his bended knee, and then tying his hands firmly to the stick – between the knees. Then the lash was laid on his back parts." Rias Body recalled that with the Rolling Jim the slave was "stretched on his stomach at full length on a large log, about eight feet long. Into holes bored in the end of this log, wooden pegs were driven. The feet were securely tied to one set of these pegs ... and the hands to the pegs at the other end. The victim was then ready to be worked on."[18]

Another common torture involved hoisting slaves up by their thumbs, with only their toes touching the ground, and beating them with a stick or whip. A victim might be "further tormented by having his wounds 'doctored' with salt and red pepper." Rhodus Walton remembered that his owner's "favorite form of punishment was to take a man (or woman) to the edge of the plantation where a rail fence was located. His head was then placed between two rails so that escape was impossible and he was whipped until the overseer was exhausted. This was an almost daily occurrence, administered on the slightest provocation." After recalling the variety of tortures inflicted on slaves, W. B. Allen, a former Alabama slave, told an interviewer, "Sir, you can never know what some slaves endured."[19]

Slaves were defined as property by slave state courts and, in the *Dred Scott* case of 1857, by the U.S. Supreme Court. As such, slaves were subject to the absolute authority of slaveholders and to whatever controls they chose to employ. As one member of the Georgia Supreme Court insisted, "Subordination can only be maintained by the right to give moderate

[17] Virginia Hayes Shepard, in Perdue et al., *Weevils in the Wheat*, 261; Delicia Patterson, *Missouri Narratives*, 272; Fannie Berry, in Perdue et al., *Weevils in the Wheat*, 42.

[18] W. B. Allen, in Rawick et al., *American Slave*, supplement, series 1, vol. 3, *Georgia Narratives*, part 1, 6–7; Rias Body, in ibid., 71.

[19] Rhodus Walton, *Georgia Narratives*, part 4, 124; W. B. Allen, in Rawick et al., *American Slave*, supplement, series 1, vol. 3, *Georgia Narratives*, part 1, 6–7.

correction – a right similar to that which exists in the father over his children."[20]

There were, however, laws limiting the abusiveness of parents over their children. Slaves enjoyed few such legal protections. And the definition of "moderate correction" was left entirely to the slaveholder. "Should death ensue by accident, while this slave is thus receiving moderate correction," recalled a British visitor, "the constitution of Georgia kindly denominates the offence justifiable homicide."[21] W. B. Allen personally knew some in bondage who were beaten, sometimes to death, for nothing more than being off the plantation without written permission. Other offenses that might result in extreme punishment were lying, loitering, stealing, and "talking back to – 'sassing' – a white person."[22]

Still, slaves resisted, most often cooperating with each other to do so. They had to balance their efforts, resisting enough to ease their burden but no so much as to bring on punishment. They organized work slowdowns. They played sick. They sabotaged or destroyed equipment to slow the pace of work. They pretended not to understand instructions. "Not that they often directly refused to obey an order," wrote one observer, "but when they are directed to do anything for which they have a disinclination, they undertake it in such a way that the desired result is sure not to be accomplished." Slaves on one plantation rid themselves of an especially cruel overseer by slipping a snake into his cabin. "Put in the snake and out went the overseer," as Mattie Logan recalled. "Never no more did he whip the slaves on that plantation. ... He was gone!"[23]

Unfortunately, mitigating cruel treatment was rarely so simple. Slavery itself was the greatest cruelty of all, and, for some slaves, the ultimate resistance, the only escape, was death. One Georgia slave took her own life by swallowing strychnine. In Covington, Kentucky, two enslaved parents "sent the souls of their children to Heaven rather than have them descend to the hell of slavery." After releasing their children's souls, they released their own. Another enslaved mother killed all thirteen of her children in

---

[20] Thomas R. R. Cobb, comp., *Reports of Cases in Law and Equity, Argued and Determined in the Supreme Court of the State of Georgia* (Athens, Ga.: Reynolds and Bro., 1855), 15: 542.

[21] James Stuart, *Three Years in North America* (Edinburgh, Scotland: Robert Cadell, 1833), 2: 164. Stuart refers to that section of Georgia's constitution that purported to give slaves protection from murder "unless such death should happen by accident in giving such slave moderate correction." See Meyers, *Empire State of the South*, 56.

[22] W. B. Allen, *Georgia Narratives*, part 1, 14–15.

[23] Frederick Law Olmsted, *A Journey in the Seaboard Slave States* (New York: Dix and Edwards, 1856), 198; Mattie Logan, *Oklahoma Narratives*, 190.

infancy to spare them a life of suffering as slaves. Two boatloads of Africans newly arrived in Charleston committed mass suicide by starving themselves to death.[24]

Sometimes slaves killed their oppressors instead. Most famous for its violence was Nat Turner's 1831 Virginia rebellion, in which more than fifty whites died. There were many others who fought back or conspired to do so. In 1800, more than a thousand slaves marched on Richmond. The governor called out armed militiamen to turn them back. There were similar efforts to gain liberty in Petersburg and Norfolk. When one slave conspirator was asked what he had to say in his defense, he calmly replied, "I have nothing more to offer than what General Washington would have had to offer, had he been taken by the British officers and put to trial by them. I have ventured my life in endeavoring to obtain the liberty of my countrymen, and am a willing sacrifice to their cause."[25]

In 1811, 400 Louisiana slaves rose up for freedom. A year later, there was rebellion in New Orleans. In 1837, slaves near that city formed a rebel band and killed several whites before being captured. Slaves fought back individually too. In 1849, a slave in Chambers County, Alabama, shot his owner. In Macon County, another slave "violently attacked with a knife and cut to pieces" his overseer. After one overseer whipped her, an enslaved Florida woman took a hoe and chopped the man "to a bloody death." When Edward Covey tried to bind and beat Frederick Douglass, he fought Covey off. From that day forward, Douglass later wrote, "I did not hesitate to let it be known of me, that the white man who expected to succeed in whipping, must also succeed in killing me."[26]

---

[24] *Cuthbert (Ga.) Reporter*, September 23, 1856; George W. Carleton, *The Suppressed Book About Slavery* (New York: Carleton Publishers, 1864), 138; C. G. Parsons, *An Inside View of Slavery* (Boston: Jewett and Co., 1855), 212; Charles Winslow Elliott, *Winfield Scott: The Soldier and the Man* (New York: Macmillian, 1937), 18.

[25] Robert Sutcliff, *Travels in Some Parts of North America in the Years 1804, 1805, and 1806* (York, England: C. Peacock, 1811), 50. See also Stephen B. Oates, *Fires of Jubilee: Nat Turner's Fierce Rebellion* (New York: Harper and Row, 1975); Kenneth S. Greenberg, ed., *The Confessions of Nat Turner and Related Documents* (Boston: Bedford/St. Martin's, 1996); Douglas R. Egerton, *Gabriel's Rebellion: The Virginia Slave Conspiracies of 1800 and 1802* (Chapel Hill: University of North Carolina Press, 1993); James Sidbury, *Ploughshares Into Swords: Race, Rebellion, and Identity in Gabriel's Virginia, 1730–1810* (Cambridge: Cambridge University Press, 1997); Michael L. Nicholls, *Whispers of Rebellion: Narrating Gabriel's Conspiracy* (Charlottesville: University of Virginia Press, 2012).

[26] *New Orleans Daily Picayune*, July 19, 1837; James Benson Sellers, *Slavery in Alabama* (Tuscaloosa: University of Alabama Press, 1964), 246–47, 248; John Henry Kemp, *Florida Narratives*, 185; Douglass, *Narrative of the Life of Frederick Douglass*, 71–73. For the

Douglass was fortunate to escape slavery before such defiance cost him his life. Most others who resisted violently were either shot or lynched. Some were burned alive.[27] What laws there were restraining whites from murdering slaves for whatever reason were in fact no restraint at all. State slave codes prevented slaves from testifying against whites in court, and few whites would testify against each other.

Aside from the brutality they sanctioned, slave codes defined legal limits for the late-antebellum South's 4 million slaves far beyond their status as chattel. No slave could lawfully carry a gun, own property, travel without a written pass, or learn to read or write. Slave gatherings, even for religious services, were forbidden without a white person present.

The South's quarter-million free blacks, most of whom lived in the upper South, labored under similar legal restrictions. They were free only in the sense that they were not chattel. But neither were they citizens. They could not vote or hold office. They could not testify against whites, could not own property in their own names, and were required to have a white guardian. Some slave states restricted their right of assembly, church services included. And they generally had to wear badges or carry papers testifying to their nonslave status. In the words of historian James Oakes, "it was like turning the Bill of Rights upside down."[28]

Slave codes also prevented municipal governments from issuing slave marriage licenses. To do so would have established a legally sanctioned bond between members of slave families, implicitly infringing on the "property rights" of slaveholders – specifically the right to deal with and dispose of slaves as the owner wished. Nevertheless, slaveholders allowed and even encouraged slaves to marry at an early age and have many children. This not only increased the slaveholder's "property" but also provided an additional means of control. Besides the constant threat of physical violence, slaveholders found the institution of the family to be an effective means of intimidation. Any slave might be pushed to the point of disregard for his or her own safety and attempt to fight back or escape. But when slaveholders threatened family members, slaves were more likely to hold their anger in check. It was another way to drive home the point that

---

1811 New Orleans uprising see Daniel Rasmussen, *American Uprising: The Untold Story of America's Largest Slave Revolt* (New York: Harper Perennial, 2012).

[27] Mabel Farrior, *Alabama Narratives*, 47; Jennie Kendricks, *Georgia Narratives*, part 3, 5.

[28] James Oakes, *Slavery and Freedom: An Interpretation of the Old South* (New York: Vintage, 1990), 69. For the most complete study of southern free blacks available see Ira Berlin, *Slaves without Masters: The Free Negro in the Antebellum South* (New York: Pantheon, 1974).

the slaveholder was master. Some did not even allow parents to name their own children, reserving that privilege for themselves.[29]

In naming the children of slave women, some slaveholders were actually exercising their own parental rights. For a planter to have any number of mistresses among his slaves was quite common. Slaveholders typically viewed rape as another method of enforcing psychological dominance within the slave community. Others simply viewed slaves as property to be used at their pleasure. The first sexual experience a planter's son had was usually with a female slave. Robert Ellett, enslaved in King William County, Virginia, recalled that "in those days if you was a slave and had a good looking daughter, she was taken from you. They would put her in the big house where the young masters could have the run of her." Pregnancy often followed. Little wonder that slaves of light complexion were present on nearly every plantation. William Craft, formerly enslaved in Georgia, wrote after his escape that "slavery in America is not at all confined to persons of any particular complexion; there are a very large number of slaves as white as any one." Harriet Jacobs, herself abused as a young woman, recalled years later that she "once saw two beautiful children playing together. One was a fair white child; the other was her slave, and also her sister. When I saw them embracing each other, and heard their joyous laughter, I turned sadly away from the lovely sight. I foresaw the inevitable blight that would fall on the little slave's heart."[30]

"Like the patriarchs of old," wrote Mary Chesnut, "our men live all in one house with their wives and their concubines, and the mulattoes one sees in every family exactly resemble the white children – and every lady tells you who is the father of all the mulatto children in everybody's household, but those in her own she seems to think drop from the clouds, or pretends so to think." As the wife of one of South Carolina's wealthiest planters, Chesnut's words carried the authority of experience. In referring to Harriet Beecher Stowe's *Uncle Tom's Cabin*, Chesnut wrote that the author "did not hit the sorest spot. She makes [Simon] Legree a bachelor."[31]

---

[29] Celestia Avery, *Georgia Narratives*, part 1, 26; Charlie King, *Georgia Narratives*, part 3, 16; Charlie Pye, *Georgia Narratives*, part 3, 187.

[30] Robert Ellett, in Perdue et al., *Weevils in the Wheat*, 84; William Craft, *Running a Thousand Miles for Freedom; or, The Escape of William and Ellen Craft from Slavery* (London: William Tweedie, 1860), 2; Harriet A. Jacobs, *Incidents in the Life of a Slave Girl*, edited by L. Maria Child (Boston: Published for the Author, 1861), 47–48. For a general treatment of enslaved women and the conditions they faced see Deborah Gray White, *Ar'n't I a Woman?: Female Slaves in the Plantation South* (New York: W. W. Norton, 1999).

[31] C. Vann Woodward, ed., *Mary Chesnut's Civil War* (New Haven, Conn.: Yale University Press, 1981), 29, 168.

"At that time it was a hard job to find a master that didn't have women among his slaves," recalled freedman Jacob Manson. "That was a general thing among the slave owners."[32] Even so, some enslaved women resisted to good effect. When a South Carolina overseer named Evans approached two women picking blackberries, he threatened to whip them if they refused his advances. As one of the women's sons later told the story,

they act like they going to indulge in the wickedness with that ole man. But when he took off his whip and some other garments, my Mammy and ole lady Lucy grab him by his goatee, *and further down,* and hist him over the middle of them black-berry bushes. With that they call me and John. Us grab all the buckets and us all put out for the "big house" fast as our legs could carry us. Ole man Evans just hollering and cussing down in them briars.

When they told their mistress what had happened, she fired Evans on the spot.[33]

An enslaved Maryland woman, taken to her owner's room to "satisfy his bestial nature," grabbed a knife and "sterilized" him. He died the next day. Fannie Berry of Virginia fought off her owner when he tried to rape her. "We tasseled and knocked over chairs and when I got a grip I scratched his face all to pieces; and there was no more bothering Fannie from him." But Fannie noted that her success was uncommon. "Honey, some slaves would be beat up so, when they resisted, and sometimes . . . the overseer would kill you. Us Colored women had to go through a plenty, I tell you."[34]

Their misery was compounded when pregnancy followed. But no matter who the father was, more children meant greater control. Not only did slaves fear for the safety of family members, there was the additional terror that they might be sold off at any time. As slaves well knew, a slaveholder's threat to sell spouses or children was not an idle one. One observer wrote that "such separations as these are quite common, and appear to be no more thought of, by those who enforce them, than the separation of a calf from its brute parent."[35]

The slaves' monetary value made threats of selling family members all the more menacing. A field hand might bring a thousand dollars. A skilled

---

[32] Jacob Manson, *North Carolina Narratives*, part 2, 97.

[33] Gus Feaster, *South Carolina Narratives*, part 2, 66. Italics added in quote.

[34] Richard Macks, *Maryland Narratives*, 53; Fannie Berry, *Virginia Narratives*, 2.

[35] James Silk Buckingham, *The Slave States of America* (London: Fisher, Son, and Co., 1842), 1: 249. The horrifying experience of being driven through the domestic slave trade system is related in Walter Johnson, *Soul by Soul: Life Inside the Antebellum Slave Market* (Cambridge: Harvard University Press, 2001), which examines the New Orleans slave market where at least 100,000 people were bought and sold.

slave brought much more. Even children commanded hefty sums. Jennie Kendricks remembered slave traders driving groups of children to market "the same as they would a herd of cattle."[36] Slaves constantly feared seeing their families put through such misery. That fear helped keep overt resistance in check. Slaves with families were also less likely to escape since that too would mean permanent separation from their loved ones. Of the many thousands who did escape bondage, most were young, single, and childless.

## CONTESTING NORTHERN SLAVERY

Those slaves who escaped north rarely found themselves welcomed. By mid-century, there were roughly a quarter-million blacks in the North, and most white northerners wanted no more. Although they opposed slavery's expansion into the western territories, hoping to keep the region free of blacks, they also tended to support slavery's continued existence in the South. Working-class whites feared job competition from migrating blacks should slavery ever end. Those fears were flamed by northern industrialists who encouraged white workers to view blacks already in the North, and not ill-treatment by management, as the source of their economic woes.[37]

Industrialists themselves generally supported slavery, fearing a sharp rise in the price of cotton should slavery ever end. Textile manufacturing was the North's leading industry, and cotton was by far the leading textile. Nearly all the North's moneyed families were invested to some extent in cotton. In 1835, participants in one of the largest assemblies ever held in Boston, led by some of the city's most prominent businessmen, pledged their complete support for slavery. They further expressed "regret and indignation" at abolitionist activity. Slavery kept blacks in the South and in the fields, just where most white northerners wanted them. On a visit to America, the English journalist Charles Mackay observed that "northern men, who talk so much of liberty, and of the political equality of all men, turn up their scornful noses at the slightest possibility of contact with an African."[38] As Mackay's observation suggests, the white North's unwelcoming attitude toward those escaping slavery had as much to do with

[36] Jennie Kendricks, *Georgia Narratives*, part 3, 1.

[37] For examples see Anthony Gronowicz, *Race and Class Politics in New York City Before the Civil War* (Boston: Northeastern University Press, 1998), xvi, 60–61.

[38] *Boston Morning Post* in *Washington Extra Globe Weekly*, September 4, 1835; Charles Mackay, *Life and Liberty in America* (London: Smith, Elder and Co., 1859), 2: 43. The financial ties between northern industrialists and southern planters are explored in

racism as economics. After his escape, Frederick Douglass lamented that "prejudice against color is stronger north than south. .... I have met it at every step the three years I have been out of southern slavery." An Indiana politician agreed: "Our people hate the Negro with a perfect if not a supreme hatred." That was why, as freedman Tom Hawkins explained, so many slaves "didn't run to no North ... 'cause them white folks up North was so mean to 'em."[39]

During the antebellum era, it was nearly as dangerous to openly oppose slavery in the North as in the South. Few white northerners called themselves abolitionists. Those who did risked their reputations and sometimes their lives. In the 1830s, William Lloyd Garrison and Elijah P. Lovejoy, leading members of the abolitionist press, learned that the hard way. After Garrison insisted on immediate freedom for enslaved Americans in his periodical, *The Liberator*, a mob assaulted him in the streets of Boston. He barely escaped with his life. Elijah Lovejoy was not so lucky. Proslavery thugs in Alton, Illinois, killed him and threw his printing press into the Ohio River. Prudence Crandall, a white teacher, nearly met the same fate when a mob attacked her school for "young Ladies and little Misses of color" in Canterbury, Connecticut.[40]

Blacks were special targets of anti-abolition violence. In July 1834, when abolitionists tried to convene in New York City, a mob broke up the meeting and went on a racist rampage. The crowd grew to several thousand, and rioting lasted for days. Soon after, there were riots in Buffalo and Palmyra; Newark, New Jersey; Norwich, Connecticut; and Columbia, Pennsylvania. There was rioting in Philadelphia as well, where white gangs roamed the streets "hunting the nigs." Philadelphia's Pennsylvania Hall was burned to the ground in 1838 following an antislavery meeting there. In 1843, Frederick Douglass had his right hand fractured when an Indiana mob shouting "Kill the nigger, kill the damn nigger!" attacked him as he tried to deliver an antislavery speech. His broken hand was improperly set, and he suffered from the injury for the rest of his life. Douglass was attacked

Anne Farrow, Joel Lang, and Jenifer Frank, *Complicity: How the North Promoted, Prolonged, and Profited from Slavery* (New York: Ballantine Books, 2005), 3–41.

[39] *Pennsylvania Freeman* (Philadelphia), October 20, 1841; George W. Julian, *Speeches on Political Questions* (New York: Hurd and Houghton, 1872), 127; Tom Hawkins, *Georgia Narratives*, part 2, 131.

[40] *Liberator* (Boston), November 7, 1835; *New York Evening Post*, November 20, 1837; *Philadelphia Public Ledger*, November 21, 1837; *Liberator*, August 3, 1833; *Newburyport (Mass.) Herald*, September 26, 1834. For various ways in which northern whites expressed hostility toward abolitionism see Farrow et al., *Complicity*, 155–77.

FIGURE 1.2. Southerners escaping slavery were rarely welcomed in the North. Their reception could be violent, even deadly. In 1834, New Yorkers broke up an abolitionist meeting and went on a rampage, killing dozens of blacks. Soon after, Philadelphia gangs roamed city streets "hunting the nigs." In 1843, Frederick Douglass, a fugitive from Maryland, had his right hand fractured when an Indiana mob attacked him as he tried to deliver an antislavery speech. Image from Frederick Douglass, *Life and Times of Frederick Douglass* (1882).

again in Harrisburg, Pennsylvania, where he confronted a crowd armed with brickbats and rotten eggs shouting "Out with the damned nigger."[41]

The law offered blacks little protection. Northern lawmen rarely intervened on behalf of blacks. Even when they did, convictions were rare. Most northern states forbade blacks to sit on juries. Several barred them

---

[41] *New York Evening Post*, July 8 and 10, 1834; *New York Spectator*, July 10 and 14, 1834; *New York Commercial Advertiser*, July 25, 1834; *Rochester Daily Advertiser* in *New York American*, August 19, 1834; *New York Emancipator*, August 12, 1834; *Washington (Penn.) Examiner*, August 2, 1834; *Columbia (Penn.) Spy* in *New York Evening Post*, August 27, 1834; *Philadelphia Inquirer*, August 2, October 16, 21, and 27, 1834; *Philadelphia National Gazette*, October 16, 1834; *Pennsylvania Freeman*, May 10, 1838; *Philadelphia Inquirer*, May 18 and 19, 1838; *Liberator*, October 13, 1843; *Liberator*, August 20, 1847. See also William S. McFeely, *Frederick Douglass* (New York: W. W. Norton, 1991), 108–12, 148. For the 1834 New York and Philadelphia riots see Linda K. Kerber, "Abolitionists and Amalgamators: The New York City Race Riots of 1834," *New York History* 48 (1967): 28–39, and John Runcie, "'Hunting the Nigs' in Philadelphia: The Race Riot of August 1834," *Pennsylvania History* 39 (1972): 187–218.

from testifying against whites. In only five northeastern states, where they were a tiny fraction of the population, could black men vote. Blacks regularly faced discrimination when seeking employment. They were almost everywhere denied access to public education. They were restricted in their use of public transportation and denied admission to hotels, restaurants, and theaters. In 1839, at a meeting of the literary and antislavery African Clarkson Association of New York City, Peter Paul Simons rose to complain that "northern freedom is nothing but a nickname for northern slavery."[42]

Simons was hardly exaggerating. As he spoke, there remained slaves held in the free states. Not until 1846 did New Jersey transfer its remaining 700 slaves to "lifetime apprentices," leaving them enslaved in all but name. Despite northern legislation dating back to the 1790s establishing gradual emancipation plans, most northern slaves were freed only by escape or death, and their children were released only after extended periods of indentured servitude or apprenticeship.[43]

The lot of blacks in the North had hardly improved by 1854. In October of that year, William Wells Brown, speaking before the Pennsylvania Anti-Slavery Society, stressed that although he had escaped slavery in the South, he felt "scarcely more free" than he had twenty years earlier working on his old master's plantation. He urged whites in the audience to fight not only against chattel slavery but also against the racial prejudice that underpinned the institution and infected whites even within the abolition movement. "Before you boast of your freedom and Christianity," he urged, "do your duty to your fellow-man."[44]

Prejudice was, in the words of black minister Theodore Wright, "the spirit of slavery." It was slavery's foundation and life force, corrupting

---

[42] *Colored American*, June 1, 1839. A valuable portrait of blacks in the antebellum North remains Leon F. Litwack, *North of Slavery: The Negro in the Free States, 1790–1860* (Chicago: University of Chicago Press, 1965).

[43] Graham Russell Hodges, *Freedom and Slavery in the Rural North: African Americans in Monmouth County, New Jersey, 1665–1865* (Madison, Wisc.: Madison House, 1997), 175; James Oliver Horton and Lois E. Horton, *In Hope of Liberty: Culture, Community, and Protest Among Northern Free Blacks, 1700–1860* (New York: Oxford University Press, 1998), 74. The earliest years of the American antislavery movement, mainly the 1770s to the 1830s, are chronicled in Richard S. Newman, *The Transformation of American Abolitionism: Fighting Slavery in the Early Republic* (Chapel Hill: University of North Carolina Press, 2001).

[44] *National Anti-Slavery Standard* (New York), November 4, 1854. Brown authored what became one of the most famous escape sagas of the age. See William W. Brown, *Narrative of William W. Brown, An American Slave* (London: Charles Gilpin, 1849).

whites North and South. For black activist J. Theodore Holly, prejudice was "the great bulwark of American slavery."[45] The Reverend Samuel Cornish, a black Presbyterian and founding member of the American Anti-Slavery Society, urged white abolitionists to combat not only slavery but prejudice as well, especially within themselves.

The time has come when the question has got to be met. When our friends must face it, if they are our friends; or do as some will, take to their heels and run. Prejudice against color, after all is the test question – at least among us. The mere and direct question of slavery is not. For every man here says – "I am as much opposed to slavery as you are. But as for these *Niggers*, we don't want them here – let them go home to their own land." This is what we hear, and this is the feeling. Here comes the tug; and here our friends have to grapple with slavery, not at arm's length, but with a back-hold. Here the slimy serpent is among them, coiled up in their own hearts and houses.

We see it, and have long seen it – the real battle ground between liberty and slavery is prejudice against color. The friends of humanity have as yet but possessed a few out-posts upon its frontiers. They have not yet undisputed possession of the field, even in their own hearts, as time will show: and we have been a little surprised that the phalanx of our friends [has] been so slow to see this.[46]

Black churches were a sustaining force in the fight against prejudice and slavery. Their ministers were leaders in the struggle. They supported abolitionist speakers, provided meeting places for abolitionist assemblies, and served as stations on the Underground Railroad. And they often did so on their own, with little or no support from white abolitionists. Although opposed to slavery, many white abolitionists also opposed equality for African Americans and even tried to limit their role in the antislavery movement. By the 1850s, disgusted blacks had abandoned the American Anti-Slavery Society, founded two decades earlier by both black and white abolitionists. In an 1855 editorial, James McCune Smith stressed that few blacks remained with the "old organization" because of racism among its white members. "The twain ought to be," Smith lamented, "but are not, one flesh."[47]

---

[45] *Utica (N.Y.) Friend of Man*, October 27, 1836; J. Theodore Holly, "Thoughts on Hayti," *Anglo-African Magazine* 1 (1859): 363.

[46] *Colored American*, June 9, 1838.

[47] *National Anti-Slavery Standard*, January 13, 1855; *Frederick Douglass' Paper* (Rochester, N.Y.), January 26, 1855. In *Frederick Douglass' Paper*, Smith signed his editorial "Communipaw," a pseudonym that he used regularly. A fine study of blacks in the antislavery movement remains Benjamin Quarles, *Black Abolitionists* (New York: Oxford University Press, 1969).

Smith was a leading light of the antislavery movement. He was the first university-trained African American to practice medicine in the United States, although no American university would accept him as a student. He earned his medical degree at Scotland's University of Glasgow, one of the finest medical schools of the day, where he graduated at the top of his class. When Smith returned to New York City, he went into private practice, served as physician at the Free Negro Orphan Asylum, and wrote extensive refutations of racist assumptions. He was a member of the American Anti-Slavery Society but became so incensed at the racism of white abolitionists that he, along with Frederick Douglass, founded the National Council of Colored People as a way to help blacks take control of their own destinies.[48]

The rift between white and black abolitionists was not entirely a racial one. Some white abolitionists, such as William Lloyd Garrison, fully supported equal rights for blacks. His differences with most black abolitionists were of a more philosophical nature. Garrison saw the U.S. Constitution as proslavery and called on free states to leave the Union. "No union with slaveholders" was a common Garrison mantra. Garrisonians also discouraged direct political activism, arguing that to support any party that supported the Constitution was to back a slave regime.

But for most black activists, the struggle against slavery and prejudice was more personal. How could northern blacks advocate political separation from the slave states, leaving nearly 4 million fellow blacks, many of them family members, in bondage? Furthermore, to stand aside from the political process seemed to blacks a self-defeating prospect. After all, it was not simply the end of chattel slavery that they wanted but equal rights as well, including the right to vote. For men like Douglass and Smith, laying claim to the Constitution and its language of liberty was the surest road to success. As Douglass put it:

The Constitution of the United States – inaugurated to "form a more perfect union, establish justice, insure domestic tranquility, provide for the common defense, promote the general welfare, and secure the blessings of liberty" – could not well have been designed at the same time to maintain and perpetuate a system of rapine and murder like slavery.[49]

---

[48] Thomas M. Morgan, "The Education and Medical Practice of Dr. James McCune Smith (1813–1865), First Black American to Hold a Medical Degree," *Journal of the National Medical Association* 95 (2003): 603–14.

[49] Frederick Douglass, *The Life and Times of Frederick Douglass* (Hartford, Conn.: Park Publishing, 1882), 323.

For blacks inclined toward political activism, it was not at all clear which party to back during the 1840s and early 1850s. Some sought to exert pressure from within the system, but neither of the two major parties, Whig nor Democrat, were antislavery in the least. Northern Democrats seemed actively supportive of slavery. Northern Whigs tried to avoid the question altogether. Freedom's best hope seemed to lie with the Liberty Party, founded in 1840 by black and white abolitionists as the nation's first antislavery organization dedicated to political activism. Prominent blacks such as Henry Highland Garnet and Samuel Ringgold Ward took leading roles as party organizers and stump speakers during the 1840 and 1844 presidential campaigns. In 1848, the New York state Liberty Party convention nominated Ward for a seat in the legislature.[50]

The year 1848 also saw the Free Soil Party founded. The United States had just taken upper Mexico after a two-year war of conquest, putting the question of slavery's expansion front and center. Mexico had abolished slavery years earlier. Would it now be reintroduced in the new U.S. territories? Northern splinter groups of both the Whigs and Democrats who trusted neither major party to resist slavery's spread reacted by forming the Free Soil Party. Although opposed to slavery's extension, the party was not antislavery. Some of its supporters were abolitionists, but many others backed the party not only as a means of keeping slavery out of the West but blacks as well. Even so, some Liberty Party men suggested casting their lot with the more broadly attractive Free Soilers. For most black abolitionists, to back a party that contained such a heavy racist element was too far a stretch. They tended to stand by the Liberty Party.[51]

The question of slavery in the new territories was pressing and divisive. For years, slaveholders had been demanding slavery's expansion, partly as a way to keep the three-fourths of southern whites who did not own slaves supporting slavery. There was only so much prime farm land in the South, and slaveholders held most of it. The noted southern commentator J. D. B. De Bow wrote in 1852, "The non-slaveholders possess generally but very small means, and the land which they possess is almost universally poor and so sterile that a scanty subsistence is all that can be derived from its cultivation."[52] Cut out of the South's dominant economic system and

---

[50] *Cortland (N.Y.) Democrat*, September 16, 1848, in C. Peter Ripley et al., eds., *The Black Abolitionist Papers* (Chapel Hill: University of North Carolina Press, 1985–1992), 4: 27–29.

[51] *Frederick Douglass' Paper*, September 25, 1851. See also Frederick J. Blue, *The Free Soilers: Third Party Politics, 1848–1854* (Urbana: University of Illinois Press, 1973).

[52] J. D. B. De Bow, *The Industrial Resources, Etc. of the Southern and Western States* (New Orleans: Offices of *De Bow's Review*, 1852), 2: 108.

denied opportunities to acquire good land, continued support for slavery among nonslaveholding whites was hardly certain.[53]

Increasing slave resistance also led slaveholders to push hard for expansion. Some did so as part of a wider demand for slavery's security, others as a means of giving slaves less free territory into which they might escape. Slave escapes – distant and local, temporary and permanent – were on the rise throughout the late antebellum period, reaching perhaps 50,000 annually during the 1850s. Should that trend continue, slavery might inevitably be doomed. To slaveholders, it was clear that slavery must expand or die.[54]

Northerners were just as firm in their opposition to slavery's expansion. Although most white northerners had few qualms about slavery where it existed, they were determined to keep slavery confined to the South. Industrialists viewed the West as a region ripe for exploitation of natural resources. Working folk saw in the West a chance to escape their dismal urban lives. Neither group wanted to compete with slaveholders for western lands. Nor did they want to live among blacks. A major reason the white North moved to abolish slavery after the Revolution was to limit the growth of its black population. And so it did. Between 1790 and 1860, blacks as a percentage of population dropped in every northern state except New Hampshire, where the 1860 black population was only 0.15 percent.[55]

---

[53] The most complete and reasoned expression of why white southerners should have opposed slavery was written by a native North Carolinian, Hinton Rowan Helper, in *The Impending Crisis of the South* (New York: Burdick Brothers, 1857). The book sent shockwaves of dread through slaveholding ranks, becoming what historian James Oakes called, "the most important single book, in terms of its political impact, that has ever been published in the United States. Even more perhaps than *Uncle Tom's Cabin*, it fed the fires of sectional controversy leading up to the Civil War." See Oakes, *Slavery and Freedom*, 76.

[54] Franklin and Schweninger, "Quest for Freedom," 38. Slaveholders did not limit their expansion demands to territories controlled by the United States. "I want Cuba," insisted Senator Albert Gallatin Brown of Mississippi in 1858. "I want Tamaulipas, Potosi, and one or two other Mexican states; and I want them all for the same reason – for the planting or spreading of slavery. And a footing in Central America will powerfully aid us in acquiring those other States. ... Yes, I want these Countries for the spread of slavery. I would spread the blessings of slavery, like the religion of our Divine Master, to the uttermost ends of the earth." See M. W. Cluskey, ed., *Speeches, Messages, and Other Writings of the Hon. Albert G. Brown* (Philadelphia: Smith and Co., 1859), 595. The best study of efforts to expand slavery south is Robert E. May, *The Southern Dream of a Caribbean Empire, 1854–1861* (Gainesville: University Press of Florida, 2002).

[55] Karen Wilson, "Safety in the Briar Patch: Enslaved Communities in the Nineteenth-Century United States," in Haggard, *African Americans in the Nineteenth Century*, 50.

Northern efforts to keep blacks at a distance were threatened by slave-holder insistence on slavery's expansion. U.S. Senator Albert G. Brown of Mississippi suggested expanding slavery even to the North.[56] Although few northerners took the threat seriously in an immediate sense, some feared that if slavery could expand anywhere, it might eventually move northward too.

The controversy over slavery's expansion had been brewing for decades. Congress reached a temporary settlement in 1820 with the Missouri Compromise. Missouri was admitted to the Union as a slave state and Maine as a free state, thus preserving the balance of free and slave states in the Senate. More significantly, a line extending westward from Missouri's southern border established a dividing line between slavery and freedom. All future states created north of the line would be free. Those south of the line would be slave. That settled the issue as far as the federal government was concerned. There was even a "gag rule" forbidding any official discussion of slavery in Congress. But as the aggressively expansive United States pushed its way to the Pacific Ocean, politicians could not ignore slavery for long.

The issue again came to a head in 1848 after the Mexican War. During the presidential campaign that year, Whigs ignored slavery, Democrats favored compromise, and Free Soilers stood against slavery's expansion, garnering more than 10 percent of the popular vote. The Liberty Party opposed both slavery's expansion and slavery itself, but barely made a showing.[57]

The successful Whig candidate, General Zachary Taylor, although elected on an evasive platform, found slavery impossible to ignore. California, part of the "Mexican Cession," asked for admission to the Union as a free state in 1849. The next year, it gained statehood under the Compromise of 1850. Although enslaving Indians was common in California, blacks were effectively kept out, and the free states now had a two-seat advantage in the U.S. Senate.[58] As compensation to slaveholders, Congress passed a Fugitive Slave Act mandating the return of slaves who escaped north. As for the remaining areas of what had been upper Mexico, "popular sovereignty" would prevail. Voters in both the New Mexico and Utah territories,

---

[56] Cluskey, *Speeches, Messages, and Other Writings of the Hon. Albert G. Brown*, 595.

[57] For Liberty Party efforts through 1848 see Rienhard O. Johnson, *The Liberty Party, 1840–1848: Anti-Slavery Third Party Politics in the United States* (Baton Rouge: Louisiana State University Press, 2009).

[58] For a brief description of Indian slavery in California see Alvin M. Josephy, *500 Nations: An Illustrated History of North American Indians* (New York: Alfred A. Knopf, 1994), 347.

encompassing the modern states of New Mexico, Arizona, Nevada, Utah, and Colorado, would make the decision on slavery themselves.

For blacks, the most worrisome aspect of the compromise was the Fugitive Slave Act. Slaves escaping northward now had to reach Canada for safety. Blacks already in the North were at increased risk. For decades, professional slavecatchers, many of them northerners, had been kidnapping free blacks into slavery. Solomon Northup of New York was taken in 1841 and spent more than a decade enslaved on a Louisiana plantation before getting word to his family. He was finally released and wrote of his experience in *Twelve Years a Slave*.[59] Most other kidnap victims were not so fortunate. With open season now declared on fugitive slaves and free blacks generally, slavecatchers were more active than ever. A young girl named Viny Frazier was snatched on her way to school and carried to Mississippi. Her family never saw her again. Charlie and Anna Dorsey were bound, gagged, and carried on a ship that took them to slavery in Florida. There they remained for the rest of their lives.[60]

### PREPARING TO MEET THE CRISIS

The Fugitive Slave Act galvanized northern blacks. It was the immediate threat and the focus of resistance, including violent resistance, throughout the 1850s. The question of whether to resist slavery with violence had been a point of debate among black abolitionists for decades. To some it seemed self-defeating, even suicidal. David Walker of Boston, in his 1829 *Appeal to the Coloured Citizens of the World*, had called for resistance by whatever means. The next year he was found dead at his door, likely poisoned by an unknown assassin. At the 1843 National Convention of Colored Citizens, in his "Address to the Slaves," Henry Highland Garnet encouraged enslaved blacks to "die freemen" rather than "live to be slaves." But Frederick Douglass opposed Garnet's call to violence, and convention members refused to adopt Garnet's views as representing their own.[61]

---

[59] Solomon Northup, *Twelve Years a Slave* (Auburn, N.Y.: Derby and Miller, 1853). For a discussion of the northern kidnapping business see Farrow et al., *Complicity*, 139–53.

[60] Rosanna Frazier, *Texas Narratives*, part 2, 63; Douglas Dorsey, *Florida Narratives*, 93. For an overview see Stanley W. Campbell, *The Slave Catchers: Enforcement of the Fugitive Slave Law, 1850–1860* (Chapel Hill: University of North Carolina Press, 1970).

[61] See Henry Highland Garnet, *Walker's Appeal, with a Brief Sketch of His Life, and also Garnet's Address to the Slaves of the United States of America* (New York: J. H. Tobitt, 1848).

The mood among northern blacks began to change in 1850. Ministers who had counseled peace and patience turned to scripture in supporting opposition to the Fugitive Slave Act by whatever means. Former slave and New York Congregational minister Samuel Ringgold Ward, speaking at a rally in Boston, told the crowd that "if the fugitive slave is traced to our part of New York State, he shall have the law of Almighty God to protect him, the law which says, 'Thou shalt not return to the master the servant that is escaped unto thee, but he shall dwell with thee in thy gates, where it liketh him best.'" William P. Newman – escaped freeman, former student at Oberlin College, and Baptist minister – renounced his Christian pacifism and declared his "fixed and changeless purpose to kill any so-called man who attempts to enslave me or mine." Frederick Douglass fully agreed. "Every slave-hunter who meets a bloody death in his infernal business, is an argument in favor of the manhood of our race."[62]

It was the same all over the North. Martin Delany, an early proponent of black nationalism, told a crowd at Allegheny City, Pennsylvania:

My house is my castle; in that castle are none but my wife and children, as free as the angels of heaven, and whose liberty is as sacred as the pillars of God. If any man approaches that house in search of a slave, – I care not who he may be, whether constable or sheriff, magistrate or even judge of the Supreme Court . . . if he crosses the threshold of my door, and I do not lay him a lifeless corpse at my feet, I hope the grave may refuse my body a resting place and righteous Heaven my spirit a home. O, no! he cannot enter that house and we both live.[63]

In Syracuse, the formerly enslaved Reverend Jermain Loguen railed against the Fugitive Slave Act. "I don't respect this law – I don't fear it – I won't obey it! It outlaws me, and I outlaw it. . . . If force is employed to re-enslave me, I shall make preparations to meet the crisis as becomes a man." Loguen called for collective resistance too, urging his audience to "stand by me . . . for your freedom and honor are involved as well as mine." Philadelphia blacks vowed "to resist this law at any cost and at all hazards." Blacks in New York promised not to allow any "blood-thirsty slaveholder" to lay hands on them "without resisting, even if need be, unto death." A meeting of Boston blacks resolved to resist the Fugitive Slave Act "at every hazard." J. B. Smith, himself a fugitive slave, urged the

---

[62] *Liberator*, April 5, 1850; *North Star* (Rochester, N.Y.), October 24, 1850; *Frederick Douglass' Paper*, June 2, 1854.

[63] Frank A. Rollin, *Life and Public Services of Martin R. Delany* (Boston: Lee and Shepard, 1868), 76.

crowd never to leave their homes unarmed "and on the head of the slave dealer be the consequences."[64]

Black men in Milwaukee, many of them fugitives, pledged protection to each other and to their escaping brethren. At a meeting in Columbus, Ohio, city blacks formed a standing "vigilant committee" and advised all "colored citizens to go continually prepared, that they may be ready at any moment to offer defence in behalf of their liberty." Blacks in Worcester, Massachusetts, determined to "brave all consequences" rather than yield themselves or any fugitive to the "threatenings of slave-drivers and women-whippers of the South, and their Northern allies."[65]

In 1855, black Bostonians petitioned the governor for weapons to arm a new militia company. When he denied their request, they armed themselves and formed the Massasoit Guards, under command of attorney Robert Morris. At an 1858 meeting of Massachusetts blacks in New Bedford, Morris promised help should anyone have trouble with slavecatchers. "You telegraph us in Boston, and we'll come down three hundred strong."[66]

The business of slavecatching became ever more dangerous as blacks organized to protect themselves. Stealth was critical for a capture to succeed. "If you want to arouse our latent manhood, and see a grand development of moral courage in opposition to public sentiment and unjust laws," thundered black abolitionist T. Morris Chester, "let it be announced that a fugitive slave is arrested by the revolting vampires who exist by sucking our blood, and you will witness a magnificent gathering together of the Afro-Americans in their physical strength."[67] Time and again, such scenes as Chester warned of played out whenever the alarm was raised. Slavecatchers, and sometimes any law officers who dared to assist them, were run down, beaten, and deprived of their captives. Many slavecatchers were fortunate to avoid being killed. Some were not so fortunate.

In September 1851, several men escaped from Maryland slaveholder William Gorsuch and headed for Pennsylvania. They sought refuge on William Parker's Lancaster County farm, not far from Christiana. Parker

---

[64] J. W. Loguen, *The Rev. J. W. Loguen as a Slave and as a Freeman* (Syracuse, N.Y.: J. G. K. Truair, 1859), 393–94; *Liberator*, November 8, 1850; *North Star*, October 24, 1850; *Boston Emancipator and Republican*, October 10, 1850.

[65] *Milwaukee Daily Sentinel and Gazette*, October 11, 1850; *Columbus Daily Ohio Statesman*, October 15, 1850; *Worcester Massachusetts Spy*, October 9, 1850.

[66] *Boston Herald*, August 25, 1855; *Boston Semi-Weekly Courier*, August 27, 1855; *Liberator*, September 14, 1855; *Liberator*, August 13, 1858.

[67] Richard Newman, Patrick Rael, and Philip Lapsansky, eds., *Pamphlets of Protest: An Anthology of Early African-American Protest Literature, 1790–1860* (New York: Routledge, 2001), 307.

FIGURE 1.3. Slaveholders had a difficult time retrieving their "property" despite the 1850 Fugitive Slave Act. Northern blacks responded to the act by forming unofficial militias and self-protection societies. In 1851, members of the Lancaster Black Self-Protection Society in Pennsylvania killed Maryland slaveholder William Gorsuch and wounded others in his party when they tried to take three fugitives by force. Image from William Still, *The Underground Railroad* (1872).

was a farmer, former slave, and founding member of the Lancaster Black Self-Protection Society. He and other society members had already thwarted several attempts to reenslave escaping blacks. Within a few days, Gorsuch, backed by perhaps half a dozen armed men and a federal deputy marshal from Philadelphia, arrived at the Parker farm to claim his slaves. Members of the Self-Protection Society were there as well. One of the men yelled to Gorsuch, "You had better go away if you don't want to get hurt." Gorsuch responded with a pistol shot. Society members returned fire and rushed the Gorsuch party. Within seconds, Gorsuch lay dead, his son was wounded, and the rest of his companions had scattered. Parker, along with his wife, fled to Canada to avoid arrest. But local officials arrested more than two dozen others and charged them with treason, riot, and murder. The effort was useless. The jury refused to convict them. Some of the jurymen later admitted that they had made up their minds to acquit before the defense even presented its case.[68]

Although a few jurors may have sympathized with the accused, such acquittals largely reflected a growing sentiment among northern whites that the Fugitive Slave Act was turning their towns and cities into battlegrounds over slavery. Some of the Christiana jurors surely hoped to send the message to slaveholders, slavecatchers, and kidnappers that they

[68] William Still, *The Underground Rail Road* (Philadelphia: Porter and Coates, 1872), 348–68; W. U. Hensel, *The Christiana Riot and Treason Trials of 1851* (Lancaster, Penn.: New Era Printing, 1911), 90. See also Thomas P. Slaughter, *Bloody Dawn: The Christiana Riot and Racial Violence in the Antebellum North* (New York: Oxford University Press, 1991).

were unwelcome. They would receive no sympathy should they be maimed or killed trying to kidnap free blacks or capture fugitives.

Such attitudes were reflected in more than sentiment. Northern states had long tried to keep the struggle over slavery beyond their borders, some by enacting personal liberty laws designed to discourage slaveholders and slavecatchers from entering their states. Pennsylvania went so far as to declare that slaves brought into the state could legally claim freedom. Such laws prevented state officials from assisting bounty hunters, forbade the use of state jails in confining captured fugitives, and provided trial by jury and the right of appeal for accused fugitives. Personal liberty laws were not always enforced, but they sent a clear signal to slaveholders and slavecatchers that northerners wanted no part of the trouble they brought.

Nor did they want more blacks in their states, likely as they were to attract slavecatchers and kidnappers. Although northern blacks accounted for barely 1 percent of the total population, that was enough for most whites. Legal restrictions and economic discrimination had for decades made it clear that blacks were unwelcome. To stress the point, during the 1850s Indiana, Illinois, and Iowa made it illegal for blacks to settle there. Other states kept blacks out by requiring proof of freedom and posting bonds to guarantee "good behavior." One Ohio congressman insisted that his state would never allow blacks to immigrate with or without a law forbidding it. "Three hundred thousand freemen of Ohio would line the banks of the Ohio river to receive them on the points of their bayonets." It was hardly an idle threat. When a group of nearly 400 free blacks from Virginia tried to settle in southern Ohio, locals quickly drove them out.[69]

That white northerners wanted blacks and slavery confined to the South was patently clear. It was not clear enough, however, to northern congressional leaders, who greatly underestimated the fears northerners held about the potential for slavery's spread. The depth of those fears became apparent after Congress passed the Kansas-Nebraska Act in 1854. In exchange for southern votes favoring organization of these territories, through which northerners hoped to build the first transcontinental railroad, they were opened to the possibility of slavery under popular sovereignty. Nebraska and Kansas both lay north of the old Missouri Compromise line, which for more than three decades had barred slavery from the area. But northern congressmen wanted their railroad, and they needed southern

---

[69] *Congressional Globe*, Thirty-first Congress, First Session (1850), Appendix, part 1, 241; *Cleveland Daily Plain Dealer*, July 13, 1846; *St. Mary's (Ohio) Sentinel* in *Liberator*, August 7, 1846.

votes to get it. Repealing the Missouri Compromise was the price for those votes. It seemed at the time a small price to pay. Most northern legislators were certain that there was no real danger of either territory becoming a slave state since the region was suited neither to large-scale cotton nor tobacco cultivation.[70]

But Kansas was just west of Missouri, a slave state. That alone was enough to concern most northerners. Free Soilers and abolitionists rushed settlers into Kansas. Proslavery men did the same. During elections for the legislature, thousands of "border ruffians" crossed over from Missouri to vote, giving the proslavery faction a victory. The territorial governor called the election a fraud but let the results stand anyway. The new proslavery legislature quickly expelled its few antislavery members and proposed a state constitution allowing slavery. Under the new government, to question slavery's legality was a felony. To aid or encourage an escaping slave was a capital offense. Antislavery men responded by forming their own competing government and drafting a constitution that excluded both slavery and free blacks from the territory.

The controversy was by no means limited to political bickering. A proslavery raid on the town of Lawrence left one man dead. In retaliation, an antislavery band led by John Brown, later of Harpers Ferry fame, killed five proslavery men along Pottawatomie Creek. Violence spread quickly. By the end of 1856, more than 200 people were dead.[71]

Bloodshed in Kansas further polarized the politics of slavery's expansion. It drove a firm wedge between the Democratic Party's northern and southern wings. It destroyed the Whigs as a national party. And it gave rise to a new political force, the Republican Party, dedicated to keeping slavery out of the territories. Republicans ran their first presidential candidate, Georgia-born John C. Frémont, in 1856. He lost to Democrat James Buchanan of Pennsylvania, but Republicans established a firm sectional base by capturing all but five of the free states.[72]

---

[70] For an excellent overview of the rising sectional controversy from the end of the Mexican War through secession see John Ashworth, *The Republic in Crisis, 1848–1861* (Cambridge: Cambridge University Press, 2012).

[71] For an overview of the Kansas issue and its national implications see James A. Rawley, *Race and Politics: Bleeding Kansas and the Coming of the Civil War* (Lincoln: University of Nebraska Press, 1979), and Paul Wallace Gates, *Fifty Million Acres: Conflicts Over Kansas Land Policy* (Norman: University of Oklahoma Press, 1997). Kansas was not admitted to the Union until 1861 after most of the slave states had seceded.

[72] Popular sovereignty's inherent shortcomings are explored in Christopher Childers, *The Failure of Popular Sovereignty: Slavery, Manifest Destiny, and the Radicalization of Southern Politics* (Lawrence: University Press of Kansas, 2012).

Although Democrats won largely on a racist platform, calling their rivals "Black Republicans" at nearly every turn, Republicans appealed to racism as well. In a speech at the 1858 Republican national convention, Senator Lyman Trumbull of Illinois assured voters that the new party was "a white man's party. . . . We wish to settle the Territories with free, white men. . . . It is better that [blacks] should not be among us."[73] A vote for Democrats, said Republicans, was a vote for blacks and slavery in the territories. Republicans promised to keep the territories free of both and to give free western land to free white men. For most white abolitionists, that platform was enough to ally them with Republicans.

Black abolitionists found the alliance harder to stomach. Many refused to support men whose distaste for slavery was limited by geography. In June 1855, black leaders such as Frederick Douglass, along with several white abolitionists, Gerrit Smith and John Brown among them, met in Syracuse, New York, and helped form the Radical Abolition Party as successor to the defunct Liberty Party. Even so, there were black leaders who saw Republicans as the more practical alternative. William J. Watkins – free-born Bostonian, abolitionist speaker, and Underground Railroad activist – saw Republicans as the best hope for at least limiting slavery. Such pragmatism seemed justified after the Radical Abolitionists garnered few votes in the 1856 presidential race.

Still, for some black activists, going Republican was going too far. Henry Highland Garnet was "deeply grieved" when a Colored Men's State Suffrage Convention at Troy, New York, backed the Republican candidate for governor in 1858. Garnet was astonished that black men could be "so blind to their best interests." He and other black leaders supported white abolitionist Gerrit Smith, former Liberty Party presidential candidate and supporter of full social and political equality for blacks, on the Radical Abolition ticket. Smith received only 5,000 votes.[74]

Equal rights supporters, Radical or not, were used to such disappointments. The previous year, they had suffered a devastating blow when the U.S. Supreme Court attempted to settle the slavery question once and for all with its *Dred Scott v. Sandford* decision. The only issue at hand had been whether Scott's temporary residence in free territory had made him a

---

[73] "Great Speech of Senator Trumbull," in *Facts for the People* (Springfield, Ill.: Daily Journal Office, 1860), 12.

[74] For letters that reflect this division see Henry Highland Garnet and James W. Duffin to Gerrit Smith, September 16, 1858, and William J. Watkins to Gerrit Smith, September 27, 1858, Gerrit Smith Papers, Syracuse University, in Ripley et al., *Black Abolitionist Papers*, 4: 398–402.

free man. The southern-dominated court ruled that it did not, but the justices went further than that. By a seven-to-two margin, they denied Scott, or any black, the right to sue in federal court. Blacks could not be U.S. citizens, they said, because the founders, when they drafted the Constitution, had not intended them to be so. Black folk, said Chief Justice Roger Taney, had no rights that whites were bound to respect. Dissenting Justice John McLean reminded his colleagues that blacks held voting rights, and hence citizenship, in ten of the thirteen states in 1789 when the Constitution was ratified, although five of those ten states later revoked or restricted black voting. Still, the notion that blacks could not be citizens was, said McLean, "more a matter of taste than of law."[75]

McLean further insisted that, by the majority's reasoning, the Court had no authority in the case at all. If Scott was not a U.S. citizen and had no access to the federal courts, then the Supreme Court had no jurisdiction. Nevertheless, hoping to lay the issue of slavery's expansion to rest, the majority cited the Fifth Amendment, which stated in part, "No person shall ... be deprived of life, liberty, or property without due process of law." Slaves were not persons but property, claimed the majority, and could not be barred from the territories. By implication, slaveholders could not be barred from taking their "property" anywhere the Constitution held force, including the free states.[76]

Ironically, the *Dred Scott* decision was a tremendous boost to the Republican Party. It pushed more northern whites into the Republican camp, and that push brought a Republican majority to the U.S. House of Representatives with the 1858 mid-term elections. Republicans were riding high on the expectation that their next presidential nominee, whomever he might be, would almost assuredly win enough of the more populous free states to become president.

For most blacks, even black Republicans, it was hard to see anything positive in the *Dred Scott* outcome. Paraphrasing Roger Taney, a gathering of New York blacks declared the ruling "a foul and infamous lie which neither black men nor white men are bound to respect." Respected or not, it was the law of the land, and blacks held little hope for positive change in the near future. William Still, a son of former slaves and chief organizer of

---

[75] Stephen K. Williams, comp., *Reports of Cases Argued and Decided in the Supreme Court of the United States*, Book 15, Lawyer's Edition (Rochester, N.Y.: Lawyer's Cooperative Publishing Company, 1884), 754.

[76] For an overview of *Dred Scott* and its impact see Don E. Fehrenbacher, *The Dred Scott Case: Its Significance in Law and Politics* (New York: Oxford University Press, 1978).

the Underground Railroad in Philadelphia, wrote that blacks in his city felt either "hopelessly doomed" or saw only a "faint prospect" that their legal status would ever improve. Charles Lenox Remond, a black Bostonian and tireless antislavery orator, nearly gave up on the United States ever becoming a true land of liberty. "We owe no allegiance to a country which grinds us under its iron hoof and treats us like dogs," Remond told a gathering at Israel Church in Philadelphia. "The time has gone by for colored people to talk of patriotism."[77]

A few black leaders even suggested that it might be time for blacks to leave the country. In the fall of 1858, Henry Highland Garnet founded the African Civilization Society to help blacks immigrate to Africa. Few took Garnet up on his offer. The great majority of African Americans had never sought immigration to any foreign land. Whatever the United States was, it was still home. But in the wake of *Dred Scott*, it seemed an increasingly hostile home.[78]

MORE CASES OF INSUBORDINATION THAN EVER

If despondency was on the rise, so was resistance. Across the North, blacks stepped up efforts to form unofficial militias, neighborhood patrols, and other self-protection societies. But it was in the South that rising resistance stoked slaveholder fears and pressed the slavery issue to a breaking point. "It is useless to disguise the fact, its truth is undeniable," wrote a Virginia newspaper editor in 1852, "that a greater degree of insubordination has been manifested by the negro population, within the last few months, than at any previous period in our history." A year later, one observer noticed that newspapers throughout the South were reporting "complaints of growing insolence and insubordination among the negroes." A South Carolina editor complained of having "seen the deadly rifle in the hands of blacks in the District, and expertness exhibited in its use that would not dishonor the famous Kentucky marksman." He called on authorities to clamp down on such dangerous conduct.[79]

Reports of rising resistance, up to and including murder, became more and more common throughout the 1850s. A Missouri slave stabbed his

[77] Ripley et al., *Black Abolitionist Papers*, 4: 391, 362; *Liberator*, April 10, 1857.
[78] Circular by the African Civilization Society, February 16, 1859, Gerrit Smith Papers, in Ripley et al., *Black Abolitionist Papers*, 5: 3–6.
[79] *Fredericksburg (Va.) Herald* in *Pennsylvania Freeman*, August 7, 1852; Olmsted, *A Journey in the Seaboard Slave States*, 29; *Spartanburg (S.C.) Spartan* in *Liberator*, June 26, 1857.

owner to death in 1853 and escaped to Canada. In 1855, another slave from Missouri slashed his owner nearly in half and fled to Iowa. An Alabama bondsman killed his owner and boasted of the murder. A Georgia slave named Lash, after some "rough handling," murdered his owner. A Florida woman chopped her overseer's head off with a hoe. In Maryland, a slave killed his owner with a knife, took flight, and was never seen again. After seeing his sister whipped, a Kentucky slave beat the overseer to death with a club and escaped on the Underground Railroad.[80]

In July 1859, *The Liberator* reported a rash of violence occurring in the spring and early summer. A slave near Grand Cone, Texas, bashed his owner's brains out with an axe, then burned the body. Another slave in Union County, Kentucky, used an axe to kill an overseer who was trying to

FIGURE 1.4. Enslaved people resisted bondage in many subtle and overt ways, becoming increasingly violent in the late antebellum era. Nat Turner's 1831 revolt saw more than fifty whites killed. More common were individual acts of violence, which were epidemic by the 1850s. One slave-state newspaper reported in 1859 that stabbing, clubbing, and death by the axe were "alarmingly frequent." Image from Samuel Warner, *Authentic and Impartial Narrative of the Tragical Scene Which Was Witnessed in Southampton County* (1831).

[80] *St. Louis Sunday Morning Republican*, October 2, 1853; Henry Clay Bruce, *The New Man: Twenty-Nine Years a Slave, Twenty-Nine Years a Free Man* (York, Penn.: Anstadt and Sons, 1895), 34–36; Martha Bradley, *Alabama Narratives*, 47; Jennie Kendricks, *Georgia Narratives*, part 3, 5; Irene Coates, *Florida Narratives*, 76; Richard Macks, *Maryland Narratives*, 55; Un-named narrator, *Kentucky Narratives*, 71. James Patrick Morgans identifies the Missouri slave as John Anderson, who eventually immigrated to Liberia. See Morgans, *The Underground Railroad on the Western Frontier* (Jefferson, N.C.: McFarland, 2010), 66–67, 203 nn. 8–15. See also Patrick Brode, *The Odyssey of John Anderson* (Toronto: University of Toronto Press, 1989).

whip him. A slaveholder in Spencer County, Kentucky, was clubbed to death after whipping two of his slaves. In Lincoln County, Missouri, an enslaved man stabbed his owner to death. An Arkansas slave crept up behind his overseer and laid on with an axe, "the blade entering the brain up to the handle, splitting the head entirely open." Commenting on one murder, a St. Louis paper remarked that reports of slaves killing whites had become "alarmingly frequent."[81]

Collective resistance was also becoming more frequent. In 1856, a North Carolina posse succeeded only in getting one of its number killed when it attacked a settlement of black escapees hiding in Big Swamp. That same year, Governor Henry Wise of Virginia moved arms into Alexandria to head off a feared insurrection. Thirty-two slaves were arrested. In Tennessee, more than sixty slaves belonging to Senator John Bell were implicated in a rebellion conspiracy. Nine were hanged – four by court order, five by a lynch mob. In Dover, Tennessee, six slaves were hanged and one was whipped to death on accusations of plotting insurrection. The incident stoked rebellion rumors throughout Stewart County, Tennessee, and neighboring Christian County, Kentucky. A newspaper editor in Galveston, Texas, wrote in 1856 that "never has there been a time in our recollection when so many insurrections, or attempts at insurrection, have transpired in rapid succession as during the past six months." In December, Georgia's *Albany Patriot* called for more slave patrols and warned that "citizens should always have their arms ready for service."[82]

In 1857, a group of Carter County, Kentucky, slaves were tried on suspicion of plotting insurrection. One was burned to death for refusing to confess. February 1858 saw a "fearful insurrection" in Arkansas. Blacks were said to have attacked two settlements and killed twenty-three whites. A newspaper editor in Franklin, Louisiana, reporting the murders of two slaveholders by their own slaves, noted that there were "more cases of insubordination among the negro population ... than ever known before." In August, more than fifty slaves on a Mississippi plantation declared that "they would die to a man before one of their party should be whipped." It took seventy-five armed whites to put down the resistance.[83]

---

[81] *Liberator*, July 8, 1859.

[82] *Wilmington (N.C.) Daily Journal*, August 14, 1856; *New York Tribune*, December 16, 1856; *Boston Herald*, December 17, 1856; *New York Tribune*, December 17, 1856; *Canton (Ky.) Dispatch* in *Philadelphia Public Ledger*, January 2, 1857; *Galveston News* in *Clarksville (Tex.) Standard*, January 17, 1857; *Albany (Ga.) Patriot*, December 25, 1856.

[83] *Liberator*, January 23, 1857, and February 12, 1858; *Franklin (La.) Sun* in *Liberator*, January 29, 1858; *Coffeeville (Miss.) Intelligencer* in *Washington National Era*, August 26, 1858.

Rebellion of another kind rocked the nation in October 1859 when John Brown and twenty other abolitionists tried to seize the federal arsenal at Harpers Ferry, Virginia, and arm local slaves. The effort failed, and a Virginia court sentenced Brown to hang for treason. Several of Brown's compatriots were killed in the raid, among them a former Virginia slave named Dangerfield Newby. Found in his vest pocket were letters from his wife, enslaved in Prince William County, Virginia, just forty miles from Harpers Ferry. The last, dated August 16, 1859, brought urgent and disturbing news.

*Dear Husband*,

your kind letter came duly to hand and it gave me much pleasure . . . I want you to buy me as soon as possible for if you do not get me somebody else will . . . it is said Master is in want of monney if so, I know not what time he may sell me an then all my bright hops of the futer are blasted for there has ben one bright hope to cheer me in all my troubles that is to be with you for if I thought I shoul never see you this earth would have no charms for me . . . I want to see you so much the Children are all well the baby cannot walk yet . . . you mus write soon and say when you think you Can Come.

Your affectionate Wife

HARRIET NEWBY

Newby attempted to buy his family and initially worked out a deal. But the owner reneged and bumped the purchase price out of Newby's reach. In desperation, he had tried to rescue his wife and children.[84]

Four other blacks were with Brown on the raid. Osborne Anderson, a fugitive slave, escaped and fled to Canada. Lewis Leary of Oberlin, Ohio, died during the raid. Shields Green and John Copeland Jr., both also of Oberlin, were captured and sentenced to hang. Shortly before his execution, Copeland wrote to his family:

Dear Parents,

my fate so far as man can seal it, is sealed, but let not this fact occasion you any misery; for remember the *cause* in which I was engaged; *remember it was a holy cause*, one in which men in every way better than I am, have suffered & died. Remember that if I must die, I die in trying to liberate a few of my poor and oppressed people from a condition of servitude against

---

[84] *Governor's Message and Reports of the Public Officers of the State* (Richmond, Va.: William F. Ritchie, 1859), 116–17.

which God in his word has hurled his most bitter denunciations. ... I am content ... I beg of you not to grieve about me. ... meet me in heaven. I remain your most affectionate son,

JOHN A. COPELAND[85]

If Harpers Ferry gave abolitionists martyrs for their cause, it gave the South's secessionist "fire-eaters" something just as valuable. After *Dred Scott* and its resulting political realignments, they knew that the next president would likely be a Republican. In that event, they were prepared to take the South out of the Union. But secessionists in the South, like abolitionists in the North, were a small minority. To build support for their cause, fire-eaters tried to paint all northerners, especially Republicans, as violent abolitionists bent on ending slavery by inciting rebellion. In the aftermath of Brown's raid, they easily played on southern whites' fears of northern-backed slave revolt. Fire-eaters pointed to Brown's black allies and described them as organized and led by "blatant freedom shriekers." There was more to come, they warned. The whole South was infested with "agents of the Black Republican Party."[86]

Although slaveholders tried to suppress the news among their slaves, word of events at Harpers Ferry quickly traveled along what Booker T. Washington later called "the 'grape-vine' telegraph." "It was impossible to keep the news of John Brown's attack on Harpers Ferry from spreading," recalled former slave George Albright of Mississippi.[87] That news was certainly welcome. Whether it spurred more resistance than there might otherwise have been is an open question, but certainly the tide of resistance that had long been rising continued to swell in the winter of 1859–60.

Fires that swept through cotton warehouses and gin presses were blamed on blacks and northern abolition agents. In November, fire destroyed six-thousand dollars' worth of corn, fodder, and cotton on one Georgia plantation. Another fire razed a gin house two miles from Columbus. A local newspaper called it "Kansas work in Georgia." There was Kansas work in Virginia too. In the Berryville neighborhood, authorities charged two slaves

---

[85] John A. Copeland Jr. to John A. Copeland Sr. and Delilah Copeland, November 26, 1859, Oswald Garrison Villard Collection, Columbia University, in Ripley et al., *Black Abolitionist Papers*, 5: 43–45.

[86] *Columbus (Ga.) Daily Sun*, October 19 and 21, 1859; *Opelika (Ala.) Southern Era*, December 6, 1859, and September 15, 1860.

[87] Booker T. Washington, *Up From Slavery: An Autobiography* (New York: Doubleday, 1901), 8; Louis Davis, in Rawick et al., *American Slave*, supplement, series 1, vol. 7, *Mississippi Narratives*, part 2, 581; George Washington Albright, in Rawick et al., *American Slave*, supplement, series 1, vol. 6, *Mississippi Narratives*, part 1, 11.

named Jerry and Joe with setting several fires. December found blacks in Bolivar, Missouri, attacking whites with stones and threatening to burn the town. Wrote one southern editor, it was all part of a northern-backed "conspiracy to murder and plunder the free white citizens of the South."[88]

This volatile atmosphere of panic and paranoia framed the 1860 presidential campaign. When Democrats could not agree on a policy regarding slavery in the territories, most southern delegates walked out. Those who stayed nominated Stephen A. Douglas of Illinois. The splinter delegates held their own convention, called themselves the Southern Rights Party, and nominated John C. Breckinridge of Kentucky. Southern politicos, many of them old-line Whigs, who refused to support the secession-leaning Southern Righters formed the Constitutional Union Party and nominated John Bell of Tennessee. The party's only platform was the "Constitution of the Country, the Union of the States, and the Enforcement of the Laws." Republicans met in Chicago and agreed on nearly everything except a candidate. Of the leading contenders, none had enough delegates to ensure nomination going into the convention. The party finally settled on Abraham Lincoln of Illinois, who seemed to be nearly everyone's second choice. As for slavery, the platform promised to halt its spread and keep it locked in the South.

Black northerners were conflicted over whether to support Republicans that year. The *Weekly Anglo-African* pointed out that Republicans constantly referred to blacks as "inferior beings." Lincoln himself, despite his distaste for slavery, had said publicly on more than one occasion, "I am not, nor ever have been in favor of bringing about in any way the social and political equality of the white and black races. ... I as much as any other man am in favor of having the superior position assigned to the white race." Lincoln vowed to enforce the Fugitive Slave Act. He stressed his support, and that of most other Republicans, for "colonizing" free blacks to Latin America or Africa. One black abolitionist wrote that voting for such a man and his party was to support slavery "where it is, and endorse a policy which looks to the expulsion of the free black American from his native land."[89]

---

[88] *Columbus (Ga.) Daily Sun*, November 5, 15, and 16, 1859; P. Williams to Gov. John Letcher, January 5, 1860, and C. C. Larue to Gov. John Letcher, January 17, 1860, Executive Papers Archives Division, Virginia State Library, Richmond, in Aptheker, *Slave Revolts*, 353; *St. Louis Missouri Democrat* in *New York Principia*, January 7, 1860; *Opelika (Ala.) Southern Era*, November 29, 1859.

[89] *Weekly Anglo-African* (New York), February 25, 1860; Speech at Columbus Ohio, September 16, 1859, in Basler et al., *Collected Works of Abraham Lincoln*, 3: 402; Ripley et al., *Black Abolitionist Papers*, 5: 71.

Those blacks who found Republicans too off-putting gravitated toward Gerrit Smith, who was again running for president on the Radical Abolition ticket. There was no hope of his winning, but, unlike Lincoln, he was an avowed abolitionist and equal rights supporter. Still, northern blacks could hardly help but look on Lincoln as a better alternative than his major rivals for the presidency. Frederick Douglass, a friend and supporter of Gerrit Smith, probably best expressed the general feeling of northern blacks when he told an audience:

While I see . . . that the Republican party is far from an abolition party, I cannot fail to see also that the Republican party carries with it the anti-slavery sentiment of the North, and that a victory gained by it in the present canvass will be a victory gained by that sentiment over the wickedly aggressive pro-slavery sentiment of the country. . . . Abolitionist though I am, and resolved to cast my vote for an Abolitionist, I sincerely hope for the triumph of that party over all the odds and ends of slavery combined against it.[90]

Southern blacks hoped for a Lincoln victory as well, believing as they did that his election would bring freedom with it. How could they think otherwise, with Southern Rights men ranting throughout the South that Lincoln meant to end slavery and bring on black equality? In September 1860, a Georgia paper complained that "every political speech that has been delivered in Macon has attracted a number of negroes, who, without entering the Hall, have managed to linger around and hear what the orators say." In Columbus, blacks attended so many public campaign rallies that white residents became alarmed at their "unusual interest in politics, and the result of the Presidential election." The mayor banned blacks from attending future rallies. In Eufaula, Alabama, "vigilant committees" kept a close watch on blacks who gathered in the streets to discuss politics. James Henry Hammond of South Carolina wrote to a friend that at least a tenth of the people attending political rallies in his area were black.[91]

Some blacks, mainly house servants, did not have to leave home to hear about the campaign. Hammond admitted that "daily at our tables and our firesides we discuss these matters with Negroes all around." What blacks heard was what slaveholders generally feared – that Lincoln was a direct

---

[90] *Douglass' Monthly*, September 1860.
[91] *Macon (Ga.) Daily Telegraph*, September 8, 1860; *Columbus (Ga.) Daily Sun*, September 27, 1860; Anne Kendrick Walker, *Backtracking in Barbour County: A Narrative of the Last Alabama Frontier* (Richmond, Va.: Dietz Press, 1941), 173; Hammond to F. A. Allen, February 2, 1861, Hammond Papers, Library of Congress, in Steven A. Channing, *Crisis of Fear: Secession in South Carolina* (New York: W. W. Norton, 1974), 39.

threat to slavery. That impression was more than enough to make enslaved people Lincoln supporters. Alabama freedman Louis Meadows remembered that slaves "hoped and prayed he would be elected. They wanted to be free and have a chance."[92]

Slaves increasingly acted on their hopes for freedom in the summer and fall of 1860. Rebellions and rumors of rebellions pervaded the South. Whatever their nature or degree, they all reflected black ambitions and white fears. Some whites blamed "black Republicans" or "abolition emissaries" for stirring up trouble. Others tried to ignore the upsurge of resistance, uncomfortable with admitting how widespread resistance really was. "We dislike to allude to the evidences of the insurrectionary tendency of things" wrote a Georgia newspaper editor in August. Nevertheless, he felt compelled to mention a conspiracy in Floyd County.[93]

There was also trouble in other Georgia towns. One "insurrectionary plot" called for slaves to burn Dalton and crash a train into Marietta. At least thirty-six slaves were implicated and imprisoned. Nearby Rome saw attempts "to incite insurrection among the slaves." Arson caused rampant fear of slave rebellion in Texas that summer as fires set by slaves swept through several towns. In September, Winston County, Mississippi, officials arrested thirty-five slaves for a rebellion plot. October found slaves in Virginia's Norfolk and Princess Anne Counties planning revolt. According to one report, they aimed to begin a war for freedom using their shovels, axes, and hoes as weapons.[94] That month in Washington County, North Carolina, authorities uncovered a planned rebellion in which 300 slaves were to

march towards Plymouth, murder and destroy all they might encounter on the road, set fire to the town, kill all the inhabitants that might oppose them, seize what money there might be, also what ammunition and weapons they might acquire, then take possession of such vessels as they required for their purpose and go in them where they might think proper.[95]

---

[92] Hammond to F. A. Allen, February 2, 1861, in Channing, *Crisis of Fear*, 39–40; Louis Meadows, in Rawick et al., *American Slave*, supplement, series 1, vol. 1, *Alabama Narratives*, 255.

[93] *Augusta (Ga.) Dispatch* in *Liberator*, August 24, 1860.

[94] Executive Committee, *Twenty-Eighth Annual Report of the American Anti-Slavery Society* (New York: American Anti-Slavery Society, 1861), 200–14. See also White, "Texas Slave Insurrection of 1860," and Reynolds, *Texas Terror: The Slave Insurrection Panic of 1860 and the Secession of the Lower South.*

[95] William S. Pettigrew to James C. Johnston, October 25, 1860, Pettigrew Papers, University of North Carolina at Chapel Hill, in Aptheker, *Slave Revolts*, 356.

### INSURRECTION AND THE KNELL OF SLAVERY

In the November presidential election, as most had expected, Lincoln carried the day. Still, he gained only a plurality of the popular vote. More than 60 percent of voters nationwide preferred candidates other than Lincoln. Even in the free states, where many white voters feared "Black Republican" intentions, 46 percent voted for someone other than Lincoln. But Lincoln's slight majorities in nearly all the free states were enough to give him an overwhelming advantage in the electoral college.

With Lincoln poised to enter the White House, slaves became ever more rebellious. Most held at least a vague assumption that Lincoln's election might mean their freedom, but they knew slaveholders would not give up slavery without a fight. If it was to be war over slavery, slaves were not waiting for Lincoln. They would start the war themselves.

At 2:30 a.m. on election day, fire consumed much of Fort Gaines, Georgia. After townspeople brought the flames under control, two blacks were shot trying to restart the blaze. Georgia newspapers also reported an election-day slave insurrection in Crawford County, just west of Macon. More than twenty slaves, perhaps many more, had gone on a rampage, intending to kill their owner "and all the white folks." Well-armed whites quickly subdued the freedom fighters and prepared to mete out summary justice. "Some will be burnt," wrote a Milledgeville paper, "others hung."[96]

There were more uprisings in the Alabama black belt counties of Montgomery, Autauga, and Marengo. They collectively involved hundreds of slaves. In December, the *Montgomery Advertiser* reported a "deep laid plan among the negroes of our neighborhood, and from what we can find out from our negroes, it is general all over the country. ... Their plan is to kill the families they live with on a certain night, and then get together and take the country." Perhaps most ominously, the editor wrote, "They look for aid from Lincoln and the Northern people." In South Carolina, according to one report, blacks formed "a secret and widespread organization of a Masonic character, having its grip, pass-word, and oath. It has various grades of leaders, who are competent and earnest men and its ultimate object is FREEDOM."[97]

[96] *Columbus (Ga.) Enquirer*, November 13, 1860; *Macon (Ga.) Daily Telegraph*, November 9, 1860; *Milledgeville (Ga.) Southern Recorder* in *Augusta (Ga.) Chronicle and Sentinel*, November 10, 1860; Executive Committee, *Twenty-Eighth Annual Report of the American Anti-Slavery Society*, 213.

[97] *Montgomery Advertiser*, December 13, 1860; Executive Committee, *Twenty-Eighth Annual Report of the American Anti-Slavery Society*, 210–11; Edmund Kirke, *Among the Pines: or, South in Secession Time* (New York: J. R. Gilmore, 1862), 90–91.

Some whites doubted the veracity of so many rebellion and conspiracy reports. They clung to the myth that slaves were loyal servants who were so lacking in intelligence that organized revolt was beyond their capability. One Virginian called news of revolt in Norfolk and Princess Anne Counties "idle reports ... manufactured out of whole cloth by those who wished to play upon the fears and anxieties of the timid and credulous." If so, it was an effective strategy. A North Carolinian wrote that fear among slaveholders had reached levels "almost inconceivable."[98] Certainly such fear played into secessionist hands. But that fear was also grounded in reality. Slaveholders knew, even if they were reluctant to admit it openly, that slaves wanted freedom. They knew that slave resistance had been on the rise for years. And they knew that slaveholders were being killed with increasing frequency. Many feared meeting the same fate.

Slave control had never been easy. By the 1850s, it was getting more difficult. A Lincoln presidency could only make it harder. Widespread fear of slave rebellion was, in fact, secessionists' most valuable ally. If the slave states remained in the Union, most slaveholders feared that their chattel would be nearly impossible to control. Outside the Union, control might be easier. Other factors helped fuel the crisis, but at its core, slaveholders' fear of their slaves was a primary force driving secession during the weeks after Lincoln's election.

South Carolina was the first to go on December 20, 1860. In its "Declaration of Immediate Causes" justifying its move, the state's secession convention frankly admitted its fear of "servile insurrection." The delegates blamed northern abolitionists for inciting slaves, but they well knew that their slaves needed little inducement from the North.[99] Abolitionism was the excuse for secession. Slave resistance was the underlying cause.

Still, slaveholders were not entirely united behind the secession movement. The same fear that led most to support secession led others to oppose it. If war followed secession, would not slaves become even more resistant? The danger seemed clear enough to Alexander Stephens of Georgia, who considered slavery "much more secure in the Union than out of it." So did Texas Governor Sam Houston. "The first gun fired in the war," he predicted, "will be the knell of slavery." Plantation mistress Mary Ann

---

[98] *Norfolk Herald* in *Christianburg (Va.) New Star*, October 13, 1860; William S. Pettigrew to James C. Johnston, October 25, 1860, Pettigrew Papers, University of North Carolina at Chapel Hill, in Aptheker, *Slave Revolts*, 356.

[99] *Declaration of the Immediate Causes which Induce and Justify the Secession of South Carolina from the Federal Union, and the Ordinance of Secession* (Charleston: Evans and Cogswell, 1860), 8–9.

Whittle wondered how slaveholders could even think of secession "when we have an enemy in our bosoms who will sho[o]t us in our beds." Raleigh's *North Carolina Standard* warned that "the negroes will know ... that the war is waged on their account. They will become restless and turbulent. ... The end will be – *Abolition!*"[100]

Nonslaveholding whites also knew that a secessionist war would be waged on slavery's account, and most of them voted against it. Although secessionists lost the popular vote, they were able to sway enough delegates in separate state conventions to take the Deep South out of the Union.[101] In February, representatives from South Carolina, Georgia, Florida, Alabama, Mississippi, Louisiana, and Texas met in Montgomery to form the Confederate States of America.

Everywhere justifications for secession were much the same. Mississippi blamed northerners for promoting "insurrection and incendiarism in our midst." Georgia's excuse was that northerners were trying to "excite insurrection and servile war among us." For Texas, northerners were attempting to "stir up servile insurrection and bring blood and carnage to our firesides."[102] There were other causes listed, but they all revolved

---

[100] Stephens to J. Henley Smith, July 10, 1860, in Urlich Bonnell Phillips, ed., *The Correspondence of Robert Toombs, Alexander H. Stephens, and Howell Cobb* (Washington, D.C.: Government Printing Office, 1913), 487; John H. Reagan, "A Conversation with Governor Houston," *Quarterly of the Texas State Historical Association* 3 (1900): 280; Whittle to Lewis Neale Whittle, December 1, 1860, Lewis Neale Whittle Papers, Southern Historical Collection, University of North Carolina at Chapel Hill, in James L. Roark, *Masters without Slaves: Southern Planters in the Civil War and Reconstruction* (New York: W. W. Norton, 1977), 4; *Raleigh North Carolina Standard*, February 5, 1861.

[101] In his seminal study of the secession crisis, David Potter looked at the popular vote for state secession conventions throughout the South and concluded: "At no time during the winter of 1860–1861 was secession desired by a majority of the people of the slave states. ... Furthermore, secession was not basically desired even by a majority in the lower South, and the secessionists succeeded less because of the intrinsic popularity of their program than because of the extreme skill with which they utilized an emergency psychology, the promptness with which they invoked unilateral action by individual states, and the firmness with which they refused to submit the question of secession to popular referenda." See David M. Potter, *Lincoln and His Party in the Secession Crisis* (New Haven, Conn.: Yale University Press, 1942), 208. A more recent examination of the ways in which secessionists maneuvered a reluctant South into secession can be found in Williams, *Bitterly Divided: The South's Inner Civil War*, 29–47.

[102] *Journal of the State Convention and Ordinances and Resolutions Adopted January 1861* (Jackson, Miss.: E. Barksdale, 1861), 87; *Journal of the Public and Secret Proceedings of the Convention of the People of Georgia* (Milledgeville, Ga.: Boughton, Nisbet, and Barnes, 1861), 112; *Journal of the Secession Convention of Texas, 1861* (Austin: Austin Printing Co., 1912), 64.

around slavery. And at their heart lay a deep-seated fear that increasingly resistant slaves, certain that they now had a friend in the White House, might be impossible to manage.

In the North, most leading black abolitionists welcomed secession. They were among the first to see it for what is was – the catalyst for a war that would surely end slavery. The last thing they wanted was to abandon their southern brethren to slavery without a fight. The time for talk was over. It was time for action. As the *Weekly Anglo-African* put it, "We want Nat Turner – not speeches; Denmark Vesey – not resolutions; John Brown – not meetings." Frederick Douglass felt the same way. "The contest must now be decided, and decided forever, which of the two, Freedom or Slavery, shall give law to this Republic. Let the conflict come, and God speed the Right."[103]

Most white northerners, including most white abolitionists, were hardly eager for war. Garrisonians, who had long urged the free North to secede, had no difficulty letting the South go. Wendell Phillips argued that if southern slaves wanted their freedom, they should rise in rebellion and fight their own battle. The North need not intervene. Many white northerners expressed relief when South Carolina cut its ties to the Union. They were glad to see the troublesome state go. The *Indianapolis Daily Journal* rejoiced. "We are well rid of South Carolina, if we are only wise enough to count it a riddance, and nothing worse. ... If all the South follows her, let it." On January 16, 4,000 people attended a mass meeting in Philadelphia carrying banners reading "NO CIVIL WAR." Horace Greeley, editor of the *New York Tribune* and one of Lincoln's staunchest supporters, wrote that if southerners were "satisfied that they can do better out of the Union than in it, we insist on letting them go in peace." It seemed clear to the *New York Herald*'s editor that "the citizens of the free States are not prepared for civil war."[104]

But northern industrialists and financiers vigorously pressed to keep the Deep South in the Union – by compromise if possible, by war if necessary. How else could they guarantee continued access to southern markets and cheap cotton? It was a question that united elites across party lines. Most

---

[103] *Weekly Anglo-African*, April 27, 1861; *Douglass' Monthly*, March 1861.
[104] Wendell Phillips, *Disunion: Two Discourses at Music Hall* (Boston: Robert F. Wallcut, 1861), 18; *Indianapolis Daily Journal*, December 22, 1860; *Philadelphia Inquirer*, January 17, 1861; *Philadelphia Evening Bulletin*, January 17, 1861, in Arnold M. Shankman, *The Pennsylvania Antiwar Movement, 1861–1865* (Rutherford, N.J.: Fairleigh Dickinson University Press, 1980), 42; *New York Tribune*, November 9, 1860; *New York Herald*, February 5, 1861.

had direct business ties to the cotton South or investments in cotton textiles. The *Boston Herald* warned that an independent South could "impose a heavy tax upon the manufactures of the North, and an export tax upon the cotton used by Northern manufacturers." Such taxes would drive up both the price of cotton and the cost of doing business in the South, thus cutting into profits and reducing stock values. Under threat of secession, stock prices in nearly four dozen textile mills had already dropped by more than 40 percent. Besides, secession would make it impossible for northern creditors to collect on the millions of dollars in debt southerners owed. And that was only a fraction of what northern businessmen stood to lose. The South pumped $60 million annually into the pockets of Boston businessmen. For New York City, the figure was $200 million. As far as these men were concerned, secession could not be allowed to stand.[105]

Congress responded with the Crittenden Compromise, which would have extended the old Missouri Compromise line between free and slave territory all the way to California. The measure failed, due mainly to Republican intransigence on expanding slavery. But Congress was able to pass the Corwin Amendment, authored by Ohio Republican Representative Thomas Corwin. This proposed thirteenth amendment would have prevented Congress, or any future amendment, from tampering with slavery in any slave state. With majority votes of slightly more than two-thirds in the Senate and an even greater margin in the House, Congress sent the amendment out to the states for ratification on March 2. Several states ratified it, but the process moved too slowly to avert war.[106]

When compromise failed, northern elites put intense pressure on the incoming president and his party. "At present," wrote a group of New York merchants to Lincoln, "there are no means of collecting any portion of [southern] debts, nor can there be, until the authority of the United States government is re-established in the rebellious states." Many such men, like Philadelphia banker Jay Cooke, had backed Republicans financially in the previous year's campaigns and now expected their payoff.[107]

---

[105] Kenneth M. Stampp, *And the War Came: The North and the Secession Crisis, 1860–1861* (Chicago: University of Chicago Press, 1968), 127; *Boston Herald*, November 12, 1860; Philip S. Foner, *Business and Slavery: The New York Merchants and the Irrepressible Conflict* (New York: Russell and Russell, 1968), 302; Potter, *Lincoln and His Party in the Secession Crisis*, 117.

[106] *Congressional Globe*, Thirty-sixth Congress, Second Session (1861), 1284; Basler et al., *Collected Works of Abraham Lincoln*, 4: 262–71.

[107] Foner, *Business and Slavery*, 302; Stampp, *And the War Came*, 220–21.

"Thus by March," as historian Kenneth Stampp writes, "it was evident that northern businessmen had carefully measured the consequences of disunion and the collapse of central authority and decided that they were intolerable."[108] So had Lincoln. Like other Republicans, he knew that to let secession stand and lose the support of financial backers would undermine the party as surely as would compromising on slavery's expansion.

In the face of widespread opposition to civil war, and in light of his silence since the November election, Lincoln's remarks in his March 4 inaugural address came as something of a surprise. Although he promised no war against slavery, he did promise war against secession. "I have no purpose, directly or indirectly, to interfere with slavery in the states where it exists," Lincoln said. "I have no lawful right to do so, and I have no inclination to do so." He had stressed the same point many times during his presidential campaign. He even announced his support for the Corwin Amendment, saying he had "no objection" to slavery and the rights of slaveholders "being made express and irrevocable." For the first time, however, he publicly made clear that secession was unacceptable. Under his administration, it would be "the declared purpose of the Union that it WILL Constitutionally defend and maintain itself."[109]

Although bitterly disappointed with Lincoln's promise to enforce the Fugitive Slave Act and his positive comments on the Corwin Amendment, leading blacks were generally supportive of his stand against secession. Most of them knew, even if Lincoln would not admit it, that war against slaveholders meant war against slavery. Blacks themselves – North and South, free and enslaved – would see to that. One enslaved South Carolinian was sure that if it came to war, the Confederacy was bound to lose. While fighting the North with one hand, it would have to hold down blacks with the other. South Carolina's governor confirmed that prediction in March 1861 when he wrote to President Jefferson Davis that in the event of war, he would need to keep enough men at home to staff local slave patrols.[110]

Now that Lincoln had proclaimed secession unacceptable, could he hold the cotton states by force? There was little popular support for such a move. "It cannot be denied," wrote the *New York Times* in March, "that

[108] Stampp, *And the War Came*, 222.
[109] Basler et al., *Collected Works of Abraham Lincoln*, 4: 262–71.
[110] *Douglass' Monthly*, April 1861, *Christian Recorder* (Philadelphia), March 9, 1861; Kirke, *Among the Pines*, 20; Gov. Francis W. Pickens to Davis, March 17, 1861, in Lynda Lasswell Crist and Mary Seaton Dix, eds., *The Papers of Jefferson Davis* (Baton Rouge: Louisiana State University Press, 1992), 7: 70–72.

there is a growing sentiment throughout the North in favor of *letting the Gulf States go.*" The *New York Herald* agreed. "Nine out of ten of the people of the Northern and Central States repudiate [Lincoln's] coercive policy." To the disappointment of black leaders, including Frederick Douglass, the North, which had put Lincoln in office, now seemed willing to "desert him and leave him a potentate without power."[111]

Although Lincoln was committed to upholding the Union, he had scant means of doing so. The army was only a few thousand strong, and volunteering was almost nonexistent. Lincoln needed men, willing men, to establish federal authority in the Deep South. To get those men, he needed an incident.

On April 12, the Confederacy obliged Lincoln by firing on Fort Sumter, providing him with the incident he had sought when he threatened to resupply the facility.[112] Lincoln immediately called for 75,000 volunteers and appealed "to all loyal citizens to ... maintain the honor, the integrity, and the existence of our National Union." Four more slave states – Arkansas, Tennessee, North Carolina, and Virginia – left the Union, but newspapers across the North echoed Lincoln's appeal. "The American Flag – the flag of our Union," cried the *Pittsburgh Post*, "has been fired into by American citizens, disloyal to the government. ... No American of true heart and brave soul will stand this. No American ought to stand it." Such words stirred thousands of young men with patriotic fervor as they rushed to uphold and redeem the honor of their flag. Pennsylvania's *Erie Weekly Gazette* wrote that the "uprising of the Northern people in response to the President's appeal for volunteers to avenge the insult to our national flag and vindicate the honor of the National character, constitute the most remarkable event of this and probably of any age."[113]

That uprising of the people did not include quite all of the people. Many remained concerned, despite Lincoln's assurance to the contrary, that the conflict might become a war against slavery. Although most white northerners now seemed willing to make war on southern slaveholders,

---

[111] *New York Times*, March 21, 1861; *New York Herald*, April 11, 1861; *Douglass' Monthly*, April 1861.

[112] For a study of Lincoln's Sumter strategy see Richard Nelson Current, *Lincoln and the First Shot* (Philadelphia: Lippincott, 1963). See also Charles W. Ramsdell, "Lincoln and Fort Sumter," *Journal of Southern History* 3 (1937): 259–88.

[113] Lincoln's Proclamation Calling Militia and Convening Congress, in David S. Heidler and Jeanne T. Heidler, eds., *Encyclopedia of the American Civil War: A Political, Social, and Military History*, vol. 5, *Documents and Appendices* (Santa Barbara, Calif.: ABC-CLIO Press, 2000), 2300–2301; *Pittsburgh Post*, April 15, 1861; *Erie Weekly Gazette*, May 2, 1861.

they had little desire to do so on behalf of slaves. The *New York Tribune*, a staunchly pro-Lincoln paper, was quick to remind its readers that this was "a War for the preservation of the Union, not for the destruction of Slavery. ... Slavery shall receive no damage from a Union triumph." Lincoln had said much the same in his inaugural address, and Congress agreed. In a near unanimous vote, it passed the Crittenden-Johnson Resolution, stressing that the war effort was not to overthrow or interfere "with the rights or established institutions" of the slave states but only "to defend and maintain the supremacy of the Constitution and to preserve the Union." Never would white soldiers be asked to put their lives on the line for blacks. The war would have no impact on slavery. It would be strictly a white man's war.[114]

Blacks had other ideas. What they wanted was freedom, and they were taking it for themselves. Within days of the firing on Fort Sumter, self-emancipated people were pouring into Union lines. Many offered their services as soldiers for the Union army. Harry Jarvis volunteered at Fortress Monroe on Virginia's Chesapeake shore, where General Benjamin Butler was in command. "I went to him," recalled Jarvis, "an' asked him to let me enlist, but he said *it warn't a black man's war.*" Jarvis replied boldly. "I tol' him it *would* be a black man's war 'fore they got through."[115] In fact, it already was.

At the height of the secession crisis, a newspaper editor in Augusta, Georgia, wrote an ominous warning. "Disguise it as we may, the greatest danger to the new confederacy arises not from without, not from the North, but *from our own people.*" Virginia's *Richmond Examiner* agreed, admitting that the South was "more rife with treason to her own independence and honour than any community that ever engaged before in a struggle with an adversary."[116] It was clear even in those early days that the Confederacy was in for a two-front war – one against northerners and another against southerners, especially those it enslaved.

[114] *New York Tribune*, May 14, 1861; *Journal of the House of Representatives of the United States*, Thirty-seventh Congress, First Session (Washington, D.C.: Government Printing Office, 1861), 58: 123; *Journal of the Senate of the United States*, Thirty-seventh Congress, First Session (Washington, D.C.: Government Printing Office, 1861), 53: 91.
[115] Mrs. M. F. Armstrong and Helen W. Ludlow, *Hampton and its Students* (New York: G. P. Putnam's Sons, 1874), 111–12. Jarvis later served with the Fifty-Fifth Massachusetts Infantry Regiment, United States Colored Troops (USCT).
[116] *Augusta (Ga.) Chronicle* in Frank Moore, ed., *The Rebellion Record: A Diary of American Events*, vol. 1 (New York: G. P. Putnam, 1861), part 2: "Documents and Narratives," 30; *Richmond Examiner*, July 19, 1861.

## 2

# "Shedding the First Blood"

## *Forcing a War for Freedom*

### THE ENEMY AT HOME

A few days before Confederates fired on Fort Sumter, the *Richmond Dispatch* assured white Virginians that there was no need to fear their slaves. "The southern negro has no sympathies with Northern abolitionists," wrote the paper's editor. Despite the looming threat of civil war, there was "perfect order and quiet among the servile classes." Newspapers across the South sent the same illusory message. But that message did little to calm slaveholder fears or to mask the reality of slave resistance. In January 1861, South Carolina plantation mistress Keziah Brevard wrote of the slaves generally, "I cannot tell whether they have any good feelings for their owners or not." By February, she had no doubt of her own slaves' feelings. Despite her efforts to "make my negroes happy," Brevard was "awakened to the fact that they *hate me* – My God – My God – what are we to expect from slaves – when mine hate me as they do – it is nothing on earth – but that I am *white* & own slaves."[1]

"We cannot sleep sound at nights for fear of the niggers," said one slaveholder early in the war. "We are compelled to mount guard at nights ... this is the only thing that keeps them in check." In April 1861, Danville, Virginia, authorities required all white males who were not in the militia to serve on local slave patrols. That same month, a terrified resident of Tippah County, Mississippi, begged Governor John Pettus not to call

[1] *Richmond Dispatch*, April 2, 1861; John Hammond Moore, ed., *A Plantation Mistress on the Eve of the Civil War: The Diary of Keziah Goodwyn Hopkins Brevard, 1860–1861* (Columbia: University of South Carolina Press, 1993), 81, 86–87.

for any more volunteers. Already blacks in the area had committed arson and attempted murder. "If there should be another call it will leave our women and children in this section exposed to the black insurgents." A resident of Jefferson County made the same request. "Nothing but eternal vigilance will keep down the enemy at home," as the writer called enslaved blacks.[2]

Even as the Confederate army called for men to fill its ranks, some slaveholders urged them to remain at home and save their families "from the horrors of insurrection." Reports from South Carolina's Prince George District convinced one correspondent that "disaffection among the slaves is more general even than I had imagined." In May, a Louisiana correspondent wrote to a friend of "very alarming disturbances among the blacks; on more than one plantation, the assistance of the authorities has been called in to overcome the open resistance of the slaves." A Louisiana slaveholder overheard his slaves plotting to kill all the area's white men and "march up the River to meet Mr. Linkum." Slave rebellion was a very real threat to the editor of southwest Georgia's *Albany Patriot*, who complained that it was no uncommon thing to see area blacks "congregate together contrary to law, *exhibit their weapons*, and no doubt devise their secret, but destructive plans."[3]

During the late spring and early summer of 1861, a rebellion hysteria swept across large parts of the South's plantation belt, southwest Georgia included. Panic spread through Decatur County in June after patrollers caught a slave named Israel away from his plantation without a pass. Israel's capture led officials to believe that a general slave revolt was about to break out. Rumors spread that blacks in the county seat of Bainbridge were collecting guns and planning to "kill all of the men and old women and children and take the younger ones for their wives." No guns were found, but two suspected insurrection leaders were imprisoned. An attempted rebellion that April near Charleston, South Carolina, resulted in seven slaves being hanged. In Monroe County, Arkansas,

[2] Allan Pinkerton, *The Spy of the Rebellion; Being a True History of the Spy System of the United Sates Army during the Late Rebellion* (New York: G. W. Dillingham, 1883), 187; Hadden, *Slave Patrols*, 173; Robinson, *Bitter Fruits of Bondage*, 49; J. D. L. Davenport to Gov. John J. Pettus, May 14, 1861, Executive Papers, Mississippi Department of Archives and History, Jackson, in Aptheker, *Slave Revolts*, 364.

[3] George W. Gayle to Jefferson Davis, May 22, 1861, in Crist and Dix, *Papers of Jefferson Davis*, 7: 175; *New York Tribune*, April 2, 1861; *London Daily News* in *New York Tribune*, July 3, 1861; Wiley, *Southern Negroes*, 82; *Albany (Ga.) Patriot*, May 23, 1861.

three slaves – two men and a girl – were hanged in June for helping plan an insurrection.[4]

Dozens of slaves in Adams County, Mississippi, tried to organize their own militia and end slavery around Natchez and Second Creek. The effort failed, and a self-appointed planter court staged a mock trial. Knowing they would be executed in any case, several of the conspirators made their feelings clear. One testified that they had planned a coordinated assault to "kill all the damn white people" when the Union army arrived. Another joined the rebellion because "master whips our children." Still another insisted that "whipping colored people would stop." Others wanted to join the Union army and see Winfield Scott, the Union's commanding general, "eat his breakfast in New Orleans." In a direct insult to southern white manhood, the slaves Simon and George told the planters that "Northerners make the South shit behind their asses." To these men, Lincoln's Union war was from the start a freedom war. And they were among the first casualties of that war. Simon, George, and at least three dozen others suffered death by hanging.[5]

In the summer of 1861, a Georgia overseer complained to his absentee employer that the slaves would not submit to physical abuse. One slave simply walked away when the overseer told him he was about to be whipped. Another Georgia slave drew a knife on an overseer who tried to whip him. His owner locked him up and forced him onto a bread and water diet. Such actions generally made slaves even more resistant. "I am satisfied that his imprisonment has only tended to harden him," one overseer wrote soon after releasing an unruly slave. "I don't think he will ever reform."[6]

Besides being terribly painful, whipping was for slaves a symbol of their lowly status. It is hardly surprising that resistance to whipping became one of the main ways enslaved people sought to demonstrate a measure of independence. Such resistance could be very dangerous. One Troup County, Georgia, planter was noted for turning his dogs on slaves who refused to be whipped. A slave on the Hines Holt plantation near

---

[4] G.H. Davis to D.C. Barrow, June 21, 1861, and J.H. Taylor to D.C. Barrow June 16, 1861, David Crenshaw Barrow Papers, University of North Carolina at Chapel Hill, in Bryan, *Confederate Georgia*, 127; *Springfield (Mass.) Daily Republican*, May 4, 1861; *The American Annual Cyclopedia and Register of Important Events of the Year 1861* (New York: D. Appleton, 1864), 25.

[5] Winthrop D. Jordan, *Tumult and Silence at Second Creek: An Inquiry into a Civil War Slave Conspiracy* (Baton Rouge: Louisiana State University Press, 1993), 291, 298, 278, 292.

[6] J.H. Taylor to D.C. Barrow, October 27, 1861, Barrow Papers, in Bryan, *Confederate Georgia*, 124–25; G.F. Bristow to Alexander H. Stephens, January 22, 1862, Alexander H. Stephens Papers, Library of Congress, in ibid., 125.

Columbus, Georgia, was shot when he resisted a whipping. He had beaten off six men who tried to hold him down.[7]

Despite such dangers, slaves continued to resist. According to freed-woman Celestia Avery of Troup County, Peter Heard whipped his slaves "unmercifully." One day while hoeing in the fields, an overseer told her grandmother Sylvia to take her clothes off when she got to the end of a fence row. She was going to be whipped for not working fast enough. When the overseer reached for her, she grabbed a wooden rail and broke it across the man's arms. A Russell County, Alabama, slave named Crecie, described as "a grown young woman and big and strong," was tied to a stump by an overseer named Sanders in preparation for whipping. He had two dogs with him just in case Crecie gave any trouble. When the first lick hit Crecie's back, she pulled up the stump and whipped Sanders and his dogs.[8]

Sanders was fortunate to escape Crecie's wrath with his life. Some were not so lucky. When a Georgia overseer began beating a young slave girl with a sapling tree, one of the older slaves grabbed an axe and killed him. Such violent retaliation was even more common during the war than before. In March 1861, an Alabama overseer ordered a slave to take off his coat and prepare to be whipped. The young man refused, drew a knife, and started to walk away. The overseer grabbed him, and both men fell to the ground. Within seconds, the overseer lay dying of a stab wound. Later that year, Mary Chesnut of South Carolina wrote that her cousin Betsey Witherspoon had been murdered by her slaves. The incident opened Mary's eyes to the danger from her own slaves. "I feel that the ground is cut away from under my feet. Why should they treat me any better than they have done Cousin Betsey?"[9]

Most threatened of all were the slaves themselves. Although some resorted to deadly retaliation, increasing numbers simply ran away. An enslaved Mississippi man, after being given 100 lashes, hid in a cave for the war's duration. After his own severe beating, a Georgia man carried his family to the woods where they lived in a cave until the war was over. Some self-emancipated refugees lived in isolated communities of several dozen. Authorities discovered a fugitive camp in the swamps near Marion, South Carolina, that was "well provided with meal, cooking utensils, blankets,

[7] Celestia Avery, *Georgia Narratives*, part 1, 24; Mary Gladdy, *Georgia Narratives*, part 2, 17.

[8] Celestia Avery, *Georgia Narratives*, part 1, 25; Samuel S. Taylor, *Arkansas Narratives*, part 4, 18.

[9] Charlie Pye, *Georgia Narratives*, part 3, 186; *Columbus (Ga.) Times* in *Macon (Ga.) Telegraph*, March 12, 1861; Woodward, *Mary Chesnut's Civil War*, 198–99.

etc." The residents had been there for some time, growing corn, squash, and peas on a fertile knoll.[10]

In Louisiana, Octave Johnson escaped early in the war and found refuge with a band of thirty men and women. They survived by appropriating livestock from nearby plantations, sometimes trading the meat to other slaves for corn meal. After living in the swamps for a year and a half, slavecatchers raided the camp. The refugees jumped into Bayou Faupron with twenty bloodhounds in hot pursuit. Aided by resident alligators that "preferred dog flesh to personal flesh," Johnson and his friends escaped and fled to Union lines in southern Louisiana. Johnson soon joined the Union army.[11]

## BLIND, UNREASONING PREJUDICE

That the Federals were allowing former slaves to serve as soldiers by the time Johnson escaped was a radical change from the war's early years. Tens of thousands of southern refugees had tried to enlist and were turned down. Northern blacks had offered their services too. When Lincoln called for volunteers in April 1861, blacks in Boston held a mass meeting at the Twelfth Baptist Church and announced their readiness to "defend the Government as the equals of its white defenders – to do so with 'our lives, our fortunes, and our sacred honor,' for the sake of freedom." Even the women were ready to take the field "as nurses, seamstresses, and warriors, if need be." In Providence, blacks formed a company and asked to be attached to the First Rhode Island Regiment. In Philadelphia, blacks organized two regiments and waited for orders telling them where to report. Jacob Dodson, a black government employee in Washington, petitioned the War Department on behalf of 300 local free blacks who were ready to "enter the service for the defense of the City."[12]

Blacks had compelling reasons to answer Lincoln's call to arms. Some associated military service with citizenship, and they meant to get a uniform

[10] Dora Franks, *Mississippi Narratives*, 51; Celestia Avery, *Georgia Narratives*, part 1, 24; *Marion (S.C.) Star*, June 18, 1861, in H. M. Henry, *The Police Control of the Slave in South Carolina* (Emory, Va.: n.p., 1914), 121.

[11] Testimony of Corporal Octave Johnson, American Freedmen's Inquiry Commission, February [?], 1864, in Berlin et al., *Destruction of Slavery*, 217.

[12] *Liberator*, April 26 and May 31, 1861, and August 22, 1862; *Douglass' Monthly*, May 1861; Jacob Dodson to Simon Cameron, April 23, 1861, United States War Department, *War of the Rebellion: A Compilation of the Official Records of the Union and Confederate Armies* (Washington, D.C.: Government Printing Office, 1880–1901), series 3, vol. 1, 107 (hereafter cited as *Official Records*).

as a means of demanding their rights. Others saw an opportunity to strike out against slaveholders. Even if the struggle was not a war against slavery, it was at least a war against slave states. For most northern blacks, many of whom had family members still enslaved in the South, that was enough for the time being. To be handed a weapon and marched south would do for the moment. All they needed was the order to do it.

Nicholas Biddle did not wait for orders. Two days after Lincoln called for volunteers, the sixty-five-year-old former slave left with his white neighbors of Pottsville, Pennsylvania, when they were ordered south to the nation's capital. Although not officially enlisted, Biddle donned a uniform and expressed his readiness to serve in whatever way he could. Along with four other Pennsylvania companies, Biddle and his comrades boarded a train for Washington. As they disembarked in Baltimore to change trains, the men marched past a jeering pro-Confederate mob. Shouts of "Nigger in uniform" rang out. Then someone yelled "Kill that —ed brother of Abe Lincoln." Suddenly Biddle was hit in the face "with a missile" so hard that it exposed his cheek bone. Lieutenant James Russell caught Biddle as he

FIGURE 2.1. Although Lincoln and Congress promised to keep the conflict a white man's war, blacks made it their fight from the start. Nicholas Biddle, a former slave living in Pennsylvania, was denied official enlistment, but he put on a uniform anyway. Passing through Baltimore, a pro-Confederate mob pelted his unit with rocks and bricks, cutting Biddle's cheek to the bone. This photo is from a wartime *carte de visite* naming Biddle as "the first man wounded in the great American Rebellion." Photo courtesy of the Library of Congress.

stumbled, and the troops hurried to their waiting train. Years later, his Pottsville friends engraved these words on a monument to Biddle:[13]

IN MEMORY OF
NICHOLAS BIDDLE.
*Died 2d Aug., 1876, aged 80 years.*
His was the proud distinction of shedding the First Blood in
The Late War for The Union. Being wounded while
marching through Baltimore with the First
Volunteers from Schuylkill County,
18th April, 1861.

Few northern whites were so generous in acknowledging the efforts of their black neighbors. For the most part, they meant to keep America a white man's country and to keep the conflict a white man's war. Neither rights for blacks nor emancipation for slaves were issues that most northern whites cared to touch. The Massachusetts legislature voted down a proposal to accept black troops. Police officials in Providence ordered local blacks to stop holding military drills, calling them "disorderly gatherings." Republican Governor William Dennison of Ohio issued an edict declaring that no black troops would be accepted into state service.[14]

Frederick Douglass was appalled at the blatant racism that lay behind refusals to accept black troops.

Our President, Governors, Generals and Secretaries are calling with almost frantic vehemence for men. – "Men! men! send us men!" they scream, or the cause of the Union is gone ... and yet these very officers, representing the people and Government, steadily and persistently refuse to receive the very class of men which have a deeper interest in the defeat and humiliation of the rebels, than all others. ... What a spectacle of blind, unreasoning prejudice.[15]

Some black leaders argued that if the government declined their services and denied them citizenship, then they owed it no allegiance. Philadelphia's *Christian Recorder*, official voice of the African Methodist Episcopal Church, made that point in a front-page editorial entitled "The Star Spangled Banner and the Duty of Colored Americans to that Flag." The writer surveyed black military service from the American Revolution to the present,

[13] Wallace, *Memorial of the Patriotism of Schuylkill County*, 77–78; Thompson, *First Defenders*, 14; Annie Wittenmyer, *Under the Guns: A Woman's Reminiscences of the Civil War* (Boston: E. B. Stills, 1895), 90–91.
[14] *Springfield (Mass.) Daily Republican*, May 25, 1861; *Liberator*, August 22, 1862; *Boston Evening Transcript*, May 8, 1861.
[15] *Douglass' Monthly*, September 1861.

stressing that "men of color" had been "right by their country's side." In return, the nation had stolen their rights and declared them noncitizens. "To offer ourselves for military service *now* is to *abandon self-respect*, and *invite insult*."[16]

If blacks could be neither citizens nor soldiers, then what was the legal status of slaves who escaped to Union lines? As far as Lincoln was concerned, the slave states were still part of the United States, subject to all laws thereof, including the Fugitive Slave Act. At the war's outset, Lincoln assured slaveholders in both the rebellious and loyal slave states that his administration would uphold their property rights. In July 1861, as Maryland slaves fled to Union army camps in northern Virginia, Lincoln sent word that they were to be returned to their owners. The same applied to escaping Virginia slaves. A Union colonel assured Virginia slaveholders, who feared that he had come to free their slaves, "The relation of master and servant as recognized in your state shall be respected. Your authority over that species of property shall not in the least be interfered with." Another Union officer in Virginia ordered his subordinates to make sure that any escaped slaves were promptly sent "back to the farm."[17]

It was the same everywhere that slaves sought refuge with Union forces. In Missouri, Union General William Harney told worried slaveholders that it was firm government policy to return slaves to their owners. General George McClellan instructed one of his field commanders in western Virginia to "see that the rights and property of the people are respected, and repress all attempts at negro insurrection." General Benjamin F. Butler promised the governor of Maryland that his forces, far from being any threat to slavery, were ready to cooperate "in suppressing, most promptly and effectively, any insurrection." George Stephens, a black correspondent employed as an army cook, wrote from Virginia that so many refugees had been hauled back to their owners by Union troops that "the slaves are almost their enemies."[18]

---

[16] *Christian Recorder*, April 27, 1861.

[17] Lt. Col. Schuyler Hamilton to Brig. Gen. [Irvin] McDowell, July 16, 1861, *Official Records*, series 2, vol. 1, 760; Du Bois, *Black Reconstruction*, 60; D. S. Miles, Endorsement, July 15, 1861, *Official Records*, series 1, vol. 2, 299–300.

[18] McClellan to Col. F. B. Kelly, May 26, 1861, *Official Records*, series 1, vol. 2, 46; Butler to Gov. Thomas H. Hicks, April 23, 1861, ibid., series 1, vol. 2, 593; *Weekly Anglo-African*, November 23, 1861. For abolitionist reaction to Butler's offer see *National Anti-Slavery Standard*, May 11, 1861.

Stephens was from an active black abolitionist family in Philadelphia. He later served with the Fifty-Fourth Massachusetts, was wounded in the assault on Fort Wagner, and rose to the rank of first lieutenant. After the war, he worked with the Freedmen's Bureau to

A Tennessee fugitive escaping to Canada reported similar abuse to a sympathetic Michigan Quaker named Willis. Willis relayed the disturbing news to Secretary of War Simon Cameron, writing that refugees were "badly treated by our officers altho the[y] offered to work or Fight for the Government, but w[e]re told to Clear out that the officers wanted no D—D Niggers about them &c &c & were actually Driven over to their old Homes." Willis stressed that such treatment of the slaves "almost Sett them Cra[z]y. the[y] Expected Friends of us in Stead of Enemys."[19]

Faced with such treatment from Union forces, some blacks decided early on that cooperation with Confederates might be the quickest way to achieve some measure of freedom. There were at least a few willing to test the possibility. In early 1861, seventy free blacks in Lynchburg, Virginia, tried to join the militia. So did sixty in Richmond, who marched to the enrollment office carrying a Confederate flag. Charles Tinsley, spokesman for a group of blacks in Petersburg, said that he and his comrades were "willing to aid Virginia's cause to the utmost extent of our ability." In New Orleans, Creoles put together a force called the Louisiana Native Guards that became part of the state militia.[20]

Blacks who tried to straddle the South's racial divide walked a fine line. Those who appeared too eager to help white Confederates ran the risk of alienating friends and family. When a black Baptist preacher offered his services and those of his sons to Virginia, his parishioners began to avoid him. Afraid of losing his congregation, the preacher insisted that he was trying to do only what was best for his flock. He finally apologized, but church members turned a deaf ear. So did whites. Except for the Louisiana Native Guards, which were enrolled by the state but barred from Confederate service, no offers from blacks to bear arms were accepted. The very notion of black soldiers seemed ridiculous to most whites. In the words of Confederate Vice President Alexander Stephens, the Confederacy's very "cornerstone" rested on the "great truth" that blacks

---

educate former slaves in Virginia. See Donald Yacovone, ed., *A Voice of Thunder: The Civil War Letters of George E. Stephens* (Urbana: University of Illinois Press, 1997).

[19] H. Willis to Cameron, December 5, 1861, in Berlin et al., *Destruction of Slavery*, 269–70.

[20] *Lynchburg (Va.) Republican* in *Alexandria (Va.) Gazette*, May 7, 1861; *Charleston (S.C.) Mercury*, April 26, 1861; *Petersburg (Va.) Express* in *Charleston (S.C.) Courier*, April 29, 1861; *New Orleans Daily Picayune*, August 29 and September 17, 1861. The Louisiana Native Guards later served in the Union army. See James G. Hollandsworth Jr., *The Louisiana Native Guards: The Black Military Experience during the Civil War* (Baton Rouge: Louisiana State University Press, 1995).

were not the equal of whites. Slavery, insisted Stephens, was the "natural and normal condition" of black folk.[21]

If Confederates would not accept blacks as citizens or soldiers, they still demanded their service as laborers. The rebel army put thousands of slaves to work building forts, digging trenches, and clearing roads. Quartermasters used blacks as teamsters, boatmen, and stable hands. Commissary officers used them as cooks, butchers, and bakers. Medical officers had them serve as nurses, orderlies, and grave diggers. All this with their families held hostage in slavery lest they escape to Union lines. Nevertheless blacks did escape, so often that officers preferred not to work them near the front. When they did, the result was predictable. One officer wrote that his fortifications were "progressing slowly, my negro force diminishing rapidly. ... Most of them have run away."[22]

### IMPOSSIBLE TO KEEP THEM OUTSIDE OUR LINES

When escaped refugees arrived at Union lines, they were often welcomed by enlisted men as cheap labor. The drudgery of camp life was made much easier by harboring runaways who could do laundry and cook meals. Besides, the soldiers reasoned, why should blacks be returned to serve traitors when loyal Union men needed their services? Officers frequently had trouble enforcing orders to turn away escaping slaves because their men refused to cooperate. As more and more slaves entered Union lines, some officers themselves began to wonder why refugees should not be put to work for the Union cause.[23]

One such officer was General Benjamin Butler, post commander at Fortress Monroe on Virginia's Chesapeake shore. Butler was a politically appointed general, a Massachusetts Democrat, and no abolitionist. He was heavily invested in the Massachusetts textile industry, which depended on southern cotton and slave labor. As a delegate to the Democratic national convention in 1860, he had voted to nominate Jefferson Davis for president. But in May 1861, finding so many potential laborers entering his lines, he was reluctant to turn them away. He badly needed their

---

[21] "The Contrabands at Fortress Monroe," *Atlantic Monthly* 8 (November 1861): 638; Henry Cleveland, *Alexander H. Stephens in Public and Private* (Philadelphia: National Publishing, 1866), 721.

[22] Capt. P. Robinson [chief engineer, Confederate Army of Mississippi] to Lt. Gen. J. C. Pemberton [commanding, Confederate Department of Mississippi and East Louisiana], January 4, 1863, in Berlin et al., *Destruction of Slavery*, 703.

[23] For examples see Berlin et al., *Destruction of Slavery*, 334, 342, 400.

FIGURE 2.2. Tens of thousands of self-emancipated people flooded Union lines in the war's early months and refused to be turned away. Each made a personal proclamation of freedom and forced the government to respond. Unable to return them to slavery, it first declared them "contraband of war" before finally recognizing that they had been right all along. They were indeed free. Pictured here are "contrabands" at Cumberland Landing, Virginia, May 1862. Photo courtesy of the Library of Congress.

help. It did little good to return them to their owners in any case. They kept coming back. Butler wrote to his superiors: "As a military question it would seem to be a measure of necessity to deprive their masters of their services." And in so doing, why not employ them for the Union? Slaves who might potentially be used by Confederates, argued Butler, should be subject to confiscation and use by the United States just as any other kind of property or "contraband of war" might be. Butler asked why Confederates should "be allowed the use of this property against the United States, and we not be allowed its use in aid of the United States?"[24]

Secretary of War Simon Cameron found the argument convincing. In fact, he had little choice but to accept the labor of escaping slaves. His only other option would be to turn the entire army into a vast slave-catching operation, an effort that would be doomed to failure. Any returned slave

---

[24] Butler to Gen. Winfield Scott [commanding general, U.S. Army], May 24, 1861, *Official Records*, series 1, vol. 2, 650.

could simply escape again. Cameron instructed Butler to employ refugees "in the services to which they are best adapted." Within weeks, Cameron issued general orders that "slaves from states in rebellion ... shall not be returned to the rebellious owners but kept and put at work." Although not held in slavery, the refugees were not legally free. Cameron told his subordinates to "consider them as Contrabands."[25] Frederick Douglass and other prominent blacks generally supported Cameron's decision but strongly objected to calling fugitives "contraband." The term, Douglass said, "will apply better to a pistol, than to a person."[26] But "contraband" stuck and remained in common use for the rest of the war.

Congress supported Cameron's decision as well, although in a more restricted way. With little debate and even less foresight, in August 1861, Congress passed the Confiscation Act. It was careful to specify that only slaves used directly to aid the Confederate war effort were subject to seizure. It made no mention of legal status, saying only that disloyal slaveholders whose "property" had been used against the United States would forfeit claim to that property, including slaves.[27]

In their haste to strike a blow against slaveholding Confederates and protect slaveholding Unionists, most congressmen failed to see the larger implications of confiscation. The act ultimately raised far more questions about slavery's future than it answered, a fact that Lincoln seemed to grasp. He signed the act, although with some reluctance because of its potential impact. A contraband order from the War Department was one thing; a confiscation act from Congress was a much larger step. Few realized at the time how far self-emancipated slaves had pushed the nation toward legal emancipation. Lincoln worried that it was much further than most northerners wished to go.[28]

Still very much in the minority, abolitionists were the only whites willing to go further. And they had been pushing hard for Lincoln to do so from the war's outset. General John C. Frémont, commander of the Western

---

[25] Cameron to Butler, May 30, 1861, in Berlin et al., *Destruction of Slavery*, 72; J. K. F. Mansfield [commanding, Department of Washington] to Mr. Justice Dunne [a District of Columbia justice of the peace], July 4, 1861, in ibid., 167.

[26] *Douglass' Monthly*, February 1862.

[27] John Syrett, *The Civil War Confiscation Acts: Failing to Reconstruct the South* (New York: Fordham University Press, 2005), 4; U.S., *Statutes at Large, Treaties, and Proclamations of the United States of America* (Boston: Little, Brown, and Company, 1863), 12: 319. For the most complete treatments of the evolution and impact of confiscation see Syrett, *The Civil War Confiscation Acts*, and Silvana R. Siddali, *From Property to Person: Slavery and the Confiscation Acts, 1861–1862* (Baton Rouge: Louisiana State University Press, 2005).

[28] Syrett, *Confiscation Acts*, 4.

Department headquartered in St. Louis, pressed further still when on August 30 he declared slaves held by active pro-Confederates in Missouri to be free. In that Lincoln and Congress had, in his view, left open the legal status of confiscated slaves, Frémont filled the gap by defining them as free. That interpretation went much too far for Lincoln. He sent word to Frémont that his freedom order must be canceled. When Frémont refused, Lincoln removed him from command.[29]

Abolitionists, especially blacks, reacted to Lincoln's decision with anger and outrage. Frederick Douglass warned that Lincoln's repudiation of Frémont could "only dishearten the friends of the Government and strengthen its enemies." To Thomas Hamilton, editor of the *Weekly Anglo-African*, Lincoln's war, far from being a war against slavery, was simply a war to keep it in the Union. Any man who would "reduce back to slavery the slaves of rebels in Missouri would order the army of the United States to put down a slave insurrection in Virginia or Georgia." So long as Lincoln pursued a policy of appeasing slaveholders, wrote Hamilton, the Union cause was doomed.[30]

Black leaders across the North repeatedly pointed out that Lincoln's oft-stated goal of preserving both the Union *and* slavery was self-defeating. Slavery and resistance to it had brought on the war. There could be no Union victory with slavery left intact. The war, as Frederick Douglass noted in May 1861, had "bound up the fate of the Republic and that of the slave in the same bundle." The editor of the *Anglo-African* agreed, writing soon after Fort Sumter fell that "no adjustment of the nation's difficulty is possible until the claims of the black man are first met and satisfied. ... If you would restore the Union and maintain the government you so fondly cherish, make way for liberty, universal and complete."[31] In August, Dr. James Pennington of New York, an escaped former slave and Presbyterian minister, headed a petition of black leaders urging Congress to end slavery. It was, they stressed, the only way to bring lasting peace.

The undersigned, Free Colored citizens of these United States, believing that African Slavery as it now exists at the South, is the prime cause of the present Crisis and that permanent peace cannot be restored until said cause be removed, most respectfully petition your honorable body to take such measures, or enact

---

[29] Proclamation, Headquarters, Western Department, August 30, 1861, in Berlin et al., *Destruction of Slavery*, 415; *Official Records*, series 1, vol. 3, 469–70, 477–78.
[30] *Douglass' Monthly*, October 1861; *Weekly Anglo-African*, September 21, 1861.
[31] *Douglass' Monthly*, May 1861; *Weekly Anglo-African*, May 11, 1861.

such a law as may, in your wisdom seem best for the immediate abolition of African Slavery.[32]

The good sense of that approach seemed obvious to Harriet Tubman, who made the same point: "God's ahead of Master Lincoln. God won't let Master Lincoln beat the South till he do the right thing."[33]

No matter how hard Lincoln tried to keep the issues of Union and slavery separate, no matter how determined white northerners were to fight only against secession, no matter how specific Congress tried to be in delineating those slaves subject to confiscation from those who were not, this war was a freedom war. It had been so from the start, as most blacks well knew. They knew it because they made it a freedom war, none more so than the tens of thousands who escaped during the war's early months and forced the government to react. Thus it was, as W. E. B. Du Bois observed, that "with perplexed and laggard steps, the United States Government followed the footsteps of the black slave."[34]

Officers charged with enforcing the Confiscation Act were especially perplexed. The act's language was fairly clear, but enforcing it proved difficult. Most field commanders simply reiterated the act to their subordinates without being very specific about procedure. Union General George McClellan, commander of the Army of the Potomac, told his officers that any slaves employed by the enemy "for military purposes" were to be detained for labor. "Those simply fugitive" were to be "dismissed from your camp."[35] But how were his men to tell which fugitives had been used by Confederates for military purposes? If dismissed, where were they to go? Back to their owners? Was the army obliged to return them? What if dismissed fugitives had escaped from behind enemy lines? What was to be done with them in such cases?

Some commanders accepted only those fugitives whose labor they needed. Others tried to exclude them entirely. General Henry Halleck attempted to "remedy this evil" of dealing with fugitives by ordering that "no such persons

---

[32] *Weekly Anglo-African*, August 17, 1861. Significantly, Pennington and his associates claimed citizenship for themselves, a status that the Supreme Court in *Dred Scott* had denied to African Americans.

[33] Tubman quoted in Lydia Maria Child to John G. Whittier, January 21, 1862, *Letters of Lydia Maria Child*, 161.

[34] Du Bois, *Black Reconstruction*, 81.

[35] Lt. Col. James A. Handie [Headquarters, Army of the Potomac] to Brig. Gen. J. Hooker [division commander, Army of the Potomac], December 1, 1861, in Berlin et al., *Destruction of Slavery*, 174.

be hereafter permitted to enter the lines of any camp, or of any forces on the march, and that any now within such lines be immediately excluded therefrom." But it was impossible to tell fugitives from free men. In the border slave states of Delaware, Maryland, Kentucky, and Missouri, free blacks numbered in the thousands and often sought employment with the army. After questioning blacks in his camp near Rolla, Missouri, one officer reported that "all claim and insist that they are *free*. Some of them, I have no question, are so; others I have as little doubt have been slaves, – but no one is here to prove it."[36]

Some commanders chaffed at the notion of giving even indirect aid to slaveholders, whom they generally viewed as pro-Confederate no matter which side of the lines they were on. An officer in Missouri complained that orders to expel fugitives from federal lines "make us Slave Catchers, instead of Soldiers." When one of his officers wrote from Kentucky asking what to do about slaveholders searching his camp for fugitives, General Ulysses S. Grant replied, "I do not want the army used as negro catchers, but still less do I want to see it used as a cloak to cover their escape." He ordered his subordinates to assist owners in recovering their slaves.[37]

In Kentucky, General William T. Sherman also assured slaveholders that state law was in full force and that fugitives would be "delivered up on claim of the owner or agent." The same was true in all slave states under federal control, even in former Confederate states or parts thereof. As General Henry Halleck moved into western Tennessee in February 1862, he told his men to show "our fellow-citizens of these States that we come merely to crush out rebellion" and not to "oppress and to plunder." Private property, including slave property, would be respected. Later that month, General Don Carols Buell made the same point when his men occupied Nashville. "We are in arms not for the purpose of invading the rights of our fellow-countrymen anywhere," he insisted, "but to maintain the integrity of the Union." When the Union military took control of New Orleans and its environs in the spring of 1862, General Benjamin Butler,

---

[36] General Orders No. 3, Headquarters, Department of the Missouri, November 20, 1861, in Berlin et al., *Destruction of Slavery*, 417; Major George E. Waring [commanding, Frémont Hussars] to Acting Maj. Gen. Asboth [commanding, Fourth Division, Department of the Missouri], December 19, 1861, in ibid., 421–22.

[37] Lt. Col. R. A. Cameron [commanding an Indiana regiment] to Hon. S. Colfax [congressman], May 11, 1862, in Berlin et al., *Destruction of Slavery*, 432–33; Brig. Gen. U. S. Grant [commanding, District of Cairo] to Col. J. Cook [commanding, Fort Holt, Kentucky], December 25, 1861, in ibid., 522.

with Lincoln's backing, assured planters that their slave property was secure.[38]

General Ambrose Burnside did the same that spring when Union forces occupied coastal North Carolina. But slaves still flocked to Union camps. Within weeks, their number had swelled to more than ten thousand. From New Bern, Burnside reported to the War Department that "the city is being overrun with fugitives. ... It would be utterly impossible if we were so disposed to keep them outside of our lines as they find their way to us through woods & swamps from every side." It was the same in Tennessee. After turning fugitives away, one commander near Nashville complained, "During the night the negroes instead of going home ... secreted themselves until they could follow the Troops and get back into my camp."[39] Their refusal to be reenslaved left officers frustrated and confused over how to proceed on both practical and legal grounds.

Secretary of War Simon Cameron had from the start worried about the Confiscation Act's ambiguity regarding refugees' legal status. Were they, as the act implied, simply government slaves-in-waiting, to be returned to their owners after the war? In the original draft of his December 1861 annual report, Cameron suggested that in light of the army's need for manpower, confiscated slaves be permanently emancipated. He even suggested that it might become necessary to enlist blacks as soldiers. Worse yet, he made the report public before Lincoln saw the document. Lincoln, still trying to keep the war a white man's affair and fearing public reaction if he did not, ordered Cameron to delete the emancipation and enlistment passages. A few weeks later, amid allegations of corruption and insubordination, Lincoln removed Cameron from office.[40]

---

[38] Sherman to Col. Turchin, October 15, 1861, *Official Records*, series 2, vol. 1, 774; General Orders No. 46, Headquarters, Department of the Missouri, February 22, 1862, ibid., series 1, vol. 8, 563–64; General Orders No. 13a., Headquarters, Department of the Ohio, February 26, 1862, ibid., series 1, vol. 7, 669–70; Butler to Sec. of War Edwin M. Stanton, June 10, 1862, ibid., series 1, vol. 15, 466; General Orders No. 41, Headquarters, Department of the Gulf, June 10, 1862, ibid., 483–84; Edwin M. Stanton to Col. George F. Shepley [military gov. of Louisiana], June 10, 1862, ibid., series 3, vol. 2, 141.

[39] Burnside [commanding, Department of North Carolina] to Edwin M. Stanton, March 21, 1862, in Berlin et al., *Destruction of Slavery*, 80–81; Brig. Gen. James S. Negley [commanding a brigade, Army of the Ohio] to Gen. Don Carlos Buell [commanding, Department and Army of the Ohio], March 9, 1862, in ibid., 524.

[40] Edward McPherson, ed., *The Political History of the United States of America, during the Great Rebellion* (Washington, D.C.: Philip and Solomons, 1865), 249. See also Erwin Stanley Bradley, *Simon Cameron, Lincoln's Secretary of War: A Political Biography* (Philadelphia: University of Pennsylvania Press, 1966).

Even as Lincoln was sacking Cameron, in part over his loose interpretation of the Confiscation Act, slaves to whom the act never applied were imposing their own interpretation. In January 1862, John Boston, a refugee from Maryland who had fled to the Union army in Virginia, wrote to his wife Elizabeth, still held in slavery. Boston twice confidently referred to himself as a free man.

My Dear Wife it is with grate joy I take this time to let you know Whare I am I am now in Safety in the 14th Regiment of Brooklyn this Day I can Address you thank god a free man I had a little truble in giting away But as the lord led the Children of Isrel to the land of Canon So he led me to a land Whare fredom Will rain in spite Of earth and hell Dear you must make your Self content I am free from al the Slavers Lash ... My Dear I Cant express my grate desire that I Have to See you I trust the time Will Come When We Shal meet again And if We don't met on earth We Will Meet in heven Whare Jesas ranes ... Dear Wife I must Close rest yourself Contented I am free I Want you to rite To me Soon as you Can Without Delay Direct your letter to the 14th Reigment New york State malitia Uptons Hill Virginea Your Affectionate Husban Kiss Daniel For me

JOHN BOSTON[41]

More and more, army officers bowed to the impossibility of keeping refugees at bay whether the Confiscation Act applied to them or not. One officer near Union City, Tennessee, gave as his excuse that "Rebel Traitors ... demanding the right to search our camp for their fugitive slaves" had "become a nuisance and will no longer be tolerated." Another officer in Kentucky insisted that he was simply too busy with the war to waste time hunting refugees.[42]

Congress bowed to the pressure as well. In March 1862, without altering its position under the Confiscation Act, Congress forbade the use of federal troops in capturing and returning fugitive slaves. The army could still confiscate those slaves used directly against the United States. And it could exclude slaves from entering its lines if commanders had the means

---

[41] John Boston to Elizabeth Boston, January 12, 1862, in Berlin et al., *Destruction of Slavery*, 357–58.

[42] General Orders No. 26, Headquarters, Mitchell's Brigade, First Division, Central Army of the Mississippi, June 18, 1862, in Berlin et al., *Destruction of Slavery*, 276; Summary of a speech by Col. Smith D. Atkins [commanding an Illinois regiment], November 1862, in ibid., 530–31.

to do so. The army was simply no longer faced with the impossible task of determining which slaves fell under protection of the Confiscation Act and returning to slavery those who did not. Escaping slaves had pushed the government a giant step further toward recognizing that they were slaves no more. General Abner Doubleday made that clear when he issued orders implementing Congress's new act. Although the act said nothing of legal status, Doubleday read it to imply that fugitives were "to be treated as persons and not as chattels."[43]

## THEY SAY THEY ARE FREE

The pressure continued to grow as more refugees, in groups large and small, made their way to Union lines. By the summer of 1862, nearly 10,000 from South Carolina had escaped to occupying Union forces along the coast.[44] At the same time, self-emancipated slaves were flocking to federal camps in southern Louisiana. General Benjamin Butler reported late that summer, "They are now coming in by the hundreds nay thousands almost daily. . . . Many plantations are deserted along the coast."[45] A planter in La Fourche Parish recorded the exodus in his diary.

> **July 7, 1862:** James Pugh's estate lost 10 negroes last night.
>
> **July 8, 1862:** There has been a perfect stampede of the negroes on some places in this vicinity.
>
> **October 28, 1862:** The negroes are in a very bad way in the neighborhood and I fear will all go off.
>
> **October 30, 1862:** Found our negroes completely demoralized. Some gone and some preparing to go. I fear we shall lose them all.
>
> **October 31, 1862:** The negroes . . . run off. It looks probable that they will all go.
>
> **November 2, 1862:** Our negroes . . . are still leaving, some every night. The plantation will probably be completely cleaned out in a week.

[43] E. P. Halsted [acting assistant adjutant-general] to Lt. Col. John D. Shaul [commanding, Seventy-Sixth New York Regiment], April 6, 1862, *Official Records*, series 2, vol. 1, 815.

[44] Edward L. Pierce, "The Freedmen of Port Royal," *Atlantic Monthly* 12 (September 1863): 299.

[45] Butler to Gen. Henry Halleck, September 1, 1862, Benjamin F. Butler Papers, Library of Congress, in William F. Messner, "Black Violence and White Response: Louisiana, 1862," *Journal of Southern History* 41 (1975): 31. See also Junius P. Rodriguez, "'We'll Hang Jeff Davis on the Sour Apple Tree': Civil War Era Slave Resistance in Louisiana," *Gulf Coast Historical Review* 10 (Spring 1995): 7–23.

**November 5, 1862:** This morning there was a rebellion among the
negroes at Mrs. G. Pugh.[46]

Very often, escaping slaves brought news of Confederate fortifications,
military movements, and troop strength. One evening near Fortress Monroe,
six Virginia slaves arrived with detailed information on Confederate deploy-
ments in the region. There were "two artillery batteries on the Nansemond
River about one and one-half miles apart – the first about four miles
from the mouth – both on the left bank. Each mounts four guns, about
24-pounders. . . . The first is garrisoned by forty men . . . the second by eight.
One gun in each fort will traverse; the chassis of the others are immovable."
The men also gave details of unit locations. "The Isle of Wight regiment is
at Smithfield. The Petersburg Cavalry Company is at Chuckatuck. There are
thirteen regiments of South Carolina troops at the old brick church near
Smithfield. . . . At Suffolk there are 10,000 Georgia troops. They have been
coming in for the past three weeks."[47]

Sometimes escaping slaves brought more than information. In May
1862, Robert Smalls ran the side-wheel steamer *Planter*, with its cargo of
ammunition and artillery, out of Charleston and turned it over to the
blockading Federals. Smalls was a skilled seaman whose owner had hired
him out to serve as the *Planter*'s assistant pilot. On the night of May 12,
after his captain and white shipmates went ashore, Smalls and other black
crewmen fired up the boilers. They headed for a nearby wharf to pick up
family members, then eased down the harbor and past Fort Sumter. Guards
at outposts along the way, even those at Sumter, suspected nothing because
Smalls knew all the proper signals. And in the darkness, no one ashore could
tell that the crewmen waving to them were all blacks.

Once past Sumter, Smalls ordered full steam and made for the Federals,
hoping they would see the old sheet he had hoisted as a white flag of truce.
As Smalls approached the first Union vessel he sighted, a lookout yelled
"All hands to quarters!" and the startled Federals brought their guns to
bear on the *Planter*. A federal seaman later recalled:

Just as No. 3 port gun was being elevated, some one cried out, "I see something that
looks like a white flag," and true enough there was something flying on the steamer
that would have been *white* by application of soap and water. As she neared us, we

---

[46] Alexander F. Pugh Diary, Alexander F. Pugh Papers, Louisiana State University, in
C. Peter Ripley, *Slaves and Freedmen in Civil War Louisiana* (Baton Rouge: Louisiana State
University Press, 1976), 17.

[47] Gen. John E. Wool to Gen. George B. McClellan, with enclosure by William J. Whipple,
November 11, 1861, *Official Records*, series 1, vol. 4, 629–31.

FIGURE 2.3. Fugitives heading for Union lines brought their labor, their knowledge, and sometimes valuable property. In May 1862, harbor pilot Robert Smalls and his enslaved comrades on the armed transport *Planter* made a daring escape. Gathering their families aboard, they ran the steamboat past Fort Sumter and out of Charleston Harbor. Smalls remained aboard and was later named captain after he saved the boat from capture. He was the first African American to command a U.S. vessel. Image from *Harper's Weekly* (New York), June 14, 1862.

looked in vain for the face of a white man. When they discovered that we would not fire on them, there was a rush of contrabands out on her deck, some dancing, some singing, whistling, jumping; and others stood looking towards Fort Sumter, and muttering all sorts of maledictions against it, and *"de heart of de Souf,"* generally.

As the *Planter* came alongside, Smalls stepped forward, took off his hat, and called out, "Good morning, sir! I've brought you some of the old United States guns, sir!"[48]

Depriving the Confederacy of much needed labor, and sometimes equipment, escaping slaves made clear how devastating their attitudes and actions were to the Confederate war effort. So many slaves were escaping by summer 1862 that Confederate General John Pemberton, commander of

---

[48] James M. Guthrie, *Camp-Fires of the Afro-American* (Philadelphia: Afro-American Publishing Co., 1899), 306–14. Reports on the *Planter* incident can be found in United States War Department, *Official Records of the Union and Confederate Navies in the War of the Rebellion* (Washington, D.C.: Government Printing Office, 1894–1922), series 1, vol. 12, 820–26. After the war, Smalls served several terms as a congressman from South Carolina. In 1899, he was appointed customs collector for Beaufort and held the position until 1913. Two years later, he died of natural causes in the home where he and his mother had once been enslaved. See Okon Edet Uya, *From Slavery to Public Service: Robert Small, 1839–1915* (New York: Oxford University Press, 1971).

the Department of South Carolina and Georgia, issued orders allowing only white soldiers to work close to Union lines. Slaves, he knew, "could not be trusted to work so near the enemy." He also diverted troops to "prevent the escape of slaves and for protection of persons and property against insubordination of negroes."[49]

It was hardly unusual to see Confederate soldiers serving as slave patrols. Elements of the Nineteenth South Carolina Regiment roamed the streets of Charleston to keep local blacks under control. Civilians too, who might otherwise have been put in the army, were paid to do patrol duty. Officials in Early County, Georgia, hired extra patrols for each of its districts. When men could not be hired for slave patrols, they were drafted. The city council of Cuthbert, Georgia, divided the town into three wards and assigned all white males between the ages of sixteen and sixty to serve on patrols. In Barbour County, Alabama, the justice of the peace assigned men to patrol companies.[50]

Although Confederate armies were constantly outnumbered by their Union counterparts by an average of two-to-one, tens of thousands of southern whites were kept at home to guard against escaping slaves and slave rebellion. To state and local officials, it seemed worth the cost. A grand jury in Baker County, Georgia, deemed slave patrollers as important as soldiers. Despite that importance, patrols were often left to incompetent or disinterested men. Consequently, patrol laws were often half-heartedly enforced or completely ignored. So badly was the job handled in Sumter County, Georgia, that slaveholders urged the local patrol commission to "appoint men to execute such duty as they know will do it in a proper manner." Slaveholders in Lowndes County, Georgia, "aggrieved that the patrol law has been so much neglected," repeatedly called for stricter enforcement. "We recommend," they wrote, "that the patrol laws be strictly enforced. In fact we deem it indispensable to the protection of property in various sections of our county." Officials in Georgia's Thomas County complained that slaves "under the present want of discipline are an absolute

---

[49] Pemberton to Col. Colquitt, June 14, 1862, *Official Records*, series 1, vol. 14, 565; Pemberton to Maj. W. P. Emanuel, June 4, 1862, ibid., 541.

[50] Special Order No. 28, August 13, 1863, Confederate States Army Records, South Carolina Historical Society, in Hadden, *Slave Patrols*, 186; *Early County (Ga.) News*, March 16, 1864; Cuthbert City Council Minutes, in Annette McDonald Suarez, *A Source Book on the Early History of Cuthbert and Randolph County, Georgia* (Atlanta: Cherokee Publishing, 1982), 130–31; Walker, *Backtracking in Barbour County*, 178.

evil" and ordered that every plantation supply the captain of the patrol commission with a list of all slaves.[51]

So resistant were nonslaveholders to serving not only on slave patrols but in the army as well that in April 1862, the Confederacy began drafting men into military service. Ultimately, conscription did the Confederacy more harm than good by helping turn southern plain folk against the war effort. They deeply resented the ways in which wealthy men avoided service, from hiring substitutes to bribing conscript officers. Most egregious was the "twenty slave law," which exempted one white male for every twenty slaves owned. Jefferson Davis stressed that the law's purpose "was not to draw any distinction of classes, but simply to provide a force, in the nature of a police force, sufficient to keep our negroes in control." But nonslaveholders generally denounced the law as a favor to planters and called the conflict a "rich man's war."[52]

Even men already in service despised the twenty slave law. "It gave us the blues," wrote Tennessee Private Sam Watkins. "We wanted twenty negroes. Negro property suddenly became very valuable, and there was raised the howl of 'rich man's war, poor man's fight.'" Watkins later recalled that "from this time on till the end of the war, a solider was simply a machine. We cursed the war ... we cursed the Southern Confederacy." Private O. Goddin of North Carolina wrote to Governor Zebulon Vance complaining of the law's "distinction between the rich man (who had something to fight for) and the poor man who fights for that he never will have. The exemption of the owners of 20 negroes & the allowing of substitutes clearly proves it."[53] One Georgia soldier called planters "the most contemptible of all our public enemies."

[51] *Albany (Ga.) Patriot*, May 30, 1861; Sumter County (Ga.) Superior Court, Minute Book, 47; Lowndes County (Ga.) Superior Court, Minute Book A, 234, 277, 291; Thomas County (Ga.) Superior Court, Minute Book 1858–1865, 494.

[52] Speech at Jackson, Mississippi, December 26, 1862, in Lynda L. Crist, Mary S. Dix, and Kenneth H. Williams, eds., *The Papers of Jefferson Davis* (Baton Rouge: Louisiana State University Press, 1997), 8: 569. For an examination of the "rich man's war" attitude's impact on the Confederate war effort see David Williams, Teresa Crisp Williams, and David Carlson, *Plain Folk in a Rich Man's War: Class and Dissent in Confederate Georgia* (Gainesville: University Press of Florida, 2002), and Williams, *Bitterly Divided: The South's Inner Civil War*.

[53] Sam R. Watkins, *Co. Aytch: Maury Grays, First Tennessee Regiment* (1882; reprint, Wilmington, N.C.: Broadfoot Publishing, 1987), 69; Goddin to Vance, February 27, 1863, Governor's Papers, North Carolina Division of Archives and History, Raleigh, in Paul D. Escott et al., eds., *Major Problems in the History of the American South*, vol. 1, *The Old South* (New York: Houghton Mifflin, 1999), 365–66.

These fellows talk loudly about *their* constitutional rights. . . . But listen again and you will hear them loud for the enforcement of the Conscript Law. Oh, yes! Their negroes must make cotton and whilst doing it the poor men must be taken from their families and put in the Army to protect their negroes. Was ever a greater wrong, or a more damning sin, perpetrated by men or devils?[54]

Reaction to the draft in general, and planter exemption in particular, was just as vicious on the home front. A Lafayette, Alabama, man warned his senator that the twenty slave law was "considered class legislation & has given more dissatisfaction than any thing else Congress has done." Many were so incensed that they simply ignored the law. One newspaper reported that not a single man appeared at the April 1862 draft call in Savannah, Georgia. The paper listed nearly 200 names of absentees. Around the same time, the entire Fourth Division of the South Carolina militia failed to report when called to service. Such displays of defiance could be dangerous. In the Alabama hill country, conscripts who declined to serve were tracked down with bloodhounds as if they were slaves. In Arkansas, General Joe Shelby sent his men after draft dodgers with orders to "use all force in your power, and when necessary shoot them down."[55]

Many deserters and draft dodgers formed anti-Confederate bands that controlled much of the southern countryside. They raided plantations, supply trains, and warehouse depots and did battle with conscript and home guard companies. By 1863, there was a full-blown inner civil war going on within the South. So violent was the conflict that a Georgia newspaper editor lamented, "We are fighting each other harder than we have ever fought the enemy."[56] To anti-Confederate southerners, the Confederacy *was* the enemy. It drafted their men, confiscated their supplies, and starved them out. It excused from the draft wealthy men, whose slaves were escaping in such numbers and taking such liberties that whites had to be forced into slave patrols.

Even with slave patrols and the twenty slave law in place, whites in high slaveholding districts constantly feared slave rebellion. A resident of Jackson County, Mississippi, begged the governor to do what he could to end

[54] *Milledgeville (Ga.) Confederate Union*, March 31, 1863.
[55] E. G. Edwards to C. C. Clay, February 19, 1863, Clement Caliborne Clay Papers, Duke University, Durham, N.C.; *Atlanta Southern Confederacy*, April 10 and 16, 1862; W. Scott Poole, *South Carolina's Civil War: A Narrative History* (Macon, Ga.: Mercer University Press, 2005), 52; Paul Horton, "Submitting to the 'Shadow of Slavery': The Secession Crisis and Civil War in Alabama's Lawrence County," *Civil War History* 44 (1998): 133; W. H. Ferrell to Col. S. D. Jackman, May 21, 1864, *Official Records*, series 1, vol. 34, part 3, 835.
[56] *Milledgeville (Ga.) Confederate Union*, November 24, 1863.

conscription. If the Confederacy kept drafting men from the county, he warned, "we may as well give it to the negroes ... now we have to patrol every night to keep them down." Governor John Milton of Florida asked Confederate Secretary of War James Seddon to exempt overseers from military service. "If left without the control of overseers ... the result will probably be insubordination and insurrection."[57]

Confederate officials rarely agreed to suspend the draft, so state governments tried to deal with slave control on their own. The Georgia General Assembly mandated death for any black person found guilty of arson. Destroying railroad bridges or obstructing rail traffic carried the same penalty. It later forbade slaveholders to let slaves hire themselves out and required slaves to reside on their owners' premises. The Alabama legislature imposed prohibitions on any sort of trade with slaves. Several times throughout the war, Alabama lawmakers increased funds awarded for the capture of runaway slaves. Other Confederate states enacted similar statutes or strengthened existing acts.[58]

Despite efforts to keep them down, enslaved blacks were increasingly claiming freedom, or some degree of it, for themselves. "They say they are free," wrote one Alabama slaveholder. "We cannot exert any authority. I beg ours to do what little is done." Some refused to work at all. A South Carolina planter complained in the summer of 1862 that "the Negroes are unwilling to do any work, no matter what it is." Some slaves demanded payment for their labor and threatened to escape if they did not get it. Others escaped to towns and cities, working as day laborers or even skilled professionals. An Alabama slave escaped and found employment as a blacksmith. By war's end, he had a trunk full of cash, albeit in worthless Confederate notes.[59]

---

[57] C. F. Howell to Gov. John J. Pettus, August 23, 1862, in Wiley, *Southern Negroes*, 36; Milton to Seddon, February 17, 1863, in Berlin et al., *Destruction of Slavery*, 746–47.

[58] *Acts of the General Assembly of the State of Georgia, 1861* (Milledgeville: Boughton, Nisbet, and Barnes, 1862), 68, 69; *Journal of the Senate of the State of Georgia, 1863* (Milledgeville: Boughton, Nisbet, Barnes, and Moore, 1863), 120; *Acts of the Called Session of the General Assembly of Alabama* (Montgomery: Shorter and Reid, 1861), 34; *Acts of the Second Called Session, 1861, and of the First Regular Annual Session of the General Assembly of Alabama* (Montgomery: Montgomery Advertiser Book and Job Office, 1862), 15–16; *Acts of the Called Session, 1863, and of the Third Regular Annual Session of the General Assembly of Alabama* (Montgomery: Saffold and Figures, 1864), 63.

[59] Susanna Clay to C[lement] Caliborne Clay, September 5, 1863, Clay Papers, Duke University; Greenwood Plantation Records [South Carolina], entry of August 8, 1862, in Wiley, *Southern Negroes*, 73–74; Magnolia Plantation Records [Louisiana], entry of August 11, 1862, in ibid., 74–75; Berlin et al., *Destruction of Slavery*, 677; W. B. Allen, *Georgia Narratives*, part 1, 12.

One white passenger on a southwest Georgia railroad wrote in 1862 of being shocked to find "crowds of slaves in gayest attire" getting on and off the trains "at every country stopping place." They held picnics, barbecues, dances, and church services. They gathered in town streets on Sunday afternoons to play games. Slaves were taking liberties in the countryside as well. They frequently took plantation stores at will, slaughtered livestock to feed themselves, and rode their owners' horses as they pleased.[60]

When a Texas planter tried to beat one of his slaves for insubordination, the bondsman "cursed the old man all to pieces," walked off to the woods, and refused to return until his owner finally promised that there would be no more whipping. Three slaves on an Alabama plantation threatened to kill the overseer if he attempted any punishment at all. A Tennessee woman wrote to her husband that "overseers generally are doing very little good and they complain of the negroes getting so free and idle, but I think it is because most every one is afraid to correct them." Such fears were well founded. On the Pugh plantation near Thibodeaux, Louisiana, slaves refused to work and assaulted Pugh and his overseer, "injuring them severely."[61]

Thankful indeed were many slaveholders who were able to avoid violent encounters with their slaves. Some were not so fortunate. In October 1862, three armed whites tracking down a fugitive camp in Surry County, Virginia, were all killed in the effort. A July 1862 insurrection on one Mississippi plantation left an overseer with his throat cut. Florida slaves became so unruly that General R. F. Floyd, commanding state troops, asked the governor to declare martial law in Nassau, Duval, Clay, Putnam, St. Johns, and Volusia Counties. It was "a measure of absolute necessity," Floyd insisted, because the region contained "a nest of traitors and lawless negroes."[62]

Even Jefferson Davis was not immune from slave insurrection. He and his brother Joseph owned a pair of plantations on a bend in the Mississippi River – Davis Bend – twenty miles south of Vicksburg. In May 1862, after Joseph moved some of the house servants to Vicksburg, the remaining

---

[60] William Harrison Ainsworth, ed., "The Negroes of the South," *New Monthly Magazine* 128 (1863): 14; Wiley, *Southern Negroes*, 75. Examples of increasing liberties that enslaved southerners took during the war can be found throughout Stephen Ash, *The Black Experience in the Civil War South* (Santa Barbara, Calif.: Preager, 2010).

[61] Lizzie S. Neblett to William H. Neblett, August 13, 1863, in Murr, *Diary and Letters of Elizabeth Scott Neblett*, 135; Wiley, *Southern Negroes*, 75–76; Brig. Gen. G. Weitzel [commanding, Reserve Brigade, U.S. Volunteers] to Maj. George C. Strong [assistant adjutant-general, Department of the Gulf], *Official Records*, series 1, vol. 15, 172.

[62] *Calendar of Virginia State Papers* (Richmond: n.p., 1893), 11: 233–36; J. W. Boyd to Gov. John J. Pettus, August 1, 1862, in Wiley, *Southern Negroes*, 82; Floyd to Gov. John Milton, April 11, 1862, *Official Records*, series 1, vol. 53, 233.

FIGURE 2.4. Black southerners increasingly took liberties during the war and resisted attempts to punish them for it. Many whites who tried were killed in the effort. "We cannot exert any authority," admitted an Alabama slaveholder. Another in Tennessee confirmed that "most every one is afraid to correct them." Still another in Texas found threats useless, "so I shall say nothing . . . I will try to feel thankful if they let me alone." From a lithograph by Henry Louis Stephens entitled "Blow for Blow" (1863). Image courtesy of the Library of Congress.

slaves forcibly took charge of the plantations. They ransacked the Davis residence, destroyed the cotton, and went to work for themselves, claiming collective ownership of the land that their families had worked for years. They managed the plantations on their own for months before federal troops arrived. In June, Davis received word from Brierfield, another of his plantations, that slaves there were ignoring the overseer, refusing to work, and generally "in a state of insubordination." Lincoln's Emancipation Proclamation was still more than six months away and already the Confederate president's own slaves, along with so many others, had effectively emancipated themselves.[63]

---

[63] Joseph E. Davis to Jefferson Davis, May 22, 1862, in Crist et al., *Papers of Jefferson Davis*, 8: 196–97; William Porterfield to Jefferson Davis, June 5, 1862, in ibid., 227; Charles J. Mitchell to Jefferson Davis, June 7, 1862, in ibid., 231–33.

Desperate slaveholders frequently turned to the Union army for protection. In southern Louisiana, Union officers were inundated with requests for help. A planter from Plaquemines Parish told General George Shepley that local slaves were in a state of insurrection and begged him to bring them under control. Commanders were sometimes conflicted over whether to intervene, although they were technically obliged to enforce state and federal laws recognizing slavery. Some officers were perfectly willing to do so. In the summer of 1862, when an insurrection broke out a few miles north of New Orleans, General Benjamin Butler informed local slaves that attacks against their owners would be repelled.[64]

On a plantation near Donaldsonville, enslaved blacks who heard that the Federals had arrived in Louisiana declared themselves free and refused to take orders. Their owner called on Union troops for help. When a federal gunboat arrived flying the U.S. flag, the blacks were overjoyed. They were sure that it was there to back them up in their claim to freedom. Instead, when they stepped forward to welcome their presumed allies, the officer in charge pointedly told them that if they thought the Union army had come to end slavery "they were very much mistaken." The officer arrested several "ringleaders" and ordered the rest back to work. As they were being led away to the plantation stocks, one of the arrested slaves exclaimed, "My God! This is more worserer than Jeff Davis."[65]

Federal help with suppressing slave resistance was not always so forthcoming. In late 1862, the wife of Confederate General Braxton Bragg appealed to Union General Godfrey Weitzel for protection from her slaves. Weitzel was inclined to help but was overruled by his superior, Benjamin Butler. A few months' experience with recalcitrant slaveholders had hardened Butler's attitude toward them. It now seemed curious to Butler that families like the Braggs were both "in rebellion against the Government" and, at the same time, "in terror seeking its protection." When such people recognized the U.S. government's authority, Butler said, he was prepared to assist. Until then, they were on their own.[66]

---

[64] See documents 71–73 in Berlin et al., *Destruction of Slavery*, 232–35; John C. P. Wederstrandt to Shepley, September 19, 1862, in ibid., 219–21; Butler to Edwin M. Stanton, August 2, 1862, *Official Records*, series 1, vol. 15, 534.

[65] William Watson, *Life in the Confederate Army: Being the Observations and Experiences of an Alien in the South During the American Civil War* (London: Chapman and Hall, 1887), 397–98.

[66] Weitzel [commanding, District of the Teche] to Maj. George C. Strong [Headquarters, Department of the Gulf], November 5, 1862 [two dispatches], and Strong to Weitzel, November 6, 1862, in Berlin et al., *Destruction of Slavery*, 225–30.

## WHAT SHALL WE DO WITH THE CONTRABANDS?

If some Union officers would not help put down slave rebellion, neither would they help blacks secure freedom. They too were on their own. Lincoln's government still recognized slavery in every slave state whether Union or Confederate. The Confiscation Act legally deprived only disloyal slaveholders of their slaves, but nearly every slaveholder professed Union loyalty as soon as federal forces arrived. So slaves took what liberties they dared and continued escaping when they could, relying on each other for help. In that sense, the Underground Railroad operated much as it had before the war, with enslaved men and women giving refugees food, shelter, and sometimes escorts from one safe house to the next.

The help did not end when they reached Union lines. Blacks established refugee aid organizations all across the North. These were especially active in border cities such as Philadelphia and Washington. Working through churches, schools, and benevolent societies, black residents provided food and shelter to escapees and helped them find jobs. In April 1862, Philadelphia's leading blacks set up an employment office for fugitives. William Still, who headed the city's Underground Railroad, led the effort. In Washington, the Reverend Richard H. Cain, minister of a local African Methodist Episcopal church, took a leading role in caring for fugitives and helping them find work.[67]

One of the most active refugee supporters was Elizabeth Keckley, a Washington seamstress who counted Mary Todd Lincoln among her clients. Keckley and forty other black women formed the Contraband Relief Association. Herself a former slave who had purchased her own freedom, Keckley led the organization in soliciting funds and supplies from dozens of black churches and relief organizations between Baltimore and Boston. She appealed for support from Wendell Phillips's Twelfth Baptist Church in Boston and Henry Highland Garnet's Shiloh Church in New York. During a stop-over in New York, Keckley told her story to a steward at the Metropolitan Hotel and raised "quite a sum of money" from the black dining room waiters. Frederick Douglass donated $200 to Keckley's effort. So did Mary Todd Lincoln.[68]

---

[67] Report by William Still, May 22, 1862, Pennsylvania Abolition Society Papers, Historical Society of Pennsylvania, Philadelphia, in Ripley et al., *Black Abolitionist Papers*, 5: 140–41; Ann J. Edwards, *Texas Narratives*, part 2, 10–11.

[68] *Christian Recorder*, August 22, 1863; Elizabeth Keckley, *Behind the Scenes, or, Thirty Years a Slave, and Four Years in the White House* (New York: G. W. Carleton and Co.,

Washington became a magnet not only for slaves escaping from Virginia and points south but also from Maryland. Claiming to be refugees from disloyal slaveholders behind Confederate lines, Maryland slaves flooded into Washington. Although subject to reenslavement under the Fugitive Slave Act, it was impossible to tell who was subject to the law. That gave Maryland escapees some degree of safety, but it put all Washington blacks in danger of enslavement. Slavecatchers often kidnapped blacks at random and sold them in Maryland slave markets. Some escaped. Others never got the chance. One Maryland owner whipped a fugitive to death as a warning example to others.[69]

So many slavecatchers roamed the streets of Washington, capturing free blacks, contrabands, and escapees without regard to status, that Congress was finally compelled to intervene. The first step toward a practical remedy, one that abolitionist leaders and "radicals" in Congress had been proposing for months, was simply to abolish slavery in the District of Columbia. In April 1862, Congress did just that. Lincoln supported the bill in principle but had reservations about the message it would send to slaveholders in the border states and occupied South. He had wanted one of the border states to lead the way and had tried without success to have Delaware make the first move. He would also have preferred a more gradual approach, expressing his sympathy for slaveholders who would "at once be deprived of cooks, stable boys &c." Nevertheless, Lincoln signed the bill into law.[70]

The act contained two provisions that Lincoln fully supported. Congress offered nothing to former slaves for their years of unpaid service, but it did offer compensation of up to $1 million from the federal treasury to slaveholders for the loss of their property. In a move toward racial cleansing, Congress also authorized $100,000 for the deportation, or colonization, of

---

1868), 111–16. Keckley's son George, whose freedom she had purchased along with her own, died in combat on a Missouri battlefield.

[69] Attorney General Edwin Bates to Maryland Gov. A. W. Bradford, May 10, 1862, in Berlin et al., *Destruction of Slavery*, 366; Gen. Charles H. Howard [assistant commissioner, District of Columbia Freedmen's Bureau] to Hon. John P. C. Shanks [congressman], [November 20] 1867, in ibid., 347–48.

[70] *Statutes at Large*, 12: 376–77; Theodore C. Pease and James G. Randall, eds., *Diary of Orville Hickman Browning* (Springfield: Illinois State Historical Library, 1925), 1: 541. For an overview of how blacks and abolitionist whites in Washington undermined slavery see Stanley Harrold, *Subversives: Antislavery Community in Washington, D.C., 1828–1865* (Baton Rouge: Louisiana State University Press, 2003). A fine collection of essays dealing primarily with how blacks contributed to and took advantage of freedom is Elizabeth Clark-Lewis, ed., *First Freed: Washington, D.C., in the Emancipation Era* (Washington, D.C.: Howard University Press, 2002). See also Kate Masur, *An Example for All the Land: Emancipation and the Struggle over Equality in Washington, D.C.* (Chapel Hill: University of North Carolina Press, 2010).

blacks to Africa or the Caribbean or anywhere else as long as it was out of the United States. Both slaveholder compensation and black colonization would become the twin pillars of Lincoln's early efforts to address the "negro question."[71]

Neither compensation nor colonization curtailed the immediate problem of fugitives from Maryland flocking into Washington. These slaves were, in effect, freeing themselves, and there were so many that little could be done to stop them. Frustrated with their own inability to act and annoyed at Maryland's constant complaints, administration officials most often turned a blind eye. When Maryland Congressman Charles Calvert asked Secretary of War Edwin M. Stanton to help retrieve fugitive slaves, the War Department's assistant secretary replied that Stanton had "more urgent and important business."[72]

Stanton's field commanders faced much the same problem. They were authorized to employ refugees, but the numbers coming in were more than they could handle. "What shall I do with my niggers?" asked the exasperated commander of Louisiana's Fort Macomb in early 1862. The commander at Fort Saint Philip was just as perplexed. "Darkies come flocking in here," he told a correspondent, and he could not feed them all. "I am placed in an awkward dilemma. . . . I cannot have them in the fort, and know not what to do." A New Hampshire officer wrote that Louisiana blacks were "coming into camp by the hundred and are a costly curse. They should be kept out or set at work, or freed or colonized, or sunk or something."[73]

General Ben Butler told the secretary of war that in light of the number of slaves escaping, trying to enforce the Confiscation Act was absurd. Of the thousands of blacks overcrowding his camps, loyal and disloyal owners had lost them alike. He had put as many to work as he could and tried to keep the rest out. "*It is a physical impossibility to take all*," Butler stressed. "I cannot feed the white men within my lines. . . . What would be the state of things if I allowed all the slaves from the plantations to quit their employment and come within the lines." Butler offered no solution beyond a growing awareness that slavery was a curse to the nation, mainly

---

[71] *Statutes at Large*, 12: 376–77. By far the best analysis of Lincoln and colonization is Phillip W. Magness and Sebastian N. Page, *Colonization after Emancipation: Lincoln and the Movement for Black Resettlement* (Columbia: University of Missouri Press, 2011).

[72] Assistant sec. of war to Calvert, April 14, 1862, in Berlin et al., *Destruction of Slavery*, 363–64.

[73] O. W. Lull to Benjamin Butler, May 11, 1862, Butler Papers, in Messner, "Black Violence," 21; *New York Times*, June 23, 1862; John M. Stanyan, *A History of the Eighth Regiment of New Hampshire Volunteers* (Concord, N.H.: Ira C. Evans, 1892), 107.

because of its "baleful effects" on whites. Butler's increasing frustration with slavery and the "negro question" was plain to see.[74]

General John Wool, commander of Virginia's Fortress Monroe, also wrote to the secretary of war asking "what am I to do with the negro slaves that are almost daily arriving at this post from the interior." The commander at Point Lookout, Maryland, complained that slaves were "continually crossing over from the Eastern shore of Va., and coming in from Md., all getting within our lines ... until the number is greater than we know what to do with." A naval officer wrote from Georgia's St. Simons Island that he could not feed all the refugees coming into his lines. The quartermaster at Helena, Arkansas, had the same difficulty. "There is a perfect 'Cloud' of negroes being thrown upon me for Sustenance & Support. ... What am I to do with them."[75]

To James Madison Bell, one of the great poets of the nineteenth century, the answer was obvious. Like so many other blacks, Bell pressed Lincoln to make freedom a Union war aim and accept the services of blacks as soldiers. In the *Pacific Appeal*, a black abolitionist newspaper based in San Francisco, Bell framed the question and added his response.

> What Shall We Do with the Contrabands?
> Shall we arm them? Yes, arm them! give to each man
> A rifle, a musket, a cutlass, a sword;
> Then on to the charge! let them war in the van,
> Where each may confront with his merciless lord,
> And purge from their race, in the eyes of the brave,
> The stigma and scorn now attending the slave.
> I would not have the wrath of the rebels to cease,
> Their hope to grow weak nor their courage to wane,
> Till the Contrabands join in securing a peace,
> Whose glory shall vanish the last galling chain,
> And win for their race an undying respect

---

[74] Butler to Edwin M. Stanton, May 25, 1862, in Berlin et al., *Destruction of Slavery*, 203–207.

[75] Wool to Simon Cameron, September 18, 1861, *Official Records*, series 1, vol. 4, 614; Capt. H. J. Van Kirk to Capt. R. W. Dawson, September 8, 1862, Records of the U.S. Army Continental Commands, in Barbara Jeanne Fields, *Slavery and Freedom on the Middle Ground: Maryland during the Nineteenth Century* (New Haven, Conn.: Yale University Press, 1985), 116; S. W. Godon [commanding, USS *Mohican*] to S. F. Du Pont [commanding, South Atlantic Squadron], March 30, 1862, in Berlin et al., *Destruction of Slavery*, 119–20; B. O. Carr [quartermaster, Helena, Ark.] to Capt. F. S. Winslow [chief quartermaster, Army of the Southwest], July 24, 1862, in Berlin et al., eds., *Freedom: A Documentary History of Emancipation, 1861–1867*, series 1, vol. 3, *The Wartime Genesis of Free Labor: The Lower South* (Cambridge: Cambridge University Press, 1990), 659 (hereafter cited as *Lower South*).

> In the land of their prayers, their tears and neglect.
> Is the war one of Freedom? Then why, tell me why,
> Should the wronged and oppressed be debarred from the fight?
> Does not reason suggest, it were noble to die
> In the act of supplanting a wrong for the right?
> Then lead to the charge! for the end is not far,
> When the Contraband host are enrolled in the war.[76]

Although Washington still insisted that ending slavery was not a war aim, growing numbers of field commanders agreed with Bell. Among them was General David Hunter. He needed soldiers, and there were plenty of blacks available to serve. That became clear to Hunter in March 1862 when he took command of the Department of the South, operating along the southeastern Atlantic coast. Two months later, he declared all enslaved people in South Carolina, Georgia, and Florida to be free and ordered conscription for all black males between the ages of eighteen and forty-five.[77]

Blacks were enthusiastic about Hunter's freedom declaration. They were less pleased, however, with his conscription order. Many were ready and willing to serve. For others, indiscriminate conscription imposed hardship on hardship. It was planting time, and families needed their men's support. To some former slaves, involuntary military service seemed like another form of slavery. They had considered themselves free well before Hunter's declaration. Now to have army press gangs force them from their homes evoked painful memories of slave traders and family separations. When one group of soldiers drafted several men on South Carolina's St. Helena Island, a witness described the scene as "strange and affecting."

Women and children gathered around the men to say 'farewell.' Fathers took the little children in their arms, while the Women gave way to the wildest expressions of grief.... a moaning and weeping, such as touches the hearts of strong men, burst forth – an evidence – and sure witness that there is a fountain of love and humanity in the hearts of the poor Negroes.[78]

When Lincoln learned of Hunter's freedom order, he issued a presidential proclamation making it "altogether void." Lincoln stressed that no field

---

[76] *Pacific Appeal* (San Francisco, Calif.), May 24, 1862.

[77] Hunter to Edwin M. Stanton, April 3, 1862, *Official Records*, series 1, vol. 6, 263–64; General Orders No. 7, Headquarters, Department of the South, April 13, 1862, in ibid., series 1, vol. 14, 333; General Orders No. 11, Headquarters, Department of the South, May 9, 1862, in ibid., series 1, vol. 14, 341; Ed. W. Smith to Gen. H. W. Benham, May 9, 1862, in Berlin et al., *Black Military Experience*, 38.

[78] G. M. Wells [plantation superintendent] to E. L. Pierce [Treasury Dept. special agent], [May 1862], in Berlin et al., *Black Military Experience*, 49–50.

commander had the authority to free slaves. Black leaders were sorely disappointed that Lincoln had once again revoked a freedom order issued by one of his generals. Could Lincoln not see that by doing so he only strengthened the rebellion and turned away the Union's warmest friends? In the *Pacific Appeal*, editor Philip Bell openly wondered whether Lincoln was in fact a slavery supporter. Bell called Lincoln's repudiation of Hunter a proslavery proclamation and alluded to Lincoln as a "Northern man with Southern principles."[79]

Although Lincoln was never proslavery, neither was he an abolitionist, at least not in an immediate sense. He wanted chattel slavery to end but feared ending it quickly. He feared opposition from whites, North and South. He feared the turmoil that might follow abrupt emancipation. He feared the consequences for the Republican Party and his own administration. He feared the question of what to do with former slaves once they were free. All that fear led him to favor a gradual approach spanning decades, with blacks yet unborn serving their parents' owners into the twentieth century. Through late 1861 and 1862, he suggested such schemes, especially to the border states, advocating federal laws to release blacks in a measured way and federal funds to compensate slaveholders for their loss. "The change," Lincoln assured slaveholders, "would come gently as the dews of heaven, not rending or wrecking anything."[80] That change need not come, as Hunter would have it, at the point of gun.

Still, if Lincoln made clear that Hunter's blacks could not be free, he dodged the question of whether they could be soldiers. He left that issue to Congress, which passed a resolution demanding to know why Hunter had enlisted "fugitive slaves" without authority. Hunter sarcastically but accurately replied that "No regiment of 'Fugitive Slaves' has been, or is being organized in this Department. There is, however, a fine regiment of persons whose late masters are 'Fugitive Rebels,' men who everywhere fly before the appearance of the National Flag, leaving their servants behind them to shift as best they can for themselves." Hunter also pointed to previous War Department orders authorizing him to "employ all loyal persons offering their services in defence of the Union and for the suppression of

---

[79] Proclamation by Abraham Lincoln, May 19, 1862, in Berlin et al., *Destruction of Slavery*, 123–25; *Pacific Appeal*, June 14, 1862.

[80] Appeal to Border State Representatives, July 12, 1862, in Basler et al., *Collected Works of Abraham Lincoln*, 5: 317–19; Annual Message to Congress, December 1, 1862, in ibid., 5: 529–30; Proclamation by Abraham Lincoln, May 19, 1862, in Berlin et al., *Destruction of Slavery*, 125. For an excellent overview see William C. Harris, *Lincoln and the Border States: Preserving the Union* (Lawrence: University Press of Kansas, 2011).

this Rebellion in any manner I might see fit." Since the orders said nothing of skin color, Hunter saw his black soldiers as federally authorized recruits. Still, the War Department refused to recognize Hunter's black regiment. Unable to pay the men or provide them with uniforms, Hunter disbanded all but one company in August 1862.[81]

Most white northerners supported keeping blacks out of the army. This was a war for Union, not against slavery, and both major parties, Republican and Democratic, had promised to keep it that way. It was, in large part, a matter of racist pride. Indiana's leading Republican newspaper, the *Indianapolis Daily Journal*, expressed a contempt for blacks common among northern whites when it wrote that Lincoln should never shame the nation by using black soldiers: "Certainly we hope we may never have to confess to the world that the United States Government has to seek an ally in the negro to regain its authority."[82]

## A NEW DEPARTURE FOR THE PRESIDENT

As the war entered its second year, white attitudes toward enlisting blacks began to change. At the April 1862 Battle of Shiloh, the largest ever fought in the Western Hemisphere to that time, Union forces suffered more than 13,000 casualties. In June, there were 5,000 more at Seven Pines. The Seven Days battles in late June and early July saw nearly 16,000 Union casualties. Losses from disease were even greater. The war for the Union was not going well, and there was no end in sight. To Samuel Kirkwood, Republican governor of Iowa, it seemed obvious that blacks should be enlisted, mainly for the sake of whites. In the summer of 1862, he wrote to General-in-Chief Henry Halleck, "When this war is over & we have summed up the entire loss of life ... I shall not have any regrets if it is found that a part of the dead are *niggers* and that *all* are not white men."[83]

There were plenty of black men willing to serve, as there had been from the war's outset. W. T. Boyd and J. T. Alston of Cleveland, both "Colard men" who had voted for Lincoln, asked permission to raise a regiment of Ohio blacks. They promised that the men "would make as patriotic and good Soldiers as any other." Captain Rufus Sibb Jones of the Fort Pitt

---

[81] Edwin M. Stanton to Hon. Galusha A. Grow [speaker of the House of Representatives], June 14, 1862, *Official Records*, series 3, vol. 2, 147–48; Hunter to Edwin M. Stanton, June 23, 1862, in Berlin et al., *Black Military Experience*, 50–53; ibid., 38–39.

[82] *Indianapolis Daily Journal*, November 26, 1861.

[83] Kirkwood to Halleck, August 5, 1862, in Berlin et al., *Black Military Experience*, 85–86.

Cadets, a black militia company in Pittsburgh, offered his men's services, assuring Secretary of War Stanton that they were "quite proficient in military discipline." G. P. Miller, a black physician from Battle Creek, Michigan, told the War Department that he could recruit up to 10,000 black men.[84]

In May 1862, a letter arrived on Stanton's desk from Garland H. White, formerly enslaved to Robert Toombs of Georgia. White was now a minister residing among fugitives in London, Canada, who wanted to return to the United States and serve as soldiers. He wrote that they were motivated by a desire to see "an eternal overthrow of the institution of slavery which is the cause of all our trouble." White had more personal motives as well. "I want to see my friends at port royal [South Carolina] & other places in the South." Like so many other exiles, White saw the war as a chance to claim for those left behind the freedom he had long claimed for himself.[85]

Although the War Department shunned such offers, David Hunter was not the only field commander to see the need for black troops and to act on it. In southern Louisiana, General Ben Butler initially argued against both the necessity and wisdom of using black troops when his forces entered the region in spring 1862. But that summer, after a Confederate offensive forced him to evacuate Baton Rouge, Butler called up the Louisiana Native Guards, a regiment of New Orleans Creoles whose offer of service he had previously turned down. They were but the first of more than 24,000 black Louisianans who would serve during the war.[86]

That summer in Kansas, Senator James H. Lane used his recruiting commission to enlist blacks. Lane was a former leader of the Jayhawkers, a Free Soil Kansas militia. Not only did he seek out the service of Kansas blacks, he also sent recruiters across the North drumming up black volunteers. Local recruiters complained that Lane's efforts were hurting their own since whites were reluctant to serve alongside blacks. Both Secretary of War Stanton and General-in-Chief Halleck denied that Lane had authority to recruit black troops, but Lane ignored them and continued mustering blacks into service.[87]

[84] Boyd and Alston to Simon Cameron, November 15, 1861, in Berlin et al., *Black Military Experience*, 80; Jones to Edwin M. Stanton, May 13, 1862, in ibid., 83–84; Miller to Simon Cameron, October 30, 1861, in ibid., 79.

[85] White to Edwin M. Stanton, May 7, 1862, in Berlin et al., *Black Military Experience*, 82–83.

[86] Butler to Edwin M. Stanton, May 25, 1862, *Official Records*, series 1, vol. 15, 441–42; General Orders No. 63, Headquarters, Department of the Gulf, August 22, 1862, in Berlin et al., *Black Military Experience*, 65–67; Testimony of Butler, American Freedmen's Inquiry Commission, May 1, 1863, in ibid., 312–15.

[87] Gov. Thomas Carney of Kansas to Abraham Lincoln, June 5, 1863, in Berlin et al., *Black Military Experience*, 44.

David Hunter also ignored the War Department. On August 5, 1862, he sent his black company under command of a white sergeant, T. C. Trowbridge, to root out rebel guerillas on Georgia's St. Simons Island. When they arrived, they found that the island's self-emancipated former slaves, led by freedman John Brown, had already been at the task for nearly two weeks. They had chased the Rebels all over the island, finally cornering them in a swamp. There the Rebels laid an ambush in which Brown was killed and several others wounded. After an exchange of gunfire, both sides withdrew. Trowbridge's men took up the search, but their quarry managed to escape in a small boat, arriving on the mainland "tattered and dirty from head to foot." The rebel band's leader later wrote to a friend, "If you wish to know hell before your time, go to St. Simons and be hunted ten days by niggers."[88]

With the war going badly for the Union, and with so many blacks eager to help, the case for black enlistment seemed clear. Its main obstacle was racism. What would placing blacks in uniform mean for their enslavement in the South and their social status nationwide? Would making blacks soldiers also make freedom a war aim? Would it make blacks citizens? Could they serve on juries, cast ballots, and hold public office? Would they have equal access to public schools, restaurants, theaters, hotels, and transportation?

Such questions were at the heart of white northern resistance to blacks having anything to do with the war. Blacks were "unfit for freedom," wrote the editor of the *Chicago Times*, "incapable of taking care of themselves as so many infants." To end slavery, predicted the editor, would send two or three million "semi-savages" heading northward to become "a pestilence more destructive than ever yet walked the earth." The *Columbus Crisis* editor was sure that ending slavery would force white northerners to "mix up *four millions of blacks* with their sons and daughters." The pro-emancipation editor of the *Chicago Tribune* admitted with regret that "the greatest ally of slaveholders in this country is the apprehension in the Northern mind that if the slaves were liberated, they would become roaming, vicious vagabonds; that they would overrun the North."[89]

The quarter-million blacks already in the North were too many for most northern whites, who tried their best to keep blacks segregated. Most schools, hospitals, theaters, and churches denied access to blacks or pushed

---

[88] Thomas Wentworth Higginson, *Army Life in a Black Regiment* (Boston: Fields, Osgood, and Co., 1870), 274–75.

[89] *Chicago Times*, October 8, 1861; *Columbus (Ohio) Crisis*, August 22, 1861; *Chicago Tribune*, August 12, 1861.

them off to inferior areas labeled "Colored." Things were much the same in the judicial and political realms. In most free states, it was illegal for blacks to testify in court against whites or to serve on juries. Even where jury service for blacks was legal, they were rarely called. Only in five New England states did adult black males have unrestricted voting rights. Blacks could vote in New York but needed substantial wealth to qualify.

Even in Massachusetts, where black men could vote and black children could attend public schools, there was debilitating racism and segregation. In an open letter to *The Liberator*, John Rock wrote that the entire country, North and South, had conspired to crush black folk.

The masses seem to think that we are oppressed only in the South. This is a mistake; we are oppressed everywhere in this slavery-cursed land. Massachusetts has a great name, and deserves much credit for what she has done, but the position of the colored people in Massachusetts is far from being an enviable one. While colored men have many rights, they have few privileges here. To be sure, we are seldom insulted by the vulgar passers by, we have the right of suffrage, the free schools and colleges are open to our children, and from them have come forth young men capable of filling any post of profit or honor. But there is no field for these young men. . . . You can hardly imagine the humiliation and contempt a colored lad must feel by graduating the first in his class, and then being rejected everywhere else because of his color. . . . Even in Boston, which has a great reputation for being anti-slavery, he has no field for his talent. . . . It is five times as difficult to get a house in a good location in Boston as it is in Philadelphia, and it is ten times more difficult for a colored mechanic to get employment than in Charleston. Colored men in business in Massachusetts receive more respect, and less patronage, than in any place that I know of. In Boston we are proscribed in some of the eating houses, many of the hotels, and all the theaters but one. . . . You know that the colored man is proscribed in some of the churches, and that this proscription is carried even to the grave yards. This is Boston – by far the best, or at least the most liberal large city in the United States.[90]

The question of social equality divided even abolitionists, mainly, although not exclusively, along racial lines. Prominent blacks such as John Rock and Frederick Douglass were relentless in their call for both freedom and the rights of equality associated with it. White abolitionists more often limited themselves to the specific goal of ending slavery. That was especially true of white abolitionists in elective office, who, knowing the racist views of their constituents and holding such views themselves, usually made their arguments on war-related grounds. Even Senator Charles Sumner of Massachusetts, a firm abolitionist of long standing, declared

[90] *Liberator*, August 15, 1862.

that emancipation should be "presented strictly as a measure of military necessity and the argument is to be thus supported rather than on grounds of philanthropy."[91]

Like Sumner, blacks had long recognized that slavery and the war were inseparable. With white northerners beginning to make the same case from whatever motive, the connection between Union victory and ending slavery seemed increasingly obvious. In Pennsylvania, a "very full meeting of the citizens of West Middletown and vicinity, without respect to party or distinction," resolved that since slavery was the war's cause, there could be no permanent peace without slavery's end.[92] In speeches and print, from town halls to the halls of Congress, more and more whites pointed out that declaring an end to slavery would cripple the Confederate war effort, deny the Confederacy foreign recognition, punish slaveholders, demoralize secessionists, further encourage slave resistance, and bring the war to a quicker end.

As for the possibility of fugitives flooding the North, such fears, argued white emancipationists, were groundless. The reason slaves were escaping North was that they wanted freedom. Give it to them in the South, and they would stay put. Presenting emancipation as a means of racial containment, George Boutwell, former governor of Massachusetts, warned that if slavery were not abolished, the North would soon be "overrun by escaped fugitives from the South." Massachusetts attorney E. H. Derby expressed the same fear, telling his readers that both the North and the West would be inundated with blacks if slavery survived the war. But end slavery and things would be different. "Once let liberty be established at the South," promised the Reverend Henry Ward Beecher, "and the North will be whiter than ever."[93]

Just a year earlier, Lincoln and the Republican Party had offered slaveholders a thirteenth amendment guaranteeing slavery forever. Now they were couching emancipation in terms of what was good for whites, appealing to northern racism in the process. It was a strategy they saw as necessary to limit the political fallout from an emancipation that was already an established fact, an emancipation that tens of thousands of fugitives had already forced on the nation. Desperate dispatches from field

---

[91] Edward Lillie Pierce, *Memoir and Letters of Charles Sumner* (Boston: Roberts Brothers, 1887–93), 4: 49.

[92] *Washington (Penn.) Reporter*, June 26, 1862.

[93] *Lowell (Mass.) Daily Citizen and News*, August 9, 1862; E. H. Derby, "Resources of the South," *Atlantic Monthly* 10 (October 1862): 508; *Cleveland Daily Plain Dealer*, December 3, 1862.

commanders had made that clear for months, stemming from ambiguities of the Confiscation Act. It had declared fugitives to be contraband of war but said nothing about their status beyond that. The result was a legal and practical mess that promoted confusion and hampered the war effort. With the war going so badly for the Union, that situation could not continue.

On July 17, 1862, Congress moved toward clearing up the mess and recognizing the inevitable. With the Second Confiscation Act, slaves belonging to disloyal slaveholders were declared "forever free of their servitude." At the same time, Congress recognized the need for black military aid with the Militia Act. It was cautious regarding how blacks should be used, specifying "for the purpose of constructing intrenchments, or performing camp service, or any other labor." But it also authorized Lincoln to use blacks "in any military or naval service for which they may be found competent," leaving the door open for their use as soldiers and seamen.[94]

Lincoln signed both acts into law with reservations, charged as he was with their enforcement. Freedom went only to slaves of disloyal slaveholders. Lincoln had "no objection" to the policy but pointed out that "a justly discriminating application of it, would be very difficult, and, to a great extent, impossible." The problem was the same that had faced the army for nearly a year – how to tell the difference between blacks formerly held by disloyal slaveholders from those belonging to Unionists.[95]

On July 13, as Congress hammered out the Second Confiscation Act, Lincoln disclosed to Secretary of State William Seward and Secretary of the Navy Gideon Welles his plan to simplify the act's implementation. He would declare all slaveholders in rebellious states, or parts thereof not under Union control, to be disloyal. Their slaves would be free. Slaveholders in Union-held territory would be deemed loyal and could keep their slaves. Claiming military necessity, Lincoln would enforce the Second Confiscation Act and end slavery, at least in part, by presidential proclamation. "We must free the slaves," Lincoln finally recognized, "or be ourselves subdued." Welles later recalled that this was "a new departure for the President," who had until then asserted that his government had no authority to interfere with slavery where it existed. But the war was not going well, and Lincoln needed all the help he could get.[96]

---

[94] *Statutes at Large*, 12: 589–92, 597–600.

[95] Lincoln to the Senate and House of Representatives, July 17, 1862, in Basler et al., *Collected Works of Abraham Lincoln*, 5: 328–31.

[96] *Diary of Gideon Welles* (Boston: Houghton Mifflin, 1911), 1: 70–71.

FIGURE 2.5. With the war going badly, recruiting at a standstill, and confusion over the legal status of "contrabands" hampering operations, in July 1862 Congress passed, and Lincoln signed, acts declaring slaves of disloyal owners free and allowing blacks to serve in the military. "Why I du declare, it's my dear old friend Sambo!" says Lincoln in the caption. "Course you'll fight for us, Sambo. Lend us a hand, old hoss, du!" Some blacks refused in protest over unequal pay and the policy against black men serving as officers. Image from *Punch* (London), August 9, 1862.

There were other factors influencing Lincoln's decision. With the lack of volunteers, there was talk that a military draft might be necessary. Lincoln hoped to avoid such a move, unpopular as it would be. Congress had taken a step toward conscription with the Militia Act, which, in addition to opening the door to black enlistment, hinted that a draft might be coming if the states did not send forward enough volunteers. Lincoln hoped that enlisting blacks might allow him to avoid conscripting whites. He also hoped that emancipation would ward off foreign recognition of the Confederacy, especially by Britain. The British Empire had outlawed slavery decades before. Making the war a freedom war would keep Britain, at least officially, out of the conflict.[97]

---

[97] The complex and conflicted attitudes of people in England toward the war are explored in Duncan Andrew Campbell, *English Public Opinion and the America Civil War* (Suffolk, Eng.: Royal Historical Society, 2003).

In late July, Lincoln told his cabinet that he intended to release a preliminary Emancipation Proclamation. It would cite the Second Confiscation Act as the basis of its authority. It would be a tentative document, giving slaveholders time to declare loyalty to the Union before it went into effect on January 1, 1863. It would be limited as well, freeing only those slaves it could not immediately reach. Slaves held in the border states would not be affected. Neither would those in former Confederate territory under Union control, such as Tennessee, northern Virginia, and southern Louisiana. The document would say nothing of plans to enlist blacks, and it would offer colonization as the ultimate solution to the "negro problem." But Lincoln could not release the Proclamation yet. Doing so after a string of Union defeats that summer would make his government appear weak and desperate. So Lincoln set the plan aside and waited for a battlefield victory.

In the meantime, Lincoln took steps to prepare whites for emancipation and blacks for deportation. Lincoln wanted northern whites to understand that when federally recognized emancipation came, it would not mean former slaves overrunning the North. If they went anywhere, it would be to some foreign land. Sending that message was in part a preemptive political tactic designed to head off criticism of his Proclamation. But colonization was not simply a ploy. Lincoln took the idea seriously. "Almost from the commencement of this administration," Navy Secretary Gideon Welles wrote in his diary, Lincoln favored "deporting the colored race." "The President was earnest in the matter; wished to send the negroes out of the country."[98]

Lincoln had Congress's support for the project. The Second Confiscation Act authorized Lincoln to colonize all blacks willing to emigrate as soon as "some tropical country" could be induced to take them. At the same time, in its *Report on Emancipation and Colonization*, a House select committee bluntly stated that "the highest interests of the white race, whether Anglo-Saxon, Celt, or Scandinavian, require that the whole country should be held and occupied by those races alone. ... The Anglo-American looks upon every acre of our present domain as intended for him, and not for the negro." Congress allocated $600,000 as a down payment on black deportation and America's racial cleansing.[99]

---

[98] *Diary of Gideon Welles*, 1: 150. Historian David Blight makes much the same point, writing that Lincoln "had long viewed colonization as the ultimate solution to America's race problem." See David W. Blight, *Frederick Douglass' Civil War: Keeping Faith with Jubilee* (Baton Rouge: Louisiana State University Press, 1989), 135.

[99] *Statutes at Large*, 12: 589–92; U.S. House of Representatives, *Report of the Select Committee on Emancipation and Colonization*, Thirty-Seventh Congress, Second Session,

As Congress called for deportation, Lincoln called for a delegation of Washington's black leaders to meet at the White House. A committee quickly formed and drew up resolutions opposing colonization, instructing five representatives to present them to Lincoln. When they met with Lincoln on August 14, they found that the president had little interest in hearing what they had to say. They had been summoned to hear Lincoln's prepared remarks, which would quickly be released to the press. Like so many white northerners, Lincoln was quick to blame slavery's victims for the nation's troubles. "But for your race among us," he told his guests, "there could not be war, although many men engaged on either side do not care for you one way or the other. Nevertheless, I repeat, without the institution of Slavery and the colored race as a basis, the war could not have an existence. It is better for us both, therefore, to be separated."[100]

George B. Vashon, a black Pittsburgh educator and later attorney for the Freedmen's Bureau, read Lincoln's remarks with disgust. In an open letter to *Douglass' Monthly*, Vashon wrote that although the black man may have brought on the war, he was not its root cause. "That cause must be sought in the wrongs inflicted upon him by the white man." Frederick Douglass made the same point, writing that "a horse thief pleading that the existence of the horse is the apology for his theft or a highway man contending that the money in the traveler's pocket is the sole first cause of his robbery are about as much entitled to respect as is the President's reasoning." Lincoln's remarks, Douglass insisted, only fueled racism rather than helping overcome it. But Lincoln's purpose was not to overcome racism. In fact, he employed racism as a means of turning opposition to his Proclamation back on its critics – to argue that emancipation was a necessary first step toward colonization, toward ridding the nation of blacks. It was necessary to undermine the Confederate war effort, preserve the Union, and avoid future civil war. The Proclamation was ultimately for the good of whites, not of blacks. But to announce the Proclamation, Lincoln needed a battlefield victory.[101]

His opportunity came on September 17 when Union forces turned back a Confederate advance in western Maryland at Antietam Creek. George

---

Report No. 148 (Washington, D.C.: Government Printing Office, 1862), 14, 16; Ripley et al., *Black Abolitionist Papers*, 5: 155 n. 1.

[100] Ripley et al., *Black Abolitionist Papers*, 5: 155 n. 1; Address on Colonization to a Deputation of Negroes, August 14, 1862, in Basler et al., *Collected Works of Abraham Lincoln*, 5: 370–75.

[101] *Douglass' Monthly*, October and September 1862; Address on Colonization to a Deputation of Negroes, August 14, 1862, in Basler et al., *Collected Works of Abraham Lincoln*, 5: 372.

McClellan, the Union commander, failed to follow up on his initial success, and the rebel army escaped into Virginia. Still, Lincoln could claim a victory. Five days later, on September 22, he issued his preliminary Emancipation Proclamation.

### A HALF-WAY MEASURE

Black leaders knew that Lincoln's primary aim was to weaken Confederates, not strengthen blacks. That his Proclamation said nothing of slavery in the Union-held South was a huge disappointment. James H. Hudson, a black abolitionist writing for the *Pacific Appeal*, called the Proclamation

a half-way measure, which purports to give freedom to the bulk of the slave population beyond the reach of our arms, while it ignores or defies justice, by clinching the rivets of the chain which binds those whom alone we have present power to redeem. The proclamation should have been made to include every bondsman on the soil of America; every chain should have been broken.[102]

If it was not the end of slavery, the Proclamation was at least a recognition that self-emancipated fugitives had pushed the issue past its tipping point. "When Virginia is a free state, Maryland cannot be a slave state," wrote Frederick Douglass. "Slavery must stand or fall together. Strike it at either extreme – either on the head or at the heel, and it dies."[103]

Reaction to the preliminary Proclamation was mixed among northern whites as well, although they leaned much more heavily toward a negative view. October and November saw huge demonstrations against emancipation in major urban areas. Mass meetings in New York and Brooklyn adopted resolutions condemning the Proclamation. The *Chicago Times* saw it as a hypocritical scheme to "save the Union ... by overriding the constitution." The editor was sure that Lincoln had "no constitutional power to issue the proclamation ... none whatever." In Philadelphia, even the Reverend Albert Barnes, president of the Pennsylvania Bible Society and a critic of slavery, preached against the Proclamation, saying that Lincoln had overstepped his authority. "Such power is not given to any individual or to any body of men under the constitution."[104]

On the front lines that summer and fall, events were taking shape that would further inflame racist fears among northern whites, supporters and

---

[102] *Pacific Appeal*, March 7, 1863.
[103] *Douglass' Monthly*, March 1863.
[104] *Chicago Times*, September 23, 1862; Albert Barnes, *The Conditions of Peace: A Thanksgiving Discourse* (Philadelphia: William B. Evans, 1863), 53.

opponents of emancipation alike. The numbers of fugitives flooding Union camps left field commanders with little choice but to seek other options for their care. In September 1862, General Ulysses S. Grant established a "Contraband Retreat" in northern Mississippi, then sent 600 of its inmates to military posts in Columbus, Kentucky, and Cairo, Illinois. With Secretary of War Stanton's approval, the post commander at Cairo tried to hire fugitives out to local employers. As word of the attempt spread, northern whites howled in protest. This was exactly what they had long feared – blacks coming north to take their jobs. Democrats used the incident to fan racist fears and gain political advantage. An Illinois Democrat insisted that the North was "in great danger of being overrun with negroes set free by our army or by the President's proclamation." Republicans feared the consequences in the upcoming elections. Stanton cancelled the fugitive employment plan, but the political damage had been done.[105]

In October, a meeting of white workers in Quincy, Illinois, issued a manifesto in which they gave

notice to those engaged in this business of attempting to ride down and crush out the free white workingmen of Illinois, by thus seeking to bring free negro labor into competition with white labor, that we cannot and will not tolerate it; that we will seek our remedy, *first*, under the law; *second*, at the polls; and *third*, if both these fail, we will redress our wrongs in such manner as shall seem to us most expedient and most practicable.

The message to blacks, with its veiled threat of violence, could hardly have been more clear.[106]

White mobs sometimes made good on such threats. In July 1862, spurred by reports of whites being thrown out of employment and wages being reduced, gangs of Irish workers attacked black laborers at the Cincinnati docks. "No d—d niggers," yelled the Irishmen, "should work on the levee." Some victims, wrote one city newspaper, turned on their attackers, "the result being several Irishmen pretty well whaled." Far outnumbered, most of the blacks took refuge on boats lining the wharves. It did little good. "On went the mob from boat to boat, in pursuit of every negro they could find. One poor 'contraband' ... was finally overtaken and pelted with boulders. His teeth were knocked out, or down his throat, while his jaw bone was fractured, eight or ten of the rowdies having pounced on him at once." Those who could get away headed for the city's black tenements. Police

[105] Berlin et al., *Lower South*, 626; Bruce Tap, "Race, Rhetoric, and Emancipation: The Election of 1862 in Illinois," *Civil War History* 39 (1993): 116.
[106] *Quincy (Ill.) Herald* in *Chicago Times*, October 26, 1862.

never responded to calls for help, reported the press, "as is usual in such cases."[107]

Even when police did respond, it was as often to help the mobs as to hinder them. One morning in September 1862, an angry crowd of thirty to forty whites in Brooklyn, New York, gathered outside a tobacco factory where a handful of blacks were employed. Soon they began hurling bricks and paving stones at the building. Before long the crowd numbered more than a thousand, many of them screaming "Down with the nagers" and "Turn out the nagers." Two police officers walking their beat happened on the scene, but, wrote the *Brooklyn Eagle*, "instead of attacking the white rioters they struck at the negroes with their clubs." The trapped blacks, five men and fifteen women, barricaded themselves on the top floor and threw anything they could find down on rioters trying to follow them. Police finally arrived in force and dispersed the mob, but not before the building was nearly gutted. Although it was only a twenty-minute walk from City Hall, police took two hours to respond.[108]

At the same time, a fugitive resettlement plan was taking shape in Virginia. General John A. Dix reported to Stanton that fugitives were suffering terribly. Poorly fed and clothed, crowded into broken-down shacks and tents, they were dying "by the hundreds and thousands." The army was simply not equipped to care for them all. So Dix asked permission to contact Governor John Andrew of Massachusetts and governors of other northern states to arrange temporary asylum and employment for the refugees. When news of the plan reached Massachusetts, whites were outraged. Opposition was especially fierce among Republicans, who accused Dix of saddling their party with the stigma of encouraging black migration North. Within weeks of Dix's request, Governor Andrew was in Washington telling administration officials face-to-face that Massachusetts would not be a haven for escaped slaves. Silence among white abolitionists confirmed the widespread hostility toward black refugees and went a long way toward defeating Dix's plan. "Massachusetts don't want them," declared the editor of the *Springfield Daily Republican*. "No free state wants them."[109]

---

[107] *Cincinnati Daily Commercial*, July 11, 1862.

[108] *Douglass' Monthly*, September 1862.

[109] For an overview of the Dix plan and reaction to it see V. Jacque Voegeli, "A Rejected Alternative: Union Policy and the Relocation of Southern 'Contrabands' at the Dawn of Emancipation," *Journal of Southern History* 69 (2003): 766–87. See page 786 for quote from the *Springfield (Mass.) Daily Republican*, November 15, 1862.

In Wisconsin that fall, when seventy-five Alabama blacks arrived at Fond du Lac to be employed as servants, the *Daily Wisconsin News* warned that the state would soon be "swarming with this black population." A West Bend newspaper editor wrote that sending blacks north "to mix with . . . and compete with . . . free labor" was "most outrageous." A Milwaukee editor agreed, insisting that "the North belongs to the free white man, not to the Negro."[110]

Republicans countered with racism of their own, insisting that emancipation would keep southern blacks *in* the South and draw northern blacks *to* the South. The North would have fewer blacks than ever before. And they used contradictory arguments that would come to characterize Lincoln and other Republicans for the rest of the war. On the one hand, they pointed out that if slavery survived the war, the issue of slavery's expansion would live on as well and would surely result in some future war. On the other hand, they stressed that the Emancipation Proclamation was a war measure only, temporary in nature, and subject to being altered or abolished at war's end. "When the rebellion is suppressed," wrote the Republican editor of Ohio's *Toledo Blade*, "the same Constitution will be operative as before. . . . Then, of course, the same rights will exist under it that existed before the war, and among these will be the right of every State to have Slavery."[111]

Democrats took full advantage of anti-emancipation sentiment in the fall 1862 elections. It was no easy task, despite widespread racist apprehensions. The nation was at war, and Republicans used patriotism as a political weapon to blast any criticism of administration policies. Democrats shot back with emotionally charged rhetoric of their own. In New York, supporters of Democratic gubernatorial candidate Horatio Seymour told the electorate that "a vote for Seymour is a vote to protect our white laborers against the association and competition of Southern negroes." Ohio Democrat William Allen told an audience that "every white laboring man in the North, who does not want to be swapped off for a free nigger, should vote the democratic ticket."[112]

Republicans had done their best to gerrymander opponents out of office. They had succeeded in some cases, which helped them retain control in Congress. Still, Democrats managed a net gain of thirty-two seats in the

---

[110] Edward Noyes, "The Negro in Wisconsin's Civil War Effort," in Martin H. Greenberg and Charles G. Waugh, eds., *The Price of Freedom: Slavery and the Civil War* (Nashville: Cumberland House, 2000), 2: 157.

[111] *Toledo Blade* in *Cincinnati Daily Gazette*, October 17, 1862.

[112] *The World and Morning Courier and New-York Enquirer*, November 4, 1862; *Springfield Daily Illinois State Register*, October 22, 1862.

House of Representatives. They also took back the governor's seats in New York and New Jersey and regained control of the Illinois and Indiana legislatures. Their victories would surely have been even greater had not the Pennsylvania and Ohio state legislative elections been scheduled for odd years and had the governors of Indiana and Illinois not been holding four-year terms that began in 1861. An unsuccessful congressional candidate from Ohio complained bitterly that Lincoln's Proclamation had come just in time to defeat him and many other Republicans. "I had thought until this year," he wrote to a friend, "the cry of 'nigger' & 'abolitionism,' were played out but they never had as much power & effect in this part of the state as at the recent elections."[113]

Stung by losses to his party that fall, Lincoln did what he could to minimize the political damage. Although he could hardly have canceled his Emancipation Proclamation, he did take steps to back-track on it before it even went into effect. On December 1, 1862, in his annual message to Congress, Lincoln proposed three Constitutional amendments. The first would promise federal compensation to states that abolished slavery by 1900, but it would not require any state to do so. The second would state that only those slaves who happened to have attained "actual freedom by the chances of war, at any time before the end of the rebellion" would legally be free and would offer compensation to all but disloyal owners for their loss. The third would require Congress to fund black colonization to any location outside the United States.[114]

Lincoln himself set the example by following through on colonization. By the end of 1862, he had contracted with a shady promoter named Bernard Kock to employ 5,000 deported blacks as timber cutters on Ile à Vache, a small island off the coast of Haiti. After evidence came to light in January 1863 that Kock was a notorious swindler, Lincoln gave up on the venture but not on the idea of colonization.[115]

---

[113] Republicans did manage a net gain of five seats in the U.S. Senate, primarily because senators were selected by state legislatures. They served staggered six-year terms, and those seats up for renewal were filled by Republican-dominated state legislatures. Only after 1913, with ratification of the Seventeenth Amendment, did the Constitution provide for election of senators by popular vote. For an examination of the 1862 congressional elections see Jamie L. Carson et al., "The Impact of National Tides and District-Level Effects on Electoral Outcomes: The U.S. Congressional Elections of 1862–63," *American Journal of Political Science* 45 (2001): 887–98.

[114] Annual Message to Congress, December 1, 1862, in Basler et al., *Collected Works of Abraham Lincoln*, 5: 529–30.

[115] *National Anti-Slavery Standard*, March 19, 1864; Lincoln to William H. Seward, January 6, 1863, in Basler et al., *Collected Works of Abraham Lincoln*, 6: 41–42.

At the same time his timber scheme was taking shape, Lincoln laid plans for sending blacks to work coal mines in Panama. Ambrose Thompson of the Chiriqui Improvement Company headed the project. Although Navy Secretary Gideon Welles and others warned that Thompson's operation was "a swindling speculation," Lincoln lobbied hard to get support for the project.[116]

Reaction among African Americans to Lincoln's colonization plan was overwhelmingly hostile. At a mass meeting in Queens County, New York, blacks drafted a letter to Lincoln informing him that "this is our native country; we have as strong attachment naturally to our native hills, valleys, plains, luxuriant forests, flowing streams, mighty rivers, and lofty mountains, as any other people." Blacks in Philadelphia felt the same way. They had "produced much of the wealth of this country," the country from which Lincoln wanted them exiled. "Shall we sacrifice this, leave our homes, forsake our birth-place, and flee to a strange land to appease the anger and prejudice of the traitors now in arms against the Government?"[117]

A. P. Smith of Saddle River, New Jersey, in a biting public letter, asked Lincoln why "must I crush out my cherished hopes and aspirations, abandon my home, and become a pander to the mean and selfish spirit that oppresses me?"

Pray tell us, is our right to a home in this country less than your own, Mr. Lincoln? . . . Are you an American? So are we. Are you a patriot? So are we. Would you spurn all absurd, meddlesome, impudent propositions for your colonization in a foreign country? So do we. . . . But you say: "Coal land is the best thing I know of to begin an enterprise." . . . Coal land, sir! If you please, sir, give McClellan some, give Halleck some, and by all means, save a little strip for yourself. . . . Good sir, if you have any nearer friends than we are, let them have that coal-digging job.[118]

Blacks also criticized Lincoln's plan to compensate slaveholders instead of slaves. At a Philadelphia meeting, they stressed that far from deporting blacks, Lincoln should be granting them the lands on which they had worked without pay for so long.[119] At a gathering in Abington, Massachusetts, John Rock asked the crowd:

---

[116] *Diary of Gideon Welles*, 1: 150–53.

[117] *Liberator*, September 12, 1862; *An Appeal from the Colored Men of Philadelphia to the President of the United States* (Philadelphia: Semi-Weekly Clarion, 1862), 4–6.

[118] *Douglass' Monthly*, October 1862. The letter refers to General George B. McClellan, commanding the Army of the Potomac, and General Henry H. Halleck, the Union army's general-in-chief.

[119] *An Appeal from the Colored Men of Philadelphia*, 6.

FIGURE 2.6. John Rock – teacher, doctor, linguist, lawyer, antislavery activist, and first African American admitted to practice before the bar of the U.S. Supreme Court – was outraged at Lincoln's efforts to compensate slaveholders for the loss of their slaves with funds from the U.S. treasury. "Compensate them for what?" Rock asked a crowd in Massachusetts. "What does society owe them? . . . It is the slave who ought to be compensated." Image from *Harper's Weekly*, February 25, 1865.

Why talk about compensating masters? Compensate them for what? What do you owe them? What does the slave owe them? What does society owe them? Compensate the master? No, never. (Applause) It is the slave who ought to be compensated. The property of the South is by right the property of the slave. You talk of compensating the master who has stolen enough to sink ten generations, and yet you do not propose to restore even a part of that which has been plundered. This is rewarding the thief. Have you forgotten that the wealth of the South is the property of the slave?[120]

George Williams of North Carolina made the same point, insisting that "the country around about me, or the Sunny South, is the entailed inheritance of the Americans of African descent, purchased by the invaluable labor of our ancestors, through a life of tears and groans, under the lash and the yoke of tyranny."[121]

[120] *Liberator*, August 15, 1862
[121] *Christian Recorder*, June 20, 1863.

Among the most disappointed in Lincoln was Frederick Douglass, especially with regard to colonization. "If the black man cannot find peace from the aggressions of the white race on this continent," Douglass wrote, "he will not be likely to find it permanently on any part of the habitable globe. The same base and selfish lust for dominion which would drive us from this country would hunt us from the world." Although Douglass had hoped for better from Lincoln, this deportation plan made it clear that the president was "quite a genuine representative of American prejudice and Negro hatred and far more concerned for the preservation of slavery, and the favor of the Border Slave States, than for any sentiment of magnanimity or principle of justice and humanity."[122]

Regardless of how Lincoln and Congress played to white racism, blacks had made huge strides in taking their own freedom and forcing recognition of that fact. And if the Emancipation Proclamation was a half-way measure, blacks would take ownership of it and expand its scope far beyond its restricted wording.

[122] *Douglass' Monthly*, September 1862.

# 3

## "Ready to Die for Liberty"

### *Expanding the Boundaries of Freedom*

THEY KNOW EVERYTHING THAT HAPPENS

Blacks throughout the country – North and South, free and enslaved – rejoiced as word of the preliminary Emancipation Proclamation spread. Despite its limited nature, it was astonishing to see such a document coming from a president who had once supported a constitutional amendment guaranteeing slavery forever. In little more than a year, blacks had forced Lincoln and the country further toward the right side of history. They still had some way to go, but black folk would continue pointing the way. The Emancipation Proclamation may have been signed with Lincoln's pen, but blacks were its author. They would take owner-ship of the document and make it much more than it was. Within days of the preliminary Proclamation's announcement on September 22, slaves were escaping to Union lines and claiming its promise of freedom months before it went into effect. The editors of the *New York Times* wrote on September 28 that there must surely be "a far more rapid and secret diffusing of intelligence and news through the plantations than was ever dreamed of at the North."

On January 1, 1863, at prayer meetings across the South and mass meetings across the North, blacks and their white abolitionist allies celebrated the day of "Jubilee." A huge crowd packed Boston's Music Hall for a celebratory concert.[1] At nearby Tremont Temple, there were three meetings that day – morning, afternoon, and evening – all of which packed the house. Among the speakers were black abolitionists William

---

[1] *Boston Evening Transcript*, January 2, 1863.

Wells Brown, John Rock, and Frederick Douglass. William C. Nell – journalist, author, and, as a Boston postal clerk, the first black ever to serve in the federal civil service – spoke of the day as a turning point in the lives of enslaved Americans. "New Year's day – proverbially known throughout the South as 'Heart-Break Day,' from the trials and horrors peculiar to sales and separations of parents and children, husbands and wives – by this Proclamation is henceforth invested with new significance and imperishable glory in the calendar of time."

Even as Nell praised the Emancipation Proclamation, he also took a jab at Lincoln's colonization plan. Although he never mentioned the word colonization, Nell's audience understood his meaning in the lines of verse he quoted.

> There's a magical tie to the land of our home,
> Which the heart cannot break, though the footsteps may roam;
> Be that land where it may, at the line or the pole,
> It still holds the magnet that draws back the soul;
> 'Tis loved by the free man, 'tis loved by the slave,
> 'Tis dear to the coward, more dear to the brave.
> Ask any the spot they like best on the earth,
> And they'll answer with pride, 'Tis the land of our birth.[2]

Frederick Douglass spoke at Tremont that afternoon, then remained waiting for news from the telegraph office that Lincoln had signed the Proclamation. Evening came but still no word. "We waited on each speaker," Douglass recalled, "keeping our eye on the door." At eleven o'clock, with no news yet, Douglass shouted to the crowd, "We won't go home till morning." "In view of the past," he later wrote, "it was by no means certain that it would come." Finally, a messenger arrived with word that the deed was done. "I never saw Joy before," said Douglass. "Men, women, young and old, were up; hats and bonnets were in the air."[3]

To spread word of the Proclamation in Mississippi, enslaved people formed an organization that freedman George Washington Albright remembered as "the 4-Ls – Lincoln's Legal Loyal League." Albright, who later served as a Mississippi state senator, was a runner for the 4-Ls, traveling "about the plantations within a certain range" and speaking at

---

[2] *Liberator*, January 16, 1863. See also Dorothy Porter Wesley and Constance Porter Uzelac, eds., *William Cooper Nell, Nineteenth-Century African American Abolitionist, Historian, Integrationist: Selected Writings from 1832–1874* (Baltimore: Black Classic Press, 2002). Nell took his verse from the nineteenth-century English poet Eliza Cook.

[3] Douglass, *Life and Times*, 428; *Douglass' Monthly*, March 1863.

"small meetings in the cabins." "The plantation owners tried to keep the news from us," said Albright, but it was no use. Such efforts as those of the 4-Ls and other grapevine telegraph operations kept slaves well informed, as they had been doing since the war's outbreak. As early as May 1861, one Louisiana planter exclaimed to a visitor, "D—n the niggers, they know more about politics than most of the white men. They know everything that happens."[4]

Even slaves in the border states and occupied South, where the Emancipation Proclamation did not apply, claimed the document as their own. Along the Union-held Virginia tidewater, more than 5,000 enslaved people, many of them from area plantations, gathered at Norfolk on January 1 to celebrate the Proclamation. A few weeks later in Tennessee, by then almost completely under federal control, one Union officer wrote of a "large number of contrabands now finding their way into our camps. ... Whole families of them are stampeding and leaving their masters." In federally controlled areas of southern Louisiana, some slaves refused to work, insisting that they were free. Others demanded wages. In Plaquemines Parish, slaves on one plantation drove off the overseer and claimed the estate for themselves. Planters in Terrebonne Parish complained to Union officers that blacks were traveling freely, sometimes by rail, and congregating on deserted plantations, all "in defiance of the orders of their masters."[5]

Weeks before the Emancipation Proclamation was official, a reporter who witnessed the scale of black resistance wrote from southern Louisiana that slavery was "forever destroyed and worthless no matter what Mr. Lincoln or anyone else may say on the subject." Within months of the Proclamation taking effect, whites in Tennessee were admitting the same. "It matters not what may have been our opinions upon this subject, or whether we prefer a different state of things," wrote twenty Tennessee slaveholders to Secretary of War Stanton. Nor did it matter that the

---

[4] George Washington Albright, in Rawick et al., *American Slave*, supplement, series 1, vol. 6, *Mississippi Narratives*, part 1, 12; *Springfield (Mass.) Daily Republican*, May 4, 1861.

[5] John Oliver to Simeon S. Jocelyn, January 14, 1863, American Missionary Association Archives, Tulane University, in Ripley et al., *Black Abolitionist Papers*, 5: 173; Gen. William Sooy Smith [commanding, First Division, Sixteenth Army Corps] to Lt. Col. Binmore [Headquarters, Sixteenth Army Corps], March 27, 1863, in Berlin et al., *Destruction of Slavery*, 303; John C. P. Wederstrandt to Brig. Gen. Shepley [military gov. of Louisiana], September 19, 1862, in ibid., 219–21; W. J. Minor et al. to Maj. Gen. Nathaniel Banks [commanding, Department of the Gulf], January 14, 1862, in Berlin et al., *Lower South*, 408–10.

Proclamation held no force in Tennessee. "The destruction of Negro Slavery in this country is an accomplished and immutable fact."[6]

In Missouri, slaves headed for the neighboring free state of Kansas by the hundreds. One witness estimated the daily out-migration in his section of the state at between fifty and a hundred. "They emigrate during the night, in squads or families, accompanied generally by a span of good mules and a lumber wagon with whatever portables they can seize upon."[7] Near Lexington, Missouri, a local man recorded the flight in his diary.

At sunrise this morning Mr Wallace came over to see if we had lost our team or any thing last night. Told us all of his negros had gone, nine, taken his oxen and wagon. In a short time Mr Bellis came by, said his waggon harness and hoarses wer stolen last night. I went in town. Doc Hassell told me all of his, two, negros wer gone, Judge Stratton lost all his (two). Brigadire General Vaughn lost two, Mr Parrner, Mr Packard, Mrs White and many others lost thare negros besides many teams wer stolen by them. Mr Musselman came in town and stated abought 80 negros passed his neighbourhood this morning on thare way to Kansas.[8]

A slave patrol tried to turn back one band of fugitives from Munroe, Missouri, but "the negroes being resolute and about to show fight," the patrol backed down.[9]

Near Paducah, Kentucky, one slaveholder complained to a Union officer of "the almost daily departure of slaves from their owners." In Maryland, slaves pretending to be refugees from behind Confederate lines poured into Washington and Baltimore. From Salisbury, Maryland, the commander of an Ohio regiment wrote to his superiors that escaping slaves were a constant annoyance. "They come to me for protection, and refuse to go back to their masters. ... The master claims them under the laws of Maryland – And they claim they are fugitives."[10]

[6] *New York Times*, October 23, 1862; John W. Bowen et al. to Stanton, September 26, 1863, in Berlin et al., *Black Military Experience*, 174–75.

[7] Lela Barnes, ed., "An Editor Looks at Early-Day Kansas: The Letters of Charles Monroe Chase," *Kansas Historical Quarterly* 26 (1960): 136.

[8] Margaret Mendenhall Frazier, trans., *Missouri Ordeal, 1862–1864: Diaries of Willard Hall Mendenhall* (Newhall, Calif.: C. Boyer, 1985), 132–33.

[9] W. A. Poillon to Dr. Martine, December 28, 1863, in Berlin et al., *Destruction of Slavery*, 476–79.

[10] A. Bradshaw to Brig. Gen. Hurlbutt [commanding, Sixteenth Army Corps], June [?] 1863, in Berlin et al., *Destruction of Slavery*, 584–85; J. P. Creager [civilian recruiting agent] to Col. William Birnie [superintendent of black recruitment in Maryland], August 19, 1863, in Berlin et al., *Black Military Experience*, 204; Col. A. L. Brown [commanding an Ohio regiment] to Captain [?], [Headquarters, Middle Department and Eighth Army Corps], June 4, 1864, in Berlin et al., *Destruction of Slavery*, 382.

FIGURE 3.1. Although the Emancipation Proclamation applied only to the Confederate South, slaves in the Union South made it their own. They headed for free states or Union camps by the tens of thousands, claiming to be from behind Confederate lines. Federal officers had no way of knowing any different. Slaveholders tried to stop the exodus, but to little effect. A slave patrol halted one band of fugitives in Missouri, but "the negroes being resolute and about to show fight," the patrol backed down. Image from William Still, *The Underground Railroad* (1872).

Slaveholders throughout the border states had much the same difficulty recovering escapees. Missouri slaveholders protested to the governor that when they saw their slaves "in camp or around the Camp, the Commander will not do anything. . . . no matter what proof the master offers, the negroes say that they belong to secessionists." Colonel C. Maxwell, commanding U.S. forces in southwestern Kentucky, freely admitted that "no distinction is made between the loyal and disloyal [slave] owner."[11]

Some slaveholders tried to take matters into their own hands. When the commander at Benton Barracks, Missouri, refused to assist in recovering slaves, the slaveholders replied "that they knew what to do." When they tried to take their "property" by force, other fugitives intervened and a wild melee broke out. The slaveholders were nearly killed. One

---

[11] John F. Ryland et al. to Gov. Hamilton Rowan Gamble, June 4, 1863, in Berlin et al., *Destruction of Slavery*, 457; Maxwell to Gen. J. T. Boyle, December 5, 1863, in ibid., 594–95.

officer stationed in Kentucky curtly remarked that slaveholders should keep their slaves at home if they wished to keep them at all.[12]

That was easier said than done. Slaves who escaped to Union camps frequently armed themselves and returned home to recover family and friends. A slaveholder in Jackson, Missouri, protested to the commander of federal forces in the state that "hundreds [of slaves] from this and the adjoining Counties have escaped and sought protection ... at Camp Girardeau." Whenever the fugitives wished to release anyone from bondage, they would "issue out from that place ... armed" and free slaves by force as they went. "Many instances of that kind have occurred."[13]

### UNOFFENDING NEGROES BRUTALLY ASSAILED

Black folk throughout the country reacted to the Emancipation Proclamation much as they had to the war itself. They made the most they could of it, forcing a response in the process. The Proclamation simply reflected that reality, with blacks welcoming the document and pushing it far beyond its stated limits.

Reaction to emancipation among many northern whites could hardly have been less welcoming. On the contrary, the Proclamation fed their racist fears. Large segments of the white working class were by no means convinced that freedom would keep blacks in the South. It might only free them to migrate north. Democrats had tapped into those fears and secured significant gains in the fall 1862 elections. When the results came in, a white New Jersey soldier took them as a happy sign "that the North is not ruled by a set of infernal fanatics and nigger worshippers." He was probably just as pleased to see New Jersey's newly elected legislature, with support from the governor, promptly declare the Emancipation Proclamation illegal.[14]

---

[12] Col. B. L. E. Bonneville [commanding, camp of instruction at Benton Barracks, Missouri] to Capt. H. C. Fillebrow[n] [Headquarters, St. Louis District], May 28, 1863, in Ira Berlin et al., eds., *Freedom: A Documentary History of Emancipation, 1861–1867*, series 1, vol. 2, *The Wartime Genesis of Free Labor: The Upper South* (Cambridge: Cambridge University Press, 1993), 570 (hereafter cited as *Upper South*); Summary of a speech by Col. Smith D. Atkins, November 1862, in Berlin et al., *Destruction of Slavery*, 530–31.

[13] Greer W. Davis to Gen. Curtis [commanding, Department of the Missouri], February 24, 1863, in Berlin et al., *Destruction of Slavery*, 449–50.

[14] E. B. Grubb to Henry Moffett, November 19, 1862, Clinton H. Haskell Collection, University of Michigan, in Randall C. Jimerson, *The Private Civil War: Popular Thought during the Sectional Conflict* (Baton Rouge: Louisiana State University Press, 1988), 39–40; William Gillette, *Jersey Blue: Civil War Politics in New Jersey, 1854–1865* (New Brunswick, N.J.: Rutgers University Press, 1995), 218–19.

Such attitudes were widespread among white Union soldiers. A New York captain wrote that his men were "much dissatisfied" with the Emancipation Proclamation. To them, the conflict had become a "nigger war," and they were all "anxious to return to their homes for it was to preserve the Union that they volunteered." An Indiana private wrote from Mississippi that his comrades "will not fite to free the niger ... there is a Regment her that say they will never fite untill the proclamation is with drawn there is four of the Capt[ains] in our Regt sent in there Resignations and one of the Liutenants there was nine in Comp. G tride to desert."[15]

One white soldier who had voted for Lincoln in 1860 threatened to desert so that "the negro worshippers might fight it out themselves." James McPherson's study of letters from Union soldiers suggests that prior to 1863, not three in ten felt that ending slavery should be a war aim. Sergeant William Pippey of Boston thought there were far fewer than that. "I don't believe there is *one abolitionist* in *one thousand* in the army." The few who held abolitionist views usually keep their opinions to themselves. When Henry Wooten, an enlisted man from New York, spoke up for abolitionism early in the war, one of his comrades shot him.[16]

For a variety of reasons, the Emancipation Proclamation among them, thousands of soldiers deserted during the winter of 1862–63. In January, when Joe Hooker took command of the Army of the Potomac, hundreds were deserting every day. His rolls showed 25 percent of the men had already left. It was the same everywhere. February's compiled reports for all Union armies showed a third of the troops absent. Private Adam Pickel of Pennsylvania wrote that month, "If it were not treason to tell the truth I would say that the whole army would run home if they had the chance."[17]

With the November 1862 elections behind him, Lincoln reacted to the wave of desertion by calling on Congress to pass a draft act. Congress had

---

[15] John Vliet to Mr. Bodge, February 2, 1863, Thomas W. Sweeny Papers, Huntington Library, San Marino, Calif., in James M. McPherson, *What They Fought For, 1861–1865* (New York: Anchor Books, 1995), 63; Simeon Royse to father, February 14, 1863, Royse Papers, Duke University, in ibid., 63.

[16] *Kittanning (Penn.) Mentor*, August 26, 1863, in Shankman, *Pennsylvania Antiwar Movement*, 110; McPherson, *What They Fought For*, 56; Pippey to A. Heath and B. Y. Pippey, July 31, 1862, William T. Pippey Papers, Duke University, in Jimerson, *Private Civil War*, 41; A. C. Wilcox to cousin Mary, May 31, 1864, New York Eighty-first Infantry Folder, United States Army Military History Institute, in Reid Mitchell, *Civil War Soldiers* (New York: Viking, 1988), 14.

[17] Ella Lonn, *Desertion during the Civil War* (Lincoln: University of Nebraska Press, 1998), 145, 151; Pickel to father, February 8, 1863, Adam H. Pickel Papers, Duke University, in Jimerson, *Private Civil War*, 232.

authorized militia drafts the previous summer, and Lincoln himself had imposed recruitment quotas on the states. Neither measure was effective enough in bringing new recruits to replace losses from death and desertion. So on March 3, 1863, Congress enacted compulsory military service.

Draft riots erupted across the North that spring and summer, fueled by white animosity toward being forced to fight in an abolition war. That wealthy men could avoid the draft by paying a $300 exemption fee when working folk barely saw such wages in a year led to cries of "rich man's war!" Democrats easily played on widespread anger, fanning the flames of antidraft sentiment and racial hatred. Republicans responded by pleading patriotism, calling those who opposed the draft traitors. Neither party expressed much sympathy for blacks.[18]

Fictitious or overblown "negro outrages" were often the focal point of racist rhetoric. Accusations ranged from assault to rape and murder, with Democrats calling such crimes the inevitable result of "Black Republican" rule. In reality, blacks were more often victims of white violence. That March, as a black man in Detroit was being taken to jail, accused of an "outrage" upon a white orphan girl, angry whites tried to grab him. After being warned off by police, the rioters, estimated at several thousand, rampaged through the city's black neighborhoods "with the cry of death and vengeance." Businesses owned by or employing blacks were special targets of the mob. One cooper shop between Fort and Lafayette streets was bombarded with brickbats and set alight. Rioters caught one of the shop's black workers and beat him nearly to death with a shovel. They chopped another to death with an axe.[19]

Blacks throughout the North felt the weight of anti-emancipation and antidraft backlash in early 1863. To make matters worse, failed labor strikes in Boston, Brooklyn, Albany, Cleveland, and Chicago

---

[18] For a concise overview of antiwar activity and draft resistance in the North see David Williams, *A People's History of the Civil War: Struggles for the Meaning of Freedom* (New York: New Press, 2005), 253–83. For urban riots see Barnet Schecter, *The Devil's Own Work: The Civil War Draft Riots and the Fight to Reconstruct America* (New York: Walker and Co., 2005); Robert D. Sampson, "'Pretty Damned Warm Times': The 1864 Charleston Riot and the 'Inalienable Right of Revolution,'" *Illinois Historical Journal* 89 (1996): 99–116; Iver Bernstein, *The New York Draft Riots: Their Significance for American Society and Politics in the Age of the Civil War* (New York: Oxford University Press, 1990); Adrian Cook, *The Armies of the Streets: The New York City Draft Riots of 1863* (Lexington: University Press of Kentucky, 1974); Lawrence H. Larsen, "Draft Riot in Wisconsin, 1862," *Civil War History* 7 (1961): 421–27; William F. Hanna, "The Boston Draft Riot," *Civil War History* 36 (1990): 262–73.
[19] *Liberator*, March 13, 1863; *Detroit Free Press*, March 7, 1863.

FIGURE 3.2. Most northerners bitterly opposed efforts to resettle refugees in their neighborhoods. "Massachusetts don't want them," reported the *Springfield Daily Republican* in 1862. "No free state wants them." In the summer of 1863, when government agents tried to draft whites to fight what many were calling a "nigger war," riots broke out all across the North. Mobs in New York City went on a week-long rampage, attacking any blacks they could find. On Clarkson Street, the rioters lynched William Jones and set his quivering body afire. Image from *New York Illustrated News*, July 25, 1863.

were all blamed on black competition. White strikers in Buffalo killed several blacks and injured many others. Irish longshoremen along New York's East River "set out upon a Negro hunt." They went after black workers along the docks, "pummeled them without mercy," then spread out through the ward attacking black porters, cartmen, and laborers. In May, violence again broke out on the docks when "a number of unoffending negroes were brutally assailed while quietly pursuing their labors."[20]

Blacks in New York City were even more brutally assailed during the draft riots that summer. In July's nearly week-long rampage, white mobs beat, burned, tortured, and killed as many blacks as they could lay their

[20] *Philadelphia Inquirer*, July 7, 1863; *New York Evening Post* in *Liberator*, April 17, 1863; *New York Principia* in *Douglass' Monthly*, June 1863.

hands on. Three blacks walking home after work on the riot's first evening were attacked on Varick Street in the Eight Ward. Two quickly escaped. The other was beaten several times – to shouts of "Kill the nigger! Kill the black son of a bitch!" – during a chase that went all the way to Clarkson Street. There the crowd caught sight of an unsuspecting black man named William Jones who had come out to buy a loaf of bread. The rioters grabbed Jones, hanged him from the nearest tree, then set his quivering body on fire. William Williams, a black seaman who stopped to ask for directions in the Ninth Ward, was beaten nearly unconscious. As he lay helpless on the street, some of the rioters threw rocks at him. One rowdy kicked at his eyes. Another picked up a heavy flagstone and slammed it down on Williams's chest. Police finally arrived, put Williams in a cart, and took him to New York Hospital where he lingered for two hours before death ended his agony.[21]

Most blacks stayed indoors, some preparing to defend themselves should the mob attack. In a house on Thompson Street, eight women banded together, determined to make their stand in the kitchen. Using several large pots, they brewed a concoction of water, soap, and ashes that they called "the King of Pain." William Wells Brown found the defiant women gathered around the boilers with dippers in their hands. "How will you manage if they attempt to come into this room," Brown asked. "We'll all fling hot water on 'em, and scald their very hearts out," came the reply. Brown further inquired, "Can you all throw water without injuring each other?" "O yes, honey," they said, "we's been practicin' all day."[22]

These women represented blacks by the hundreds of thousands who were ready to fight – in or out of the army. The army was where Lincoln needed them, and his Proclamation had its intended effect on black men. They flooded into recruiting offices across the North and flocked to Union lines across the South, tens of thousands of them eager to enlist.

## WE WILL FIGHT FOR OUR RIGHTS AND LIBERTY

Frederick Douglass was among the most enthusiastic supporters of black enlistment. "The iron gate of our prison stands half open," he told northern blacks as he urged them to arms. "One gallant rush ... will fling it wide." Two of Douglass's sons joined that rush. So did nearly 200,000

---

[21] Cook, *Armies of the Streets*, 82, 97–98.
[22] William Wells Brown, *The Rising Sun; or, Antecedents and Advancement of the Colored Race* (Boston: A. G. Brown and Co., 1874), 385.

other black men, along with at least a dozen black women disguised as men, who enlisted in the Union's army and navy. The vast majority were former slaves.[23]

Despite the eagerness of so many to serve, some former slaves were reluctant to exchange one kind of servitude for another, much less fight for a government whose commitment to their freedom seemed so tentative. They were sometimes given no choice but to enlist. Recruiting companies in New Orleans seized blacks off the streets and forced them to serve. In York County, Virginia, a shoemaker with a wife and three children to support was taken by force. General David Hunter so often resorted to heavy-handed coercion in trying to get recruits in South Carolina that some of the conscripts deserted. Others were more resigned to their fate. Jacob Forrester of Union-occupied Fernandina, Florida, told recruiters that "if I was compelled to go, I would go, for I was no better to die than any other man." Still, resentment persisted. Solomon Lambert, drafted in Arkansas at the age of fifteen, was sure that emancipation came not because of any altruistic motive white northerners had but only because Union ranks began "to get slim."[24]

When blacks voluntarily enlisted, they did so for their own reasons. "Liberty is what we want and nothing shorter," wrote a Louisiana man. "We will fight for our rights and liberty we care nothing about the union we have been in it Slaves for over two hundred And fifty years."[25] At a "war meeting" of former slaves on St. Simons Island, Georgia, a northern correspondent witnessed several speakers, including one black man, trying to draw new recruits.

They were asked to enlist for pay, rations and uniform, to fight for their country, for freedom and so forth, but not a man stirred. But when it was asked them to fight for themselves, to enlist to protect their wives and children from being sold away from them, and told of the little homes which they might secure to themselves and their

---

[23] Broadside entitled "Men of Color, To Arms!" (Rochester, N.Y.), March 21, 1863, in Foner, *Life and Writings of Frederick Douglass*, 3: 319.

[24] Maj. George B. Drake [Headquarters, Department of the Gulf] to Gen. T. W. Sherman [commanding defenses of New Orleans], August 15, 1864, in Berlin et al., *Black Military Experience*, 164; Jane Wallis [Virginia freedwoman] to Prof. Woodbury [northern missionary], December 10, 1863, in ibid., 138; General Orders No. 119, Headquarters, Department of the South, August 16, 1864, *Official Records*, series 3, vol. 4, 621; Affidavit of Jacob Forrester, April 28, 1863, in Berlin et al., *Black Military Experience*, 57–58; Solomon Lambert, *Arkansas Narratives*, part 4, 231.

[25] Statements of A Colored man and one of the union Colored friends, [September ? 1863], in Berlin et al., *Black Military Experience*, 154–55.

families in after years, they all rose to their feet, the men came forward and said "I'll go," and the women shouted, and the old men said "Amen."[26]

That blacks tended to enlist more for personal than patriotic reasons had much to do with the way they viewed whites in general, not just slaveholders. The treatment many received at the hands of Union soldiers did little to alter their suspicion of northern whites. Most northerners blamed not only slaveholders but slaves as well for the war. The weight of that resentment could fall hard on blacks who sought refuge with the Federals. For some it could be deadly. James W. Hildreth of the Fourth New York Heavy Artillery believed that blacks were better off in slavery. Outside slavery, it was best simply to kill them. His comrades agreed. When a black man showed up in their camp, he was met with the cry "Kill him!" The soldiers almost clubbed the poor man to death.[27]

In most cases, mistreatment of blacks by white Union soldiers was more casual, although hardly less cruel. Drunken Federals occupying Alexandria, Virginia, shot blacks in the streets for amusement. Some Indiana soldiers entertained themselves by shoving a black child into a large cask of molasses. The boy nearly suffocated before he could clear his nostrils and mouth. One white company set up camp on a plantation and found entertainment locking terrified black children in a dark store room. A bemused sergeant recalled that "such a yell of terror as they set up, Pandemonium never heard! They shrieked, groaned, yelled, prayed, and pulled their wool!"[28]

Freedman Sam Word of Arkansas recalled years after the war his mother's first disappointing encounter with federal troops. Although she had little of value in her shack, among her few prized possessions were her quilts. "One day a Yankee soldier climbed in the back window and took some of the quilts. He rolled em up and was walking out of the yard when mother saw him and said, 'Why you nasty, stinkin' rascal. You say you come down here to fight for the niggers, and now you're stealin' from em.'"

[26] *Boston Commonwealth*, February 21, 1863.

[27] Hildreth to mother, November 23, 1862, and January 4, 1863, Flinbaugh Collection and Harrisburg Civil War Round Table Collection, United States Army Military History Institute, in Mitchell, *Civil War Soldiers*, 123.

[28] Robert Goldthwaite Carter, *Four Brothers in Blue: or Sunshine and Shadows of the War of the Rebellion, a Story of the Great War from Bull Run to Appomattox* (1913; reprint, Austin: University of Texas Press, 1978), 89–90; Oscar Osburn Winther, ed., *With Sherman to the Sea: The Civil War Letters, Diaries, and Reminiscences of Theodore F. Upson* (Bloomington: Indiana University Press, 1958), 135; John Frederic Holahan, Civil War Diary, April 26, 1862, Pamplin Historical Park, Petersburg, Va., in Mitchell, *Civil War Soldiers*, 122–23.

The thief yelled back, "You're a G— D— liar, I'm fightin' for $14 a month and the Union."[29]

To supplement their meager income, soldiers occasionally captured fugitive slaves and sold them to slavecatchers. John Oliver, a free black carpenter from Virginia who had moved north before the war, witnessed such kidnappings in Norfolk. Working as a teacher among Virginia fugitives in 1863, Oliver wrote to his sponsors at the American Missionary Association that he was himself afraid to walk the streets after dark for fear of Union soldiers. "Human life," said Oliver, "is most terabely insecure in Norfolk, for the Colored people."[30]

For black women, there was the additional danger of rape. From early in the war, as Union forces moved into Confederate territory, black residents began reporting "outrages." One complaint from South Carolina detailed a rape committed by three drunken officers. In another case, Private Adolph Bork raped a "woman of color" named Susan. When she refused his advances, as Susan testified, Bork "took out his revolver and said, 'God damn you, I will force you to do it.' He said he would blow me to pieces if I didn't let him do it." Bork was eventually executed by firing squad, not for the crime of rape but for shooting another soldier.[31]

Rape or attempted rape of a woman with any degree of African ancestry was hardly considered a crime at all. Private Patrick Manning of New Hampshire assaulted a "quadroon" named Clara Grier, who testified at his court-martial, "He took hold of me and attempted to throw me down and I hollered and he kicked me. He asked me if I wanted five dollars. I said no. He asked me if he could stay with me. I said no." The court found Manning not guilty of attempted rape, but for other crimes sentenced him to three years at hard labor wearing a ball and chain.[32]

Whether by intent or neglect, rarely were any soldiers brought to justice for abusing blacks. And the higher one's rank, the less likely was prosecution. When General William T. Sherman's army marched through Georgia, a single column reported 17,000 blacks trailing behind. That so

---

[29] Sam Word, *Arkansas Narratives*, part 7, 239–40.

[30] Ripley et al., *Black Abolitionist Papers*, 5: 136 n. 4; John Oliver to Simeon S. Jocelyn, January 14, 1863, in ibid., 5: 172–73.

[31] Report of William E. Park [plantation superintendent, St. Helena Island, S.C.], March 18, 1862, in Berlin et al., *Lower South*, 166–68; Rev. Abram Mercherson [South Carolina black minister] to Maj. Gen. J. G. Foster [commanding, Department of the South], August 12, 1864, in ibid., 314.

[32] Thomas P. Lowry, *The Story the Soldiers Wouldn't Tell: Sex in the Civil War* (Mechanicsburg, Penn.: Stackpole Books, 1994), 124–25. The term "quadroon" generally referred to anyone of one-quarter African ancestry.

many slaves took flight to follow Sherman was more a reflection of their desire for freedom than of any love they had for Union troops. Few were under any illusion that "Uncle Billy," as Sherman's men affectionately called him, held any great affection for them. If any did, they were soon disappointed. With Confederate cavalry hot on their heels, Sherman pulled up his pontoon bridges after crossing Ebenezer Creek near Savannah, leaving more than 500 terrified refugees stranded on the opposite bank. Some were shot down by pursuing Rebels. Others, with children clinging to their backs, jumped into the swollen creek and drowned. Survivors were rounded up and carried back to their owners. Reflecting on the callousness of his army's role in the affair, one appalled Union soldier asked, "Where can you find in all the annals of plantation cruelty anything more completely inhuman and fiendish than this?" Such expressions of sympathy for blacks were infrequent among white Union soldiers.[33]

What they did frequently express was a deep aversion to serving in the army with black soldiers. As one Pennsylvania sergeant wrote, "We don't want to fight side and side by the nigger. We think we are too superior a race for that." A Michigan corporal insisted that white men were "superior to niggers" and that he did not want "to go through the rough life of a soldier and perhaps get shot, for a d—d nigger." After white Union soldiers at Plymouth, North Carolina, heard rumors that black troops were being sent from Massachusetts, they threatened to "throw down their arms." An Indiana private wrote home to his parents that "if old Abe arms them niggers I will quit and go South."[34] Few went South, but many did desert.

Of those who stayed, most came to abolitionism grudgingly. Some refused to call themselves abolitionists at all. "I am no abolitionist," insisted an Ohio soldier, "in fact dispise the word." But, as did so many others, he came to see that "as long as slavery exists ... there will be no permanent peace for America. ... Hence I am in favor of killing slavery."

---

[33] Paul D. Escott, "The Context of Freedom: Georgia's Slaves during the Civil War," *Georgia Historical Quarterly* 58 (1974): 85; Joseph T. Glatthaar, *The March to the Sea and Beyond: Sherman's Troops in the Savannah and Carolinas Campaigns* (New York: New York University Press, 1985), 64.

[34] Felix Brannigan to sister, July 16, 1862, Felix Brannigan Papers, Library of Congress, in Jimerson, *Private Civil War*, 93; Marion Munson to Joshua Van Hoosen, February 19, 1863, Joshua Van Hoosen Papers, University of Michigan, in ibid., 95; H. G. Spruill to Josiah Collins, March 16, 1863, Josiah Collins Papers, North Carolina Division of Archives and History, Raleigh, in Wayne K. Durrill, *War of Another Kind: A Southern Community in the Great Rebellion* (New York: Oxford University Press, 1990), 173; Charles H. Sowle to parents, January 26, 1863, Charles H. Sowle Papers, Duke University, in Jimerson, *Private Civil War*, 41.

An Indiana sergeant wrote to his wife that he would support freeing the slaves "if it will only bring the war to an end any sooner I am like the fellow that got his house burned by the guerillas he was in for emancipation subjugation extermination and hell and damnation. We are in war and anything to beat the south."[35]

Jacob Allen, a white abolitionist in the Union army, knew how his comrades felt about blacks and worried that their new antislavery feelings might not last. "Though these men wish to abolish slavery," he wrote to William Lloyd Garrison, "it is not from any motive outside of their own selfishness; and is there not a possibility that at some not very distant day, these old rank prejudices, that are now lulled to sleep by selfish motives, may again possess these men and work evil?"[36] Frederick Douglass was worried too. What the government could do, it could try to undo. Might emancipation be in danger if the political winds turned against it? Barely a month after the Emancipation Proclamation took effect, Douglass voiced his concern before an assembly in New York.

Much as I value the present apparent hostility to Slavery at the North, I plainly see that it is less the outgrowth of high and intelligent moral conviction against Slavery, as such, than because of the trouble its friends have brought upon the country. I would have Slavery hated for that and more. A man that hates Slavery only for what it does to the white man, stands ready to embrace it the moment its injuries are confined to the black man.[37]

For the moment, however, proslavery Confederates were the much greater threat.

### ENTERING THE ARMY BY HUNDREDS AND THOUSANDS

On January 5, 1863, four days after Lincoln signed the Emancipation Proclamation, Jefferson Davis issued an enslavement proclamation under

---

[35] Henry Henney to family, n.d. [late December 1862], United States Army Military History Institute, in McPherson, *What They Fought For*, 62; Amory K. Allen to My Dear Companion [Mary Delphany Allen], January 8, 1863, in "Civil War Letters of Amory K. Allen," *Indiana Magazine of History* 31 (1935): 361. For an examination of how soldiers on both sides viewed slavery see Chandra Manning, *What This Cruel War Was Over: Soldiers, Slavery, and the Civil War* (New York: Alfred A. Knopf, 2007).

[36] Allen to Garrison, October 23, 1862, Garrison Papers, Boston Public Library, in McPherson, *Struggle for Equality*, 92.

[37] *Douglass' Monthly*, March 1863.

the heading "An Address to the People of the Free States." White north-erners, he charged, had "degraded" themselves by allying with blacks. His government would redeem white honor by robbing all blacks of their freedom. As of February 22, 1863, Davis declared, "all free Negroes in the Southern Confederacy shall be placed on the slave status, and be deemed to be chattels, they and their issue forever." Any black Union soldier captured in combat would be subject to enslavement.[38]

The threat of enslavement was little deterrence to those whom the Confederacy already considered slaves. Blacks continued escaping by the tens of thousands and enlisting with the Federals. Charles Grandy of Virginia saw the war as answering his prayers for freedom. As soon as he saw a chance to get away, he and a friend headed for Union lines. After several narrow escapes, they made it to Norfolk and enlisted. When an Alabama slave named Ned prayed aloud for freedom and was severely beaten for it, he escaped and joined the Union army. Soon after, Ned sent a letter to his former owner, Tom White, telling him where he was and daring White to come and take him.[39]

Slavery was still legal in the border states, and only free blacks could legally enlist. But that did not stop slaves from enlisting. So badly were their services needed that all they had to do was show up at a recruiting station claiming to be free. Enrollment officers trying to meet their quotas simply accepted blacks at their word. Union forces in Missouri were in such need of recruits that they accepted any able-bodied black man of military age, free or slave, promising freedom for those still enslaved and compensation for their owners. Much the same policy applied in Maryland. Slaveholders protested bitterly, claiming that their slaves were faithful and would not leave "unless enticed or forced

[38] Broadside entitled "An Address to the People of the Free States by the President of the Southern Confederacy," January 5, 1863, Printed Ephemera Collection, Portfolio 245, Folder 13, Rare Book and Special Collections Division, Library of Congress. The danger for captured black soldiers included execution as well as enslavement. In a joint resolution that spring, the Confederate Congress authorized Davis to turn captured black soldiers over to state governments, all of which had laws mandating execution for rebellious blacks. Furthermore, white officers in black regiments, if captured, were also subject to execution. Because the Confederacy feared retaliation against its own troops held captive in the North and because many Confederate commanders found the orders distasteful, Richmond did not press enforcement. See Confederate States Congress, Joint Resolutions, April 30–May 1, 1863, *Official Records*, series 2, vol. 5, 940–41; Berlin et al., *Black Military Experience*, 567–68.

[39] Charles Grandy, *Virginia Narratives*, 22; Mingo White, *Alabama Narratives*, 417.

away." "This is a delusion," wrote General William Birney of Camp Stanton, Maryland. "I have yet to see a slave of this kind."[40]

To appease Kentucky slaveholders, Lincoln exempted their state from efforts to recruit blacks, but that hardly mattered to the enslaved. Freedwoman Mary Crane, born in Kentucky, recalled that her father "and most all of the other younger slave men left the farms to join the Union army." Freedman George Washington Buckner recalled the night that his mother awoke her children and said "Get up and tell your uncles goodbye. . . . They were starting away to fight for their liberties, and we were greatly impressed."[41]

Since they could not legally enlist in Kentucky, escapees headed for neighboring states. A group of Todd County slaveholders complained to Kentucky's federal adjutant-general that several hundred slaves had escaped to the nearby town of Clarksville, Tennessee, where many of them enlisted. "They are still going," grumbled the slaveholders, "in large numbers." It was the same on Kentucky's northern border, so much so that it seemed slavery might soon expire in the state. "The Great Deep of Slavery in Kentucky is broken up," wrote a resident of Evansville, Indiana, "and the fragments are rapidly drifting northward across the Ohio River. The *Men* are entering the Union Army by hundreds and thousands – their *wives and children*, following their husbands."[42]

Kentucky slaveholders tried to save some remnant of slavery by hiring armed patrols to intercept runaways. One slave in Taylor County was caught and "badly whipped." Another in Adair County was "subjected to the most unmerciful beating" for trying to enlist. In Nelson County, patrols killed a number of blacks trying to escape and join the Union army. Blacks were not the only victims of proslavery vigilantes. A deputy provost marshal in Spencer County was severely beaten for seeking black recruits. An enrolling agent in LaRue County, was, according to one report, "stripped, tied to a tree and cow-hided for enlisting slaves."

[40] General Orders No. 135, Headquarters, Department of the Missouri, November 14, 1863, *Official Records*, series 3, vol. 3, 1034–36; Thomas Clagett Jr. et al. to Hon. Reverdy Johnson [U.S. senator from Maryland], October 28, 1863, in Berlin et al., *Black Military Experience*, 213–14; Endorsement by Birney [superintendent of black recruitment in Maryland], January 28, 1864, in ibid., 215.

[41] Mary Crane, *Indiana Narratives*, 10; George Washington Buckner, ibid., 30.

[42] Adjutant Gen. [Lorenzo Thomas] to Edwin M. Stanton, February 1, 1864, in Berlin et al., *Black Military Experience*, 253–54; H. G. Petree et al. to Lorenzo Thomas, August 1864, in Berlin et al., *Destruction of Slavery*, 601; A. L. Robinson [surveyor of customs at Evansville, Ind.] to Sec. of the Treasury W. P. Fessenden, October 10, 1864, in Berlin et al., *Upper South*, 680.

Trying to curb the violence, and because the recruits were badly needed, the War Department ended Kentucky's black recruiting exemption in early 1864. Violence continued, but so did black volunteering. Nearly 60 percent of Kentucky's military-aged black men enlisted, the largest proportion of any slave state.[43]

Black men from the free states, unhampered by slaveholders, joined the army at even higher rates. Seventy percent of all northern black men of military age served, roughly three times the percentage for northern whites. Despite continuing objections to blacks serving in the military, some northern governors saw in black recruits an opportunity to help fill their draft quotas and reduce casualties among whites. Governor John Andrew of Massachusetts took a leading role, even casting his recruiting net out of state. Pennsylvania, which lagged in forming black regiments, became a prime recruiting ground. One black abolitionist enrolled dozens of men for Massachusetts regiments, much to the dismay of Pennsylvania whites. In April 1863, the *Chambersburg Valley Spirit*, a Democratic paper that had only weeks earlier voiced opposition to enlisting blacks, now wrote that "we scarcely like the idea of their being credited to Massachusetts, and thus filling up her quota under the last draft, while Pennsylvania was compelled to fill her quota, under the same draft, with free white male citizens." Pennsylvania eventually furnished more black men for the Union army than any other free state, although many served in units from other states.[44]

Although a few blacks had earlier joined existing white units, in January 1863, Secretary of War Stanton ordered that black recruits be placed in all-black regiments. A further stipulation, one that black leaders vigorously protested, was that only whites could be commissioned as officers in black regiments, although the Louisiana Native Guards already had black officers. Stanton and other administration officials justified the white officers only restriction by arguing that since blacks officially had no prior military service, there were no blacks qualified to oversee training.

[43] Lt. Col. A. Jacobson [investigating officer] to Maj. Gen. W. S. Rosecrans [commanding, Department of the Missouri], February 17, 1864, in Berlin et al., *Black Military Experience*, 240–41; Capt. James M. Fidler, historical report, June 15, 1865, in ibid., 257; Table 1. Black Soldiers in the Union Army and Black Male Population of Military Age in 1860, by State, in ibid., 12.

[44] *Cincinnati Commercial* in *Washington National Daily Intelligencer*, April 24, 1863; Ripley et al., *Black Abolitionist Papers*, 5: 179; Edward Ayers, William G. Thomas III, and Anne Sarah Rubin, "Black and on the Border," in Boritt and Hancock, *Slavery, Resistance, Freedom*, 72–73.

But that reasoning did not apply to white regiments. Stanton failed to acknowledge that hundreds of inexperienced whites served as officers, some even as generals. Nor would Stanton recognize that since 1850, when Congress passed the Fugitive Slave Act, northern blacks had formed any number of unofficial militias, effectively led and well-trained by black officers.[45]

The injustice of having blacks serve in separate units led by white officers so enraged some Boston blacks that they organized a campaign against enlistment. So effective were their efforts that most of Boston's eligible black men refused to serve in the state's first black regiment, the Fifty-Fourth Massachusetts Infantry. For others, military service seemed to offer an opportunity to press their struggle forward by some degree even if it was not to the degree they wished. Despite their disgust at the army's inequitable treatment, leading black New Englanders such as James McCune Smith, William Wells Brown, Charles Lenox Remond, Martin Delany, and John Langston became active recruiters for the Fifty-Fourth and Fifty-Fifth Massachusetts Infantry regiments, the Twenty-Ninth Connecticut Infantry, and the Fourteenth Rhode Island Heavy Artillery.[46]

The objection of most whites to appointing blacks as officers stemmed more from racism than anything else. To officially recognize any black man as "an officer and a gentleman" would not only elevate his status above that of white enlisted men, but it might also potentially place him in authority over whites. Although blacks could serve as noncommissioned officers (corporals and sergeants) within their own units, the army sought to maintain the distinction between "man" and "gentleman" along racial lines.[47]

Black soldiers vigorously spoke out against the injustice of denying them any hope of being led by black officers or becoming officers themselves. "We want black commissioned officers," wrote a sergeant to *The Liberator*. Although there were some white officers who treated

---

[45] L. Thomas to Gov. [William Sprague] of Rhode Island, January 15, 1863, *Official Records*, series 3, vol. 3, 16; Order of Edwin M. Stanton, January 26, 1863, ibid., 20–21; L. Thomas to Capt. Silvey, February 10, 1863, ibid., 38–39.

[46] *Weekly Anglo-African*, February 28, 1863; *Boston Press and Post*, March 30, 1863; *Liberator*, February 27, 1863; Berlin et al., *Black Military Experience*, 75. For the enlistment boycott in Boston see Stephen Kantrowitz, *More Than Freedom: Fighting for Black Citizenship in a White Republic, 1829–1889* (New York: Penguin Press, 2012), 2–3, 282–88.

[47] General Orders No. 143, War Department, May 22, 1863, *Official Records*, series 3, vol. 3, 215–16; Berlin et al., *Black Military Experience*, 304.

their black troops with respect, many others did not. "We want men whose hearts are truly loyal to the rights of man. . . . we want simple justice. . . . Can [we] have confidence in officers who read the Boston *Courier* [an anti-emancipation newspaper] and talk about 'Niggers'?" Two sergeants of the Fifty-Fourth Massachusetts boldly wrote to Stanton asking permission to raise a field artillery unit to be led by black officers.[48]

Some few white officers who supported black efforts to gain commissions ignored protocol and granted them field promotions. After an inspection tour, one officer reported that Captain James M. Williams, heading the Fifth Kansas Cavalry Regiment, had black officers leading one of his companies. "Laying aside the question as to the policy or propriety of making soldiers of the Negroe," he wrote, "I must say that the inspection was highly satisfactory – They exhibit a proficiency in the manual and in company evolutions truly surprising and the best company is the one officered by black men."[49]

Stanton refused to be influenced by earnest petitions and glowing reports. During 1863 and 1864, he authorized commissions for only about two dozen blacks as surgeons and chaplains. Surgeons carried the rank of major. Chaplains held an undefined rank, usually understood to be between the ranks of major and captain. Whatever the case, both positions were outside the chain of command. Even those commissions were granted reluctantly and sparked loud complaints from white officers and enlisted men. Still, some blacks did gain field commissions from local commanders eager for their services as recruiters among emancipated former slaves. Through it all, blacks served well as noncommissioned officers on combat duty. So lauded were they by their white officers and so persistent were their demands for promotion that in the war's closing weeks, Stanton finally relented and authorized more black commissions.[50]

Although tens of thousands of black troops eventually proved themselves under fire, so strong was prejudice against their abilities that it seemed at first that they might never be used for anything but menial labor. William T. Sherman bluntly told a recruiter that blacks were "not the equal of the white man." According to Sherman, blacks should "be used for some side purposes and not be brigaded with our white men."

---

[48] *Liberator*, October 7, 1864; First Sergeant J. H. W. N. Collins and Sergeant John Shaffer to Edwin M. Stanton, September 11, 1864, in Berlin et al., *Black Military Experience*, 339–40.

[49] Col. N. P. Cipman [chief of staff, Department of the Missouri] to Gen. Samuel R. Curtis [commanding, Department of the Missouri], October 16, 1862, in Berlin et al., *Black Military Experience*, 70–72.

[50] Berlin et al., *Black Military Experience*, 307–309.

Most other officers felt the same way. They set black soldiers to building fortifications, hauling carts, or digging latrines – anything that might rob them of an opportunity to earn the respect that came with combat service. In some regiments, the colonel was "Ole Massa." Squads were "work gangs," and their officers "nigger drivers." The soldiers may as well have been slaves.[51]

Such attitudes persisted even in the face of early reports lauding the value of black soldiers. As early as January 1863, Colonel T. W. Higginson, commanding a regiment of former slaves recruited mainly along the southeastern tidewater, found black troops indispensable. "They know the country, while white troops do not," he wrote after a successful raid along the Georgia-Florida coast.

Instead of leaving their homes and families to fight they are fighting for their homes and families, and they show the resolution and the sagacity which a personal purpose gives. It would have been madness to attempt, with the bravest white troops, what I have successfully accomplished with black ones. Everything, even to the piloting of the vessels and the selection of the proper points for cannonading, was done by my own soldiers. Indeed the real conductor of the whole expedition up the Saint Mary's was Corporal Robert Sutton of Company G, formerly a slave upon the Saint Mary's River, a man of extraordinary qualities, who needs nothing but a knowledge of the alphabet to entitle him to the most signal promotion. In every instance when I followed his advice the predicted result followed, and I never departed from it, however slightly, without finding reason for subsequent regret.

The men's performance was such that "no officer in this regiment now doubts that the key to the successful prosecution of this war lies in the unlimited employment of black troops."[52]

The value of black troops also became obvious to Union officers at Washington, North Carolina, after Confederates began siege operations. They did not have enough white soldiers to man their defensive perimeter, so they armed all the town's able-bodied black men and put them on the line. "This was our first experience with armed negroes," wrote one Union

---

[51] Sherman to John A. Spooner [recruiter], July 30, 1864, in Berlin et al., *Black Military Experience*, 110–111; Sherman to John Sherman, April 26, 1863, William Techumseh Sherman Papers, Library of Congress, in V. Jacque Voegeli, *Free But Not Equal: The Midwest and the Negro during the Civil War* (Chicago: University of Chicago Press, 1969), 101; D. Densmore to Benjamin [December 1864], and to "Dear Friends at Home," December 18, 1864, Benjamin Densmore Family Papers, Minnesota Historical Society, in Wilson, *Campfires of Freedom*, 39.

[52] Higginson to Brig. Gen. [Rufus] Saxton, February 1, 1863, *Official Records*, series 1, vol. 14, 195–98.

soldier, who recalled "how quietly it was submitted to by many whites who had loudly declared 'they never would fight side of a nigger!' Whitworth shots, exploding shells, and bullet tz-z-zps were wonderfully persuasive arguments on such a question."[53]

Despite the obvious need for black troops and clear evidence of their skill, strong prejudice against using them remained. So certain were some departments that their black troops would never see combat that no weapons were issued. "Instead of the musket," complained one black soldier, "it is the spad and the Whelbarrow and the Axe." Charlie Davenport, a Mississippi freedman, recalled that when his father enlisted at Vicksburg, "they put a pick in his hand instead of a gun. . . . He worked a heap harder for his Uncle Sam than he'd ever done for the master." An elderly slave named Moses told a Union officer that "some of our bucks run away and enlisted board a gun-boat, and expected to be treated just like white men. They put those bucks to shovel coal and working before a hot fire, and didn't even give them good hog and hominy." "If I had my way," he insisted, "I'd be on the Canada side. The colored man is safe there."[54]

"The duty performed is of the hardest kind," wrote Captain Edmund Fowler of the "very arduous fatigue duty" his black company was ordered to perform. "The men are nearly used up. I have quite a number sick, at times I have had to put the sick on duty in order to make out the number called for."[55] Such treatment, even for the sick, was hardly uncommon. Nor was it uncommon for sick men to be worked literally to death. A black soldier who had been working with his comrades in what he called "the most horable swamps in Louisiana stinking and misery," wrote to President Lincoln asking for justice.

We are treated in a Different maner to what others Rigiments is. . . . Men are Call to go on thes fatiues wen sum of them are scarc Able to get Along the Day Before on the sick List And Prehaps weeks to And By this treatment meney are throwen Back in sickness wich thay very seldom get over. . . . Meney of them old and young was Brave And Active. But has Bin hurried By and ignominious Death into Eternity.

[53] William P. Derby, *Bearing Arms in the Twenty-Seventh Massachusetts Regiment of Volunteer Infantry During the Civil War, 1861–1865* (Boston: Wright and Potter, 1883), 168–69.

[54] Unsigned to My Dear Friend [and] Pre. [Lincoln], August 1864, in Berlin et al., *Black Military Experience*, 501; Charlie Davenport, *Mississippi Narratives*, 41; Admiral David Dixon Porter, *Incidents and Anecdotes of the Civil War* (New York: D. Appleton and Co., 1885), 90–91.

[55] Fowler to Lt. Col. A. G. Bennett [commanding, Twenty-First Regiment, USCT], August 3, 1863, in Berlin et al., *Black Military Experience*, 491–92.

But I hope God will Presearve the Rest Now in existence to Get Justice and Rights.[56]

A medical review board found that more than a third of the men in three black Missouri regiments had died of unknown illness, brought on mostly by overwork and physical abuse. Most of those left alive were in a sorry state. The board recommended that almost 200 men be discharged on account of poor health. A newly appointed post commander improved conditions. He provided better sanitation and diet and reduced "heavy labor, in mud and water." For most of the original volunteers, it was too late. They were either dead or their health ruined, some beyond recovery.[57]

In spite of the prejudicial obstacles, some commanders of black regiments were committed to earning respect for their men and pushed hard for combat assignments. One officer wrote to his superior from Fort Scott, Kansas, "These men have been recruited with the promise that they were to fight, not work as common laborers, that they were to be treated in every way as soldiers . . . that they would have an opportunity to strike a blow for the freedom of their brothers."[58] The men made the most of such opportunities when they came.

### WE DID OUR DUTY AS MEN

On May 27, 1863, Union regiments attacked Confederate fortifications on the Mississippi River at Port Hudson, twenty-five miles north of Baton Rouge. They included the First and Third Louisiana Native Guards, led mainly by black company officers. In an after-action report, a white officer admitted that he had entertained some fears as to his men's "pluck."

But now I have none. . . . Valiantly did the heroic descendants of Africa move forward cool as if Marshaled for dress parade, under a most murderous fire . . . these men did not swerve, or show cowardice. I have been in several engagements, and I never before beheld such coolness and daring. Their gallantry entitles them to a special praise. And I already observe, the sneers of others are being tempered into eulogy.[59]

---

56 Unsigned to My Dear Friend [and] Pre. [Lincoln], August 1864, in Berlin et al., *Black Military Experience*, 501–502.

57 Berlin et al., *Black Military Experience*, 487.

58 Col. N. P. Chipman [chief of staff, Department of the Missouri] to Gen. Samuel R. Curtis [commanding, Department of the Missouri], October 16, 1862, in Berlin et al., *Black Military Experience*, 71.

59 Capt. Elias D. Strunke [officer in a Louisiana black regiment] to Brig. Gen. Daniel Ullmann [commanding, Fifth Regiment, U.S. Volunteers, later Eighty-Second Regiment, USCT], May 29, 1863, in Berlin et al., *Black Military Experience*, 528–29.

A few days later, on June 7, two regiments of former slaves helped fend off attacking Rebels at Milliken's Bend, a federal stronghold on the Mississippi River just north of Vicksburg. "Here ensued a most terrible hand to hand conflict," reported one officer, "our men using the bayonet freely and clubbing their guns with fierce obstinacy, contesting every inch of ground." So doggedly did they resist the Rebels that Captain M. M. Miller wrote afterward, "I never more wish to hear the expression, 'The niggers won't fight.'" One official reported that "the sentiment of this army with regard to the employment of negro troops has been revolutionized by the bravery of the blacks in the recent Battle of Milliken's Bend. Prominent officers, who used in private to sneer at the idea, are now heartily in favor of it."[60]

The notion that blacks lacked the discipline for soldiering was dealt a further blow on July 16 when the Fifty-Fourth Massachusetts fought off a rebel charge on James Island just south of Charleston, South Carolina. "It is not for us to blow our own horn," Corporal James Henry Gooding wrote home to Boston, "but when a regiment of white men gave us three cheers as we were passing them, it shows that we did our duty as men should." An even tougher test came two days later when the Fifty-Fourth led an assault on Fort Wagner, guarding the southern approach to Charleston Harbor. Gooding later recalled that when the charge sounded,

we went at it, over the ditch and onto the parapet through a deadly fire; but we could not get into the fort. We met the foe on the parapet of Wagner with the bayonet – we were exposed to a murderous fire from the batteries of the fort, from our Monitors and our land batteries, as they did not cease firing soon enough. . . . The color bearer of the State colors was killed on the parapet. Col. [Robert Gould] Shaw seized the staff when the standard bearer fell, and in less than a minute after, the Colonel fell himself. When the men saw their gallant leader fall, they made a desperate effort to get him out, but they were either shot down, or reeled in the ditch below.[61]

See also Edward Cunningham, *The Port Hudson Campaign, 1862–1863* (Baton Rouge: Louisiana State University Press, 1963).

[60] Brig. Gen. Elias S. Dennis [commanding, District of Northeast Louisiana] to Col. John A. Rawlins [Headquarters, Department of the Tennessee], June 12, 1863, in Berlin et al., *Black Military Experience*, 533; Miller to aunt, June 10, 1863, *Official Records*, series 3, vol. 3, 452–53; Charles A. Dana [special commissioner, War Department] to Edwin M. Stanton, June 22, 1863, *Official Records*, series 1, vol. 24, part 1, 105–106.

[61] Corporal James Henry Gooding, *On the Altar of Freedom: A Black Soldier's Civil War Letters from the Front*, ed. Virginia M. Adams (Amherst: University of Massachusetts Press, 1991), 36–39. In February 1864, Gooding was wounded and captured at the Battle of Olustee in Florida. He died later that year at Georgia's Andersonville prison. Gooding's letters constitute one of the few collections written by a black soldier ever to see print. A similar collection from a variety of black soldiers is found in Edwin S. Redkey, ed., *A Grand Army of Black Men: Letters from African-American Soldiers in the Union Army, 1861–1865* (Cambridge: Cambridge University Press, 1992).

Six hundred men of the Fifty-Fourth went in on the assault. Nearly half were captured, killed, or wounded. One of the most severely injured was Sergeant William H. Carney, a refugee from slavery in Virginia. When a color sergeant went down, Carney grabbed the flag, planted it on Wagner's parapet, fought off attempts to capture it, and carried it away with him despite wounds to his head, chest, right leg, and arm. On arriving at a field hospital, he passed the colors to a regimental officer, reporting, to the cheers of his wounded comrades, "Boys, the old flag never touched the ground." Carney became one of twenty-three black Civil War servicemen awarded the Congressional Medal of Honor.[62]

The value of black troops became increasing apparent as they gained more combat assignments. To one white soldier serving in Louisiana, it was clear that blacks would indeed fight. "It has been proved where ever they have had a chance." They proved it again at Petersburg, Virginia, when four untested black regiments sent veteran Confederates in headlong retreat. "The majority of the whites expected that the colored troops would run," according to a correspondent on the scene, "but the sable forces astonished everybody by their achievements. With a wild yell that must certainly have struck terror into the hearts of their foes [they] charged, under a hot fire of musketry and artillery, over the rebel ditch and parapet, and drove the enemy before them." Not content with simply taking their objective, members of the Twenty-Second Regiment laid hold of a captured cannon, swung it around, and fired into the fleeing Confederates.[63]

---

[62] Return of Casualties in the Union Forces, *Official Records*, series 1, vol. 28, part 1, 210; Col. E. N. Hallowell [commanding, Fifty-Fourth Massachusetts Regiment] to Gen. Truman Seymour, November 7, 1863, ibid., series 1, vol. 28, part 1, 362–63. See also Peter Burchard, *One Gallant Rush: Robert Gould Shaw and His Brave Black Regiment* (New York: St. Martin's Press, 1965), 137–141.

    The Carney quote is from Robert Stewart Davis, "Three Months Around Charleston Bar; or The Great Siege as We Saw It," *United States Service Magazine* 1 (1864): 282. Carney's Medal of Honor, like most of those won by black servicemen, was awarded long after the war. Carney's came in 1900, eight years before his death at age sixty-eight. Since his was the earliest engagement for which the medal was awarded, Carney is sometimes credited with being the first black serviceman to win the Medal of Honor.

[63] Benjamin Stevens to mother, August 12, 1863, in Richard N. Ellis, ed., "The Civil War Letters of an Iowa Family," *Annals of Iowa* 39 (1969): 582; *Frank Leslie's Illustrated Newspaper*, July 9, 1864; Col. Samuel A. Duncan [commanding, Second Brigade, Third Division, Eighteenth Army Corps] to Capt. Solon A. Carter [acting assistant adjutant-general], *Official Records*, series 1, vol. 51, part 1, 266. See also Samuel P. Bates, *History of Pennsylvania Volunteers, 1861–5* (Harrisburg: B. Singerly, 1871), 5: 991–92.

FIGURE 3.3. The Twenty-Second Regiment, United States Colored Troops (USCT), at Petersburg, driving Confederates from their fortifications and into the woods beyond. Not content with simply taking their objective, the men laid hold of a captured cannon, swung it around, and fired into their retreating foe. This assault of June 15, 1864, was the opening salvo of the Siege of Petersburg, which marked the beginning of the end for the Confederacy. Image from *Frank Leslie's Illustrated Newspaper* (New York), July 9, 1864.

After the Battle of Nashville, where blacks and whites had advanced together "while the fire of the enemy poured upon them in torrents," an officer rode over the field in front of the dislodged Confederate positions. "Black and white dead lay side by side," he wrote. "Death had known no distinction of color, nor had Valor, for the blacks were as near the enemy's line as were the whites."[64]

If death did not discriminate, white officers often did by placing blacks in the vanguard of attacks, where casualties were always highest. Just before the assault on Fort Wagner, General Quincy Gillmore, commanding the Department of the South, asked his operational subordinate General Truman Seymour how he planned to organize his forces. Seymour replied, "Well, I guess we will let Strong lead and put those d—d niggers from Massachusetts in the advance; we may as well get

[64] Col. Reuben D. Mussey [commissioner for the organization of black troops in middle and east Tennessee] to Capt. C. P. Brown [Headquarters, Tennessee Black Troops], December 21, 1864, in Berlin et al., *Black Military Experience*, 560–62.

rid of them one time as another." William Ball "Soldier" Williams, a former slave and Union veteran, recalled with bitterness that white soldiers "put us in front to shield themselves." He considered quitting the army but "didn't know how to get out."[65]

Field commanders used blacks as cannon fodder so frequently that their superiors became increasingly sensitive to accusations of callousness. Just before the Battle of the Crater, in which Union forces attempted to break the Confederate lines at Petersburg with a massive explosion, General Ulysses S. Grant changed an order that had blacks leading the attack. He later testified before a congressional committee that he and his subordinates had feared being charged with "shoving those people ahead to get killed because we did not care anything about them." Nevertheless, when blacks were finally ordered into the fray, they attacked along the right crest of the crater and captured a number of rebel prisoners. Others were ordered directly into the crater, where they became entangled with a mass of white troops unable to move up the other side. There, like the whites, they suffered huge casualties. Recalled one commander of black troops, "Had it not been for the almost unpassable crowd of troops, Cemetery Hill would have been our's, without a falter upon the part of my Brigade. . . . Too much praise cannot be awarded to the bravery of both officers and men."[66]

There were individual as well as collective acts of bravery. Albert Jones, a Virginia freedman who had escaped with his brother to join the Union army, remembered that in one battle the Rebels "sent a bullet through my hand. . . . But that didn't stop me. I had it bandaged and kept on fighting." He never regained full use of his wounded hand. At Dalton, Georgia, just before black troops were sent into the attack, a white lieutenant warned, "it may be slavery or Death to some of you today." One of the men, Henry Prince, responded, "Lieutenant, I am ready to die for Liberty." And so he

---

[65] Excerpt from testimony of Nathaniel Paige, special correspondent of the *New York Times*, before the American Freedmen's Inquiry Commission [February ? 1864], in Berlin et al., *Black Military Experience*, 534–36; William Ball Williams, *Arkansas Narratives*, part 7, 191. Seymour was referring to General George Crockett Strong, whose brigade contained the Fifty-Fourth Massachusetts Regiment. Both Seymour and Strong were wounded during the second day's assault on Wagner. Strong died twelve days later of tetanus. Paige added that Seymour later became an "ardent admirer" of black soldiers.

[66] U.S. Congress, *Report of the Joint Committee on the Conduct of the War: Battle of Petersburg*, Senate Reports, Thirty-Eighth Congress, Second Session, no. 142, 111, in Berlin et al., *Black Military Experience*, 522 n. 5; Col. J. K. Sigfried [commanding a black brigade] to Capt. George A. Hicks [Headquarters, Fourth Division, Ninth Army Corps], July 31, 1864, in ibid., 549–51.

did. "The vows were scarce uttered," recalled the regiment's commander, who singled Henry out for praise, "until a ball pierced his heart and he was dead!"[67]

In March 1863, two companies of whites near Washington, North Carolina, trying to escape attacking Confederates by river found one of their transports stuck fast in the mud from the weight of the soldiers. As an eyewitness recalled, they "were saved from death or capture by the self-sacrifice of a gallant negro, who, seeing the boat aground ... jumped overboard and pushed the flat into the river." Hit by enemy fire, "the brave man fell lifeless into the water, but the launch floated away to a place of safety."[68]

Blacks sometimes received grudging admiration even from Confederates. After the engagement at Milliken's Bend, one rebel officer wrote that his black foes fought "with considerable obstinacy, while the white or true Yankee portion ran like whipped curs." Such observations provide evidence that the respect soldiers often displayed across the lines could be displayed toward black soldiers as well. One Federal wrote of his surprise when Confederates agreed to a picket-line truce with black soldiers facing them. "The rebels and our colored soldiers now converse together on apparently very friendly terms, and exchange such luxuries as apples, tobacco, and hard tack, by throwing them to each other. It was hardly deemed possible that the enemy could be induced to refrain from firing on black troops wherever they could be seen."[69]

Rebel commanders usually wanted their men to do precisely that – to kill as many black troops as possible, at times including those who could have been taken prisoner. Despite the government's official policy that captured blacks be enslaved, the unofficial policy of many Confederate officers was that blacks in uniform be shot on sight, even those trying to surrender. Still, some Rebels balked at such barbarism. At Milliken's Bend, they took blacks prisoner rather than murder them in cold blood. One officer recalled hearing his men shout during the battle that surrendering blacks should be spared. When General Edmund Kirby Smith

---

[67] Albert Jones, *Virginia Narratives*, 42–43; Col. Thomas J. Morgan to Col. R. D. Mussey, October 8, 1864, in Berlin et al., *Black Military Experience*, 556.

[68] Derby, *Bearing Arms in the Twenty-Seventh Massachusetts Regiment*, 168.

[69] Gen. Henry D. McCulloch [commanding a Confederate brigade] to Maj. R. P. Maclay [assistant adjutant and inspector general], June 8, 1863, *Official Records*, series 1, vol. 24, part 2, 467; R. J. M. Blackett, ed., *Thomas Morris Chester, Black Civil War Correspondent: His Dispatches from the Virginia Front* (Baton Rouge: Louisiana State University Press, 1989), 115.

heard that so many blacks had been captured alive, he told one of his commanders, "I hope this may not be so, and that your subordinates who may have been in command of Capturing parties may have recognized the propriety of giving no quarter to armed negroes and their officers." A rebel deserter later testified that three days after the battle, he witnessed the hanging of one white officer and several black soldiers taken at Milliken's Bend.[70]

Such atrocities took place in numerous engagements, often on direct orders of rebel officers. The colonel of an Alabama regiment told his men "to shoot, wherever and whenever captured, all negroes found armed." In Louisiana, one Texas colonel ordered his cavalry brigade to charge a fort held by black soldiers and to "take none with uniforms on." In Arkansas, at the Battle of Poison Springs, eyewitnesses reported black prisoners being "murdered on the spot." The same occurred at the Battle of Saltville in Virginia, where Confederates "brutally murdered" black prisoners. During the Battle of the Crater, Rebels ran bayonets through wounded black soldiers.[71]

After rebel forces captured Plymouth, North Carolina, Sergeant Samuel Johnson put on civilian clothes and passed himself off as a slave, an act that saved his life. Captured and placed in servitude, he finally escaped and told a harrowing story.

All the negroes found in blue uniform or with any outward marks of a Union soldier upon him was killed – I saw some taken into the woods and hung – Others I saw stripped of all their clothing, and they stood upon the bank of the river with

---

[70] Richard Lowe, "Battle on the Levee: The Fight at Milliken's Bend," in Smith, *Black Soldiers in Blue*, 125; Smith [commanding, Confederate Department of the Trans-Mississippi] to Gen. R. Taylor [commanding, Confederate District of Louisiana], June 13, 1863, in Berlin et al., *Black Military Experience*, 578; Lt. Commander E. K. Ewen [Union naval officer] to Adm. David D. Porter [commanding, Mississippi Squadron], June 16, 1863, in ibid., 581.

[71] Col. Jno. R. F. Tattnall [commanding, Alabama Confederate regiment] to Capt. S. Croom [Headquarters, Confederate District of the Gulf], November 8, 1862, in Berlin et al., *Black Military Experience*, 570–71; Gregory J. W. Urwin, "'We Cannot Treat Negroes . . . as Prisoners of War': Racial Atrocities and Reprisals in Civil War Arkansas," in Gregory J. W. Urwin, ed., *Black Flag Over Dixie: Racial Atrocities and Reprisals in the Civil War* (Carbondale: Southern Illinois University Press, 2004), 141; Col. James M. Williams [First Kansas Colored Infantry Regiment] to Capt. William S. Whitten [assistant adjutant-general], April 24, 1864, *Official Records*, series 1, vol. 34, part 1, 746; Col. James S. Brisbin [superintendent of the organization of Kentucky black troops] to Gen. L. Thomas, October 20, 1864, in Berlin et al., *Black Military Experience*, 558; Bryce A. Suderow, "Battle of the Crater: The Civil War's Worst Massacre," in Urwin, *Black Flag Over Dixie*, 203–209.

their faces riverwards and then they were shot – Still others were killed by having their brains beaten out by the butt end of the muskets in the hands of the Rebels.[72]

When nearby Fort Williams fell to the Rebels, a Union lieutenant recalled that "the negro soldiers who had surrendered, were drawn up in line at the breastwork, and shot down as they stood."[73]

At Tennessee's Fort Pillow, former slaves and white southern Unionists were outnumbered four to one by attacking Confederates under General Nathan Bedford Forrest. The defenders tried to surrender, but most were ruthlessly cut down. Confederate Sergeant Achilles Clark vividly recalled the massacre.

The slaughter was awful. Words cannot describe the scene. The poor deluded negroes would run up to our men fall upon their knees and with uplifted hands scream for mercy but they were ordered to their feet then shot down. The white men fared but little better. Their fort turned out to be a great slaughter pen. Blood, human blood stood about in pools and brains could have been gathered up in any quantity.

A few Confederate officers, and Clark himself, tried to stop the killing but got no support from their commander. "Gen. Forrest," Clark wrote, ordered the prisoners to be "shot down like dogs." After the massacre, an enthused Forrest called Fort Pillow a clear demonstration that "negro soldiers cannot cope with Southerners."[74]

After the Battle of Olustee, west of Jacksonville, Florida, victorious Confederates roamed among wounded Federals shooting every black soldier they could find. When William Penniman of the Fourth Georgia Cavalry rode up to ask what the men were doing, an officer replied, "Shooting niggers, Sir." Penniman protested that it was shameful to murder wounded prisoners, but the killings continued. Another Georgia soldier who was at Olustee later recalled, "How our boys did walk into the niggers, they would beg and pray but it did no good." Next day,

[72] Affidavit of Samuel Johnson, July 11, 1864, in Berlin et al., *Black Military Experience*, 588–89.

[73] Lieutenant Alonzo Cooper, *In and Out of Rebel Prisons* (Oswego, N.Y.: R. J. Oliphant, 1888), 34. For an overview of the Plymouth Massacre see Weymouth T. Jordan and Gerald W. Thomas, "Massacre at Plymouth, April 20, 1864," in Urwin, *Black Flag Over Dixie*, 153–202.

[74] John Cimprich and Robert C. Mainfort Jr., eds., "Fort Pillow Revisited: New Evidence about an Old Controversy," *Civil War History* 28 (1982): 299; Forrest to Lt. Col. Thomas M. Jack [assistant adjutant-general], April 15, 1864, *Official Records*, series 1, vol. 32, part 1, 610. See also John Cimprich, *Fort Pillow, a Civil War Massacre, and Public Memory* (Baton Rouge: Louisiana State University Press, 2005).

Penniman rode over the battlefield. "The results of the previous night became all to[o] apparent. Negroes, and plenty of them, whom I had seen lying all over the field wounded, and as far as I could see, many of them moving around from place to place, now ... all were dead. If a negro had a shot in the shin, another was sure to be in the head."[75]

Ultimately, the take-no-prisoners policy worked more against Confederates than for them. When word of the murders spread, black soldiers began to fight with a rage that astonished friend and foe alike. Rebel prisoners, recalled one Union officer, "told me that they would rather fight two Regiments of White Soldiers than one of Niggers. ... [They] fear them more than they would fear Indians." A white cavalryman from Maine wrote home of black troops shooting captured Confederates. "The officers had hard work to stop them from killing All the prisoners," he recalled. "When one of them would beg for his life the niggers would say remember port hudson." After a company of black cavalrymen surrounded a band of Confederate guerrillas, someone shouted "Remember Fort Pillow." The blacks captured seventeen prisoners, then shot them all dead. A white officer in one black regiment wrote to his wife that his men had killed five captured Confederates. "Had it not been for Ft Pillow," he lamented, "those 5 men might be alive now. ... It looks hard but we cannot blame these men much."[76] Indeed, few of their comrades faulted black soldiers for giving no quarter to men they believed would give them none. The general rule was kill or be killed.

Even when some degree of humanity prevailed and blacks survived initial captivity, life as a prisoner of war was always brutal and often brief. Private Joseph Howard of the 110th Regiment, United States Colored Troops (USCT), wrote of his after-capture experience, "We were kept at hard labor and inhumanly treated. If we lagged or faltered or misunderstood an order we were whipped and abused. ... For the slightest causes we were ubjected to lash." Medical care for black prisoners was poorly provided or nonexistent. An inmate at Georgia's Andersonville prison witnessed the treatment of 200 black captives, many of them wounded, who survived the slaughter at Olustee: "One fellow had a hand shot off and some enraged brutes had cut off his ears and nose, and

---

[75] William Penniman reminiscences, 60–62, William Penniman Papers, Southern Historical Collection, University of North Carolina at Chapel Hill, in David J. Coles, "'Shooting Niggers Sir': Confederate Mistreatment of Union Black Soldiers at the Battle of Olustee," in Urwin, *Black Flag Over Dixie*, 74–75.

[76] Benjamin Stevens to mother, August 12, 1863, in Ellis, "Civil War Letters of an Iowa Family," 582; Glatthaar, *Forged in Battle*, 157.

otherwise mutilated him. The doctors refused to dress his wounds, or even amputate his shattered arm; he was naked in the prison, and finally died from his numerous wounds." Blacks held in Confederate prison camps died at a rate of 35 percent, more than twice the average for white captives.[77]

## THEY TREAT THE MEN LIKE DOGS

The treatment black soldiers received from their own comrades was nearly as appalling, especially when it came to medical care. One black soldier complained in a letter to the secretary of war, "My Left Leg is very Badley [in]fected from an old cut." He had told the surgeon that the leg "was getting worse but he will driv Me off Like a dog and Say That he cant do any thing for Me." The soldier was sure that such treatment had everything to do with the color of his skin. "Sir, if I was a white Man I would be discharged Sum time a go." Samuel Johnson, a Florida slave who escaped to join the Union army, changed his mind when he saw the "feeble medical attention" given to wounded members of the Fifty-Fourth Massachusetts.[78]

Blacks were assigned the worst doctors and received the least medical attention. An inspector general reported that the surgeon who ran one black hospital "did not evince much knowledge of his duties." Other surgeons attached to black regiments were described as simpletons and even murderers. When one black soldier reported for sick call, the surgeon had him bucked and gagged on suspicion of faking the illness. Next day, the soldier was dead. Another surgeon kicked a black patient for leaving his tent without permission. The man had needed to relieve himself. He died that evening. As a dying black soldier lay moaning in pain, one surgeon yelled, "god damn him if he was a going to die and don't [make] So much fuss about it." "The officers see all this," wrote one black soldier, "and don't Seem to pay any attention to it." Small wonder that the rate of death from disease for black soldiers was more than twice that of whites.[79]

[77] Statement of Private Joseph Howard, January 30, 1865, *Official Records*, series 2, vol. 8, 153; S. S. Boggs, *Eighteen Months a Prisoner Under the Rebel Flag* (Lovington, Ill.: n.p., 1880), 26–27; Lonnie R. Speer, *Portals to Hell: Military Prisons of the Civil War* (Mechanicsburg, Penn.: Stackpole Books, 1997), 108.

[78] Colored [soldier] to [Edwin M. Stanton], January 21, 1865, in Berlin et al., *Black Military Experience*, 646–47; Samuel Johnson, *Florida Narratives*, 179–80.

[79] Unsigned to Sir [unidentified Washington official], August 20, 1864, in Berlin et al., *Black Military Experience*, 640–41. For contrast of death from disease between black and white soldiers see Margaret Humphreys, *Intensely Human: The Health of the Black Soldier in the American Civil War* (Baltimore: Johns Hopkins University Press, 2008), 11.

If the death rate was higher, basic pay for blacks was lower – $10 a month instead of the normal $13. And the army withheld $3 more for the cost of their uniforms. Even for those blacks who rose in the ranks, there were no corresponding pay increases as there were for whites. Still, the need for income among black soldiers' families was no less than for whites. As one soldier expressed the need, "Our families – hundreds, nay thousands, of helpless women and children – are this day suffering for the natural means of subsistence, whose husbands and fathers have responded to the country's call." For soldier Solomon Steward, not being able to support his family was especially painful. Writing from Union-held Fernandina, Florida, his wife Emma informed him that an "administering angel Has Come and borne My Dear Little babe To Join In Tones with Them sweet and pure as angels whispers. My babe only Live one day It was

FIGURE 3.4. Despite their dedicated and much-needed service, blacks were treated worse and paid less than white soldiers. "We have done a soldier's duty," wrote Corporal James Henry Gooding of the Fifty-Fourth Massachusetts to President Lincoln. "Why can't we have a soldier's pay?" Letters from soldiers' families were filled with news of suffering for lack of income. One general commanding black troops reported to headquarters, "The effects of such letters on the minds of the enlisted men of these regiments may be easily imagined." Photo of unknown soldier and family courtesy of the Library of Congress.

a Little Girl. Her name Is alice Gurtrude steward I am now sick In Bed and have Got nothing To Live on." Such letters made clear the impact of discriminatory pay.[80]

"I have a wife and 3 Children ... and my wife is sick," wrote a black soldier to President Lincoln. "She has sent to me for money ... I have No way of geting Eney money to send to her Because I cant Get my Pay."[81] He had been in the army seven months and had received no funds. It was an all too common experience. The commanding general of the Union's Northern District, Department of the South, wrote to his superiors from Folly Island, South Carolina:

Letters have been constantly arriving for six months in these regiments, in which the wives of the enlisted men describe their sufferings, and the sufferings of their families – children have died because they could not be supplied with proper food, and because the Doctor could not be paid, or medicines obtained from the Druggist. Mothers advise their sons to throw down the musket and come home. ... The effects of such letters on the minds of the enlisted men of these regiments may be easily imagined.[82]

Even when soldiers were paid, to many the principle of equal pay was as important as its practicality. Black soldiers had fought and died just as whites had. Were their lives worth less? In a letter to Lincoln, Corporal James Henry Gooding reminded him that "when the war trumpet sounded o'er the land, when men knew not the Friend from the Traitor, the Black man laid his life at the Altar of the Nation – and he was refused." But when the need for more soldiers became so great that blacks had to be called upon, how did they respond? "Let their dusky forms, rise up, out the mires of James Island, and give the answer. Let the rich mould around Wagners parapets be upturned, and there will be found an Eloquent answer. ... We have done a Soldiers Duty. Why cant we have a Soldiers pay?"[83]

If they could not have a soldier's pay, many refused to take any at all. In a show of support for their men, neither did some white officers. Colonel Robert Gould Shaw refused to have anyone in his regiment paid until all

[80] *Christian Recorder*, May 21, 1864; Emma to husband John, February 8, 1864, in Thomas Wentworth Higginson, "Intensely Human," *Atlantic Monthly* 93 (1904): 596–97.

[81] George Rodgers et al. to Mr. President, August 1864, in Berlin et al., *Black Military Experience*, 680–81.

[82] Brig. Gen. A. Schimmelfennig [commanding, Northern District, Department of the South] to Capt. W. L. M. Burger [Headquarters, Department of the South], June 2, 1864, in Berlin et al., *Black Military Experience*, 397–98.

[83] Gooding to A. Lincoln, September 28, 1863, in Berlin et al., *Black Military Experience*, 385–86.

his men received equitable pay. Captain A. W. Heasley told his company, "Boys, stand up for your full pay! I am with you, and so are all the officers." Unfortunately, not all officers were so supportive. When soldiers of Pennsylvania's Thirty-Second Regiment, USCT, declined to accept reduced pay, the officers were "very much put out." One soldier reported that "they began to treat the men like dogs. The least thing that the men would do, they were bucked and gagged, and put on knap-sack-drill, and made to stand in the hot, broiling sun for four hours at a stretch; in consequence of which, a few of the men got sun-struck."[84]

Several black regiments threatened mutiny or desertion over the pay issue. In a letter to President Lincoln, seventy-four soldiers of the Fifty-Fifth Massachusetts demanded "imediate Discharge Having Been enlisted under False Pretence." They warned that if "imediate steps are not taken to Relieve us we will Resort to more stringent mesures." Threats sometimes turned to action, especially when officers would not support their men. When their officers failed to petition the government on their behalf, several black units stacked arms and refused to do any service until they received equal pay. When a black artillery company declined to fall out for inspection in protest over pay, fourteen men were sent to a remote prison in the Florida Keys. The army court-martialed Sergeant William Walker of the Third South Carolina Regiment for "leading the company to stack arms before their captain's tent, on the avowed ground that they were released from duty by the refusal of the government to fulfill its share of the contract." Walker was sentenced to execution.[85]

The frequent and intense complaints, petitions, and protests finally forced Congress to equalize pay in June 1864. Still, discrimination was present in the act. Men who had been free before the war would receive back pay to the time of their enlistment. Those who had been enslaved would receive back pay only to January 1, 1864. Some soldiers got

---

[84] Col. E. N. Hallowell [commanding, Fifty-Fourth Massachusetts Volunteers] to Gov. John A. Andrew, November 23, 1863, in Berlin et al., *Black Military Experience*, 387; Shaw to brother Clem., July 1, 1863, in Russell Duncan, ed., *Blue-Eyed Child of Fortune: The Civil War Letters of Colonel Robert Gould Shaw* (Athens: University of Georgia Press, 1992), 367–68; Taylor, *Reminiscences*, 16; *Christian Recorder*, July 30, 1864.

[85] Sgt. John F. Shorter et al. to President of the United States, July 16, 1864, in Berlin et al., *Black Military Experience*, 401–402; Capt. Thomas W. Fry to [?], September 21, 1864, in William H. Chenery, *The Fourteenth Regiment Rhode Island Heavy Artillery (Colored) in the War to Preserve the Union, 1861–1865* (Providence, R.I.: Snow and Farnham, 1898), 66; Statement of Sgt. William Walker, January 12, 1864, in Berlin et al., *Black Military Experience*, 392–94.

around the restriction by taking a "Quaker Oath" concocted by Colonel Edward Hallowell of the Fifty-Fourth Massachusetts. His troops simply stated that from the war's outset, "no man had the right to demand unrequited labor" of them. From the perspective of former slaves, that had always been the case.[86]

There was discrimination too in equipping black soldiers. In April 1864, long after the percussion cap Springfield rifle became standard issue, one officer wrote to the War Department following an inspection of a black field unit, "This Regiment, like most of this class of soldiers, have the old flintlock muskets, altered to percussion, which have been used for a long time. The muskets of this Regiment were condemned once, and have been condemned by an Inspector a second time." Some whites were reluctant to trust blacks with even these antiquated weapons. Several officials suggested that blacks be armed only with pikes.[87]

Just as discouraging as the abuse blacks suffered through official channels was the unofficial abuse they suffered from white soldiers. Despite their steadfast combat service, blacks were verbally insulted, physically abused, and socially degraded. "Our boys don't think much of them," wrote a white Indiana volunteer. "They still say this is a *White Mans War*." At one point, roughly forty white soldiers assaulted a group of black enlisted men, injuring several.[88] Colonel James S. Brisbin witnessed various forms of abuse just before blacks were sent into combat at the First Battle of Saltville in southwestern Virginia.

On the march the Colored Soldiers as well as their white Officers were made the subject of much ridicule and many insulting remarks by the White Troops and in some instances petty outrages such as the pulling off the Caps of Colored Soldiers, stealing their horses etc was practiced by the White Soldiers. These insults as well as the jeers and taunts that they would not fight were borne by the Colored Soldiers patiently or punished with dignity by their Officers but in no instance did I hear Colored soldiers make any reply to insulting language used toward [them] by the White Troops.

---

[86] U.S., *Statutes at Large, Treaties, and Proclamations of the United States of America* (Boston: Little, Brown, and Company, 1866), 13: 129–30; Luis Fenollosa Emilio, *History of the Fifty-Fourth Regiment of Massachusetts Volunteer Infantry, 1863–1865*, second ed. (Boston: Boston Book Company, 1894), 220–21.

[87] Lorenzo Thomas to Edwin M. Stanton, April 7, 1864, in Quarles, *Negro in the Civil War*, 204–205; Robert Gould Shaw to brother Clem., July 1, 1863, in Duncan, *Blue-Eyed Child of Fortune*, 367–68.

[88] Winther, *With Sherman to the Sea*, 149; Ripley, *Slaves and Freedmen in Civil War Louisiana*, 124–25.

Of the 400 blacks who went into battle that day, more than 100 were killed or wounded. "On the return of the forces," recalled Brisbin, "those who had scoffed at the Colored Troops on the march out were silent."[89]

The most degrading aspect of military life for some black troops was the way they were often used as slave labor for white troops. Colonel James C. Beecher, commanding a regiment of former North Carolina slaves, complained to superiors about his men being

put to work laying out and policing camps of white soldiers. . . . they are regarded as, and called "d – d Niggers" by so-called "gentlemen" in uniform of U.S. Officers, but when they are set to menial work for white regiments what those Regiments are entitled to do for themselves, it simply throws them back where they were before and reduces them to the position of slaves again.[90]

As they had resisted inequitable pay, black soldiers also resisted inequitable treatment – especially treatment that reminded them too much of slavery. When one captain had a soldier tied up, just as a plantation overseer might have done, two of the victim's comrades freed him. Being free had to mean that one could not be bound, else what was the point of being free? One private cut a friend loose and exclaimed, "No white son of a bitch can tie a man up here." Such resistance constituted mutiny and could have severe consequences. Although blacks accounted for roughly 10 percent of Union servicemen, almost three-fourths of those executed for mutiny were black. And those were the ones who received at least the formality of a hearing. Many did not. Robert Gould Shaw wrote of Colonel James Montgomery, who commanded another regiment of blacks in the same brigade, "He shoots his men with perfect looseness, for a slight disobedience of orders." So did Lieutenant Francis Bichinel of the Thirty-Sixth Regiment, USCT, who shot a black soldier named Silas Holley for nothing more than "alleged stubbornness" and "manifesting a mutinous spirit." Had such traits been capital crimes, nearly every soldier, black or white, would have been executed. From the officers' perspective, almost all soldiers were guilty of these shortcomings at one time or another.[91]

[89]  Brisbin [superintendent of the organization of Kentucky black troops] to Gen. L. Thomas, October 20, 1864, in Berlin et al., *Black Military Experience*, 557–58.
[90]  Beecher to Brig. Gen. Edward A. Wild [commanding brigade], September 13, 1863, in Berlin et al., *Black Military Experience*, 493.
[91]  Glatthaar, *Forged in Battle*, 115; Gary Kynoch, "Terrible Dilemmas: Black Enlistment in the Union Army During the American Civil War," in Greenberg and Waugh, *Price of Freedom*, 1: 121; Shaw to Charley Morse, July 3, 1863, in Duncan, *Blue-Eyed Child of Fortune*, 369; Blackett, *Thomas Morris Chester*, 115.

White officers in black regiments were a mixed lot. Although some treated their men with respect and advocated their advancement, many others did not. The problem stemmed from lax officer review boards that failed to question prospective officers about their racial attitudes or their motives for applying for positions in black regiments. Some did so to avoid combat, sure their men would never be used in battle. Others sought only the privileges and pay of higher rank. Some had been, and still were, slaveholders, certain that they knew how to "handle" blacks better than nonslaveholding officers.[92]

Army regulations required that superiors behave "with kindness and justice to inferiors." Officers were "forbidden to injure those under them by tyrannical or capricious conduct, or by abusive language." But those prohibitions were not well-enforced when it came to black troops. An army chaplain in Louisiana wrote to the commander of his brigade of the "abuses practised by officers upon the men, such as cursing and vilifying, in the most shameful language, striking and kicking," all of which was "practised habitually." Most of the soldiers had until recently been enslaved, and the chaplain pointed out that military service "ought to present to them a contrast to the irresponsible cruelties of slavedriving, instead of a too faithful reproduction of them." He wished that such behavior could be eradicated but doubted that there was "a disposition in the governing powers of the army to take cognizance of this class of offences, and enforce a better principle."[93]

That was all too clear to David Washington of the Third U.S. Colored Cavalry. After his captain struck him, Washington reported the incident to headquarters. He was told to wait for his captain to be called up. When the captain finally arrived two days later, he accused Washington of desertion. For that crime, Washington was sentenced to a year imprisonment at hard labor without pay. Washington wrote directly to President Lincoln, telling his commander-in-chief, "I am a good solger all ways has done what is right. . . . I ought not to be in pr[i]son if I had [justice] done me I am a colerd man I have no edication I don't know nothing at all abought law. . . . pleas doe all you can fer me." There was no reply.[94]

[92] Berlin et al., *Black Military Experience*, 408–409.
[93] *Revised United States Army Regulations of 1861* (Washington, D.C.: Government Printing Office, 1863), 9; Chaplain Saml. L. Gardner to Gen. Daniel Ullmann, December 19, 1864, in Berlin et al., *Black Military Experience*, 417–18.
[94] Washi[ng]ton to Mr. A. Linco[l]n, November 26, 1864, in Berlin et al., *Black Military Experience*, 455.

Private Newton Rucker wrote to his commanding general about a Lieutenant Brown, complaining that he "daily treats the men of company [A] with such excesive cruelty that they can no longer submit to the degredation heaped upon them." Rucker himself had been forced "to walk a '*beat*' untill I have deposited the excrement of my body in my pants." After a white officer, Augustus Benedict, whipped two drummer boys of the Fourth Louisiana Regiment, soldiers staged a mutiny and threatened to kill Benedict. Most of the men were former slaves who had been promised that, in accordance with army regulations, they would never be whipped. Eight of the mutineers went to prison for the crime of insisting that regulations be evenly applied.[95]

Poorly as most black soldiers were treated, it is a testament to fortitude that their desertion rate was only slightly above the average for whites. For those who did desert, a frequent complaint was that they had been treated not as soldiers but as slaves. In September 1864, Private Spencer Brown of the Fifth Regiment, USCT, deserted. His comrades had heard him remark with disgust "that he was no better treated in the army than he was by his former master."[96]

Still, there were small signs that black soldiers' sacrifices were having at least some impact on northern white attitudes. For the most part, those attitudes remained deeply racist and paternalistic. Many remained downright hostile. In Baltimore, whites attacked a black army surgeon, commissioned as a major, tearing the rank insignia from his uniform. Thugs in Zanesville, Ohio, nearly killed a black soldier who walked into a barbershop for a haircut. Such violence against blacks, even black soldiers, was hardly uncommon.[97]

But there were also scenes that a year before would have been unimaginable. In February 1864, the same month that the Zanesville incident occurred, New York City saw its first black regiment formed, the Twentieth Regiment, USCT. Before it left for the front, supporters insisted on having the Twentieth parade down streets where blacks had been brutally beaten and murdered just seven months earlier during the draft riots. Now black soldiers marched boldly down those same streets, greeted, as one witnessed recalled, with "waving handkerchiefs,

---

[95] Rucker to Gen. T. W. Sherman [commanding defenses of New Orleans], December 6, 1864, in Berlin et al., *Black Military Experience*, 456; Excerpts from proceedings of a military commission convened at Fort Jackson, La., December 12–13, 1863, in ibid., 442–49.

[96] Lonn, *Desertion during the Civil War*, 149–50; Blackett, *Thomas Morris Chester*, 115.

[97] *Christian Recorder*, May 30, 1863; *Anglo-African*, February 13, 1864 (the *Weekly Anglo-African* had become the *Anglo-African* by 1864).

flowers [and] acclamation." The *New York Times* saw the event as symbolic of a "prodigious revolution which the public mind everywhere is experiencing."[98]

Opposition to using blacks in the army was indeed crumbling rapidly in 1864 as Pennsylvania, Ohio, Michigan, Indiana, Illinois, Connecticut, and New York organized black troops by the thousands. In the army too, attitudes were changing. Much as they had resisted it, most white soldiers gradually came to accept emancipation and black soldiers as a necessary part of the war effort. Some even took pride in it. To one Massachusetts private, there was no question that it was "worth dying to attain ... the freedom of every human being over whom the stars and stripes wave." Most took a more practical view of blacks in uniform. "I don't care if they are one ½ mile thick in front in every Battel," wrote one soldier. "They will stop Bullets as well as white people."[99] Charles G. Halpine, who served for a time on General David Hunter's staff, penned the following verse under the pseudonym Private Miles O'Reilly, mimicking Irish brogue.

> Some tell us 'tis a burnin' shame
> To make the naygers fight;
> And that the thrade of bein' kilt
> Belongs but to the white:
> But as for me, upon my sowl!
> So liberal are we here,
> I'll let Sambo be murthered instead of myself,
> On every day in the year.
> On every day in the year, boys,
> And in every hour of the day;
> The right to be kilt I'll divide wid him,
> And divil a word I'll say.[100]

Some white soldiers' changing views reflected a more appreciative attitude. Near the war's end, an officer remarked after a march through southern Alabama that he had never seen such friendly conduct between white and black troops. "During the whole march I have not heard a word of reproach cast upon a colored soldier. But on the other hand, I have seen the two divisions exchange gifts, and talk with each other with apparent

[98] Henry O'Rielly, *First Organization of Colored Troops in the State of New York to Aid in Suppressing the Slaveholders' Rebellion* (New York: New York Association for Colored Volunteers, 1864), 15–18; *New York Times*, March 7, 1864.

[99] James E. Glazier to parents, January 16, 1863, Glazier Papers, Huntington Library, in McPherson, *What They Fought For*, 57; Isaac Marsh to wife, May 12, 1863, Isaac Marsh Papers, Duke University, in Jimerson, *Private Civil War*, 96.

[100] Halpine, *Life and Adventures*, 55.

equality." In northern Alabama, when the Fourteenth Regiment, USCT, distinguished itself during operations near Decatur, the regiment's commander, Colonel Thomas Morgan, noted that their action "elicited praises and cheers from *all* who witnessed it – It is no small event for a black regiment to receive three hearty cheers from a regiment of white men; and yet the 14th deserved the compliment." Two companies of the regiment that had never been under fire before conducted themselves "like Veteran Soldiers." Morgan expressed his pride in the regiment, telling the men that he "would not exchange its command for that of the best white regiment in the U.S. service."[101]

One officer from Massachusetts had been described by those who knew him as "a bitter pro-slavery man, violent in his talk against abolitionists and 'niggers.'" But after serving with blacks in Louisiana, he was so impressed that he returned home a committed abolitionist. On a Boston train, as a black soldier in uniform stepped onto the car, someone yelled, "I'm not going to ride with niggers." The officer, in full uniform, rose from his seat for all to see and called out, "Come here, my good fellow! I've been fighting alongside of people of your color, and glad enough I was to have 'em by my side. Come sit by me."[102]

## LITTLE AID FROM THE GOVERNMENT

Beyond their service in combat, another way in which the army's freedmen sought respect was by learning to read and write. More than 80 percent of black servicemen had been slaves before the war and forbidden to become literate, although a few managed to achieve the skill. Now, as soldiers, they also tended to be eager students. E. S. Wheeler, chaplain of a black regiment in Louisiana, reported that "a majority of the men seem to regard their books as an indispensable portion of their equipments, and the cartridge box and spelling book are attached to the same belt."[103]

Regimental chaplains, pressed by black soldiers, took a leading role in establishing schools, acquiring books, and soliciting teachers for the men. Those few blacks in the chaplain corps were especially insistent on educating black troops. Henry McNeal Turner, an active abolitionist and

---

[101] Chaplain C. W. Buckley to Gen. L. Thomas, April 1, 1865, in Berlin et al., *Black Military Experience*, 563–65; General Order No. 50, Headquarters, Fourteenth Regiment, USCT, November 23, 1864, in ibid., 559.

[102] Lydia Maria Child to Eliza Scudder, [n.d.] 1864, *Letters of Lydia Maria Child*, 180.

[103] Wheeler to Brig. Gen. Daniel Ullmann, April 8, 1864, in Berlin et al., *Black Military Experience*, 618–19.

the army's first black chaplain, organized schools and harangued his superiors for time and tents in which to study. Chaplains also gained the support of missionary societies, which sent supplies and teachers, white and black.[104]

Some white company and regimental officers were also supportive, even organizing schools themselves and holding out promotion to sergeant as a reward for literacy. Such efforts were more the exception than the rule. Most white officers outside black regiments, and many within, believed blacks to be inferior beings and saw no point in trying to educate them. When support was not forthcoming, the men pooled their resources, purchased books, and paid teachers. When teachers were unavailable, they taught themselves. With limited time and little backing, their struggle for literacy was an uphill struggle. By war's end, most black soldiers remained functionally illiterate. But for the first time in their lives, many could not only sign their names but read and write as well.[105]

Of more immediate concern to formerly enslaved black soldiers was seeing friends and family released from slavery. Often without orders, blacks made raids behind Confederate lines to rescue enslaved loved ones. In later life, freedman Claude Wilson of Lake City, Florida, told of the day a six-mule team pulled up to his mother's cabin driven by a black soldier who told them they were free. "I been praying for this a long time," his mother exclaimed. They loaded the wagon with what furniture they had and headed for Union-held Jacksonville. In Edenton, North Carolina, black troops freed a number of slaves and "threatened to have the town shelled if they were interfered with." One officer recalled a young man named Moore who enlisted for the sole purpose of getting his parents and siblings out of slavery. Free them he did, but he later died in combat. His last words to his family were "I know I shall fall, but you will be free."[106]

Black soldiers extended freedom even to areas where the Emancipation Proclamation did not apply. Under the guise of recruiting volunteers, black servicemen regularly swept through central Kentucky's plantation belt, emancipating slaves as they went. In Louisiana, members of the Native

---

[104] Turner to adjutant-general, U.S. Army, June 29, 1865, in Berlin et al., *Black Military Experience*, 626–27.

[105] Berlin et al., *Black Military Experience*, 612, 613; General Order No. 31, Headquarters, Sixty-Second Regiment, USCT, July 3, 1864, in ibid., 617.

[106] Claude Augusta Wilson, *Florida Narratives*, 360; Edward Stanly [military gov. of N.C.] to Maj. Gen. Foster [commanding, Department of North Carolina], January 20, 1864, in Berlin et al., *Destruction of Slavery*, 87–88; Testimony of Col. George H. Hanks, American Freedmen's Inquiry Commission, February 6, 1864, in Berlin et al., *Lower South*, 519.

Guards received permission to go on recruiting detail. They had more on their minds than recruiting soldiers. With signed passes in hand, they marched across southern Louisiana freeing slaves and taking them to New Orleans. At one plantation in St. Bernard Parish, five soldiers showed up at their former owner's place and freed their wives. When slaveholders protested that they were loyal Unionists in Union-held territory and that the Emancipation Proclamation had no force there, the soldiers leveled their rifles and threatened to shoot anyone who stood in their way.[107]

In Missouri, Private Spotswood Rice wrote to his daughter's owner warning that he was coming to claim his right as a father. "Mary is my Child and she is a God given rite of my own and you may hold on to hear as long as you can but I want you to remember this one thing that the longor you keep my Child from me the longor you will have to burn in hell and the qwicer youll get there." A Louisiana soldier made plain to his commanding officer that he intended to have his children. "I am in your service; I wear military clothes; I have been in three battles; I was in the assault at Port Hudson; *I want those children*; they are my flesh and blood." To him, his service entitled his family to the rights of free people.[108]

Slaveholders who suffered only the loss of their slaves at the hands of black soldiers could count themselves fortunate. Some suffered worse. William Harris of the First Regiment, USCT, gave his former Virginia owner a lashing so violent that blood flew at every stroke. Harris then turned the whip over to three female ex-slaves who "took turns in settling some old scores." Fortunately for slaveholders, such retribution was unusual. Most black soldiers were far more concerned with ending slavery than taking revenge. When slaveholders found themselves at the mercy of their former slaves, violence rarely came of it.[109]

---

[107] J. L. Seaton [western Kentucky Unionist] to Hon. Lush. [Lucian, often misspelled Lucien] Anderson [Kentucky congressman], February 1864, in Berlin et al., *Black Military Experience*, 255; Capt. George G. Davis [provost marshal, St. Bernard Parish, Louisiana] to Gen. James Bowen [provost marshal general, Department of the Gulf], August 21, 1863, in ibid., 157–58; Col. H. N. Brisbie [commanding a Louisiana black brigade] to Lt. O. A. Rice [Headquarters, Post of Morganzia, Louisiana], September 24, 1864, in ibid., 511.

[108] Rice to Kittey Diggs, September 3, 1864, in Berlin et al., *Black Military Experience*, 690; Testimony of Col. George H. Hanks, American Freedmen's Inquiry Commission, February 6, 1864, in Berlin et al., *Lower South*, 519.

[109] *Christian Recorder*, May 28, 1864; Brig. Gen. Edward A. Wild [commanding a black brigade] to Maj. Robert S. Davis [Headquarters, Department of Virginia and North Carolina], May 12, 1864, in Berlin et al., *Destruction of Slavery*, 99–97. See also Glatthaar, *Forged in Battle*, 202.

Major William Holden learned that first-hand, much to his relief. Henry, a former slave of Holden's who had run off to join the Union army after being whipped, came marching back one day leading a dozen black soldiers. As a young slave who witnessed the homecoming later recalled:

Now ole Major was sitting in his favorite chair on the porch when he saw Henry coming with those soldiers and he like to fell, he was that scairt. . . . poor ole Major thought Henry remembered that whipping. But Henry drew the men up in front of ole Major and he said, "This is my master, Major Holden. Honor him, men." And the men took off their caps and cheered old Major. And he nearly like to fell again – such a great big burden was off his shoulders then.

Henry and the other soldiers took their seats at Holden's dining room table where his wife served them a roast chicken feast. For a former slave to be served at his former owner's table brought a satisfaction that few but those once held in bondage could understand. For Henry, it was an image he would forever hold as a sign that his freedom was real.[110]

Another sign of freedom, among the first that soldiers demanded once their families were out of bondage, was a wedding ceremony with legal standing. Having a marriage certificate in hand reading that loved ones were lawfully joined in wedlock was tangible evidence that wives could not be sold from husbands, husbands from wives, nor children from their parents. It meant that husbands no longer had to see their wives raped by slaveholders. A. B. Randall, chaplain of a black regiment, reported twenty-five weddings in a single month. Another chaplain wrote that the "marriage relation" of forty-three couples of his regiment had been legalized. Some of them had been together for as long as thirty years, living precariously as husband and wife without the protection of a legally sanctioned marriage.[111]

Married or not, soldiers' families who followed their men to camp were left to support themselves, as one report noted, "with but little aid from the government by washing, ironing, cooking, making pies, cakes &c. for the troops." Freedman John Finnely recalled that as a boy, he carried water for

[110] Ira Berlin, Marc Favreau, and Steven F. Miller, eds., *Remembering Slavery: African Americans Talk about Their Personal Experiences of Slavery and Freedom* (New York: New Press, 1998), 255–56.

[111] Randall to Brig. Gen. L. Thomas, February 28, 1865, in Berlin et al., *Black Military Experience*, 712; Chaplain Jas. Peet to Brig. Gen. L. Thomas, September 30, 1864, in ibid., 604.

the soldiers. Women sometimes found work in government hospitals at wages of $4 a month.[112]

As more blacks fled to army posts, it became increasingly difficult to accommodate them. Some officers sent the refugees farther north to already overcrowded contraband camps. In February 1864, Captain Newton Flagg wrote to Secretary Stanton of "extreme want and destitution" among the refugees in Quincy, Illinois. About 400 were "scattered over the city in miserable hovels and stables" with little in the way of food or clothing. During the previous three months, local citizens had contributed $1,500 and "large amounts of clothing," but those resources were now exhausted. Flagg implored Stanton to send help, but what little came could not meet the need. Conditions continued to deteriorate for the rest of that year and into the next. During the winter of 1864–65, between four and seven fugitives died each week in Quincy.[113]

Things were even worse that winter at a refugee camp in Nashville, Tennessee, where the death rate was thirty per day. In January 1865, Lieutenant Colonel Joseph Putnam of the Forty-Second Regiment, USCT, in Chattanooga wrote to his superiors that "the men of my command appeal to me for relief from such treatment." He told of one soldier whose wife and six children had been sent to Nashville several weeks earlier by order of the post commander. "Today the children were brought back, – how or by whom I cannot learn. They are nearly starved, their limbs are frozen, – one of them is likely to loose both feet, – Their mother died in the camp at Nashville." Putnam requested that measures be taken to relieve suffering refugees.[114]

Soldiers did more than appeal for their families' relief. They took matters into their own hands, deserted their posts, and delivered relief themselves. From Knoxville, Tennessee, Major John Shannon wrote to headquarters of being constantly annoyed by soldiers with suffering families "asking permission to be absent for the purpose of providing for them ... many absent themselves without permission." He would

[112] Vincent Colyer [former superintendent of the poor, Department of North Carolina] to Hon. Robert Dale Owen [chairman, American Freedmen's Inquiry Commission], May 25, 1863, in Berlin et al., *Upper South*, 124; John Finnely, *Texas Narratives*, part 2, 39.

[113] Flagg [quartermaster at Quincy, Illinois] to Edwin M. Stanton, February 5, 1864, in Berlin et al., *Upper South*, 586; ibid., 587.

[114] Putnam to Brig. Gen. W. D. Whipple [headquarters, Department of the Cumberland], January 30, 1865, in Berlin et al., *Upper South*, 460–61.

continue to lose men and be unable to recruit more unless the army provided for the men's families.[115]

Black soldiers who rescued their families from bondage and brought them to camp could, and often did, see them hauled back into slavery. Officers who were unwilling to aid the fugitives simply turned them over when their former owners showed up to claim them. One captain in Missouri complained that such treatment impeded efforts to recruit black soldiers. He was told that "no remedy is known for the evils complained of" since the Emancipation Proclamation did not apply in the border states.[116]

In July 1864, General S. S. Fry of Kentucky's Camp Nelson issued a circular informing local slaveholders that women, children, and men unfit for service would be "delivered up to their owners upon application." By late that year, Fry was expelling soldiers' families from the camp whether their owners applied for them or not. On November 23, Joseph Miller of the 124th Regiment saw his wife and children driven out into the bitter cold. Shortly after, Miller filed a complaint. "I told the man in charge of the guard that it would be the death of my boy I told him that my wife and children had no place to go." The guards threatened to shoot them all if they did not leave, so leave they did. That night, without leave, Miller went in search of his family. He found them a few miles away in "an old meeting house belonging to the colored people."

The building was very cold having only one fire. My wife and children could not get near the fire, because of the number of colored people huddled together. ... I found my wife and children shivering with cold and famished with hunger They had not received a morsel of food during the whole day. My boy was dead ... killed by exposure to the inclement weather. ... I dug a grave myself and buried my own child.

Knowing he could be shot for desertion if he did not report back to Camp Nelson, Miller left his family at the meeting house and filed his complaint as quickly as he could. Other soldiers complained as well. After several were published in the abolitionist press, embarrassed army officers ceased their policy of turning out soldiers' families. Barracks were built to

[115] Maj. John A. Shannon [commanding a Tennessee black regiment] to Lt. W. W. Deane [headquarters, chief of artillery, Department of the Ohio], March 6, 1864, in Berlin et al., *Upper South*, 444.
[116] Capt. John Gould [commissary officer] to Edwin M. Stanton, January 21, 1864, and Endorsement, Headquarters, Department of the Missouri, in Berlin et al., *Black Military Experience*, 247–48.

house the refugees at Camp Nelson, but the army supplied little else. By February 1865, about half of the roughly 600 women and children were ill, mostly with pneumonia and smallpox. One witness described the sick as "huddled together in rags and dirt" waiting to die.[117]

On December 4, 1864, a black Kentucky soldier named George Washington wrote to President Lincoln demanding a discharge. His wife and four children were still held in slavery, suffering at the hands of an abusive owner. Washington asked that the president free them and release him from service so that he could care for them himself. He could hardly do so if he remained a soldier since the army had not paid him for some time.[118]

The volume of such demands and the outrage they expressed grew so great that finally, in March 1865, only weeks before the war's end, Congress passed legislation providing that the wife and children "of any person that has been, or may be, mustered into the military or naval service of the United States, shall, from and after the passage of this act, be forever free."[119]

---

[117] Brig. Gen. Speed S. Fry [post commander], Circular, Camp Nelson, Kentucky, July 6, 1864, in Berlin et al., *Upper South*, 672; Affidavit of Joseph Miller, November 26, 1864, in Berlin et al., *Black Military Experience*, 269–71; Marion B. Lucas, "Camp Nelson, Kentucky, During the Civil War: Cradle of Liberty or Refugee Death Camp?" *Filson Club History Quarterly* 63 (1989): 448. For the impact of apathy, neglect, and outright cruelty on the health of blacks during and after the war see Jim Downs, *Sick from Freedom: African-American Illness and Suffering during the Civil War and Reconstruction* (New York: Oxford University Press, 2012).

[118] Washington to Lincoln, December 4, 1864, in Berlin et al., *Destruction of Slavery*, 608.

[119] *Statutes at Large*, 13: 571.

# 4

## "Full Equality before the Law"

### *Claiming the Rights of Freedom*

#### THE "FAITHFUL SLAVE" IS ABOUT PLAYED OUT

As the war entered its latter phase, enslaved southerners continued taking freedom for themselves – some outright, others by degree. In the summer of 1863, an Alabama newspaper editor complained of blacks becoming "so saucy and abusive that a police force has become positively necessary as a check to their continued insolence." In Georgia, legislators had already introduced a bill "to punish slaves and free persons of color for abusive and insulting language." Along with freedom of speech, blacks were taking freedom of assembly as well. In Blakely, Georgia, the *Early County News* reported that blacks were "almost nightly running around where they have no business." A slaveholder in Columbus, Georgia, feared that blacks were forgetting their second-class status. "It is not uncommon," he wrote, "to see two or three in one whiskey shop."[1]

Although cause for concern, slaves taking small liberties were among the least of slaveholder worries. Tension between slaves and slaveholders hung over the South like a storm cloud whose lightning could strike nearly anywhere, any time. Despite their public insistence that slaves were generally content, slaveholders knew better than anyone except the slaves themselves that discontent was the norm. July 1863 found one Alabama

---

[1] *Selma (Ala.) Morning Reporter*, August 29, 1863; *Milledgeville (Ga.) Southern Recorder*, November 25, 1862; *Early County (Ga.) News*, March 16, 1864; B. W. Clark to Gov. Joseph E. Brown, January 30, 1864, Governor's Incoming Correspondence, Georgia Department of Archives and History, Morrow.

slaveholder frankly admitting to another that "the 'faithful slave' is about played out."[2]

That was certainly clear to Jane Eubanks of Columbia County, Georgia, who wrote to Governor Joe Brown about needing more men assigned to slave patrols. There were 400 slaves in her vicinity and few white men to keep them subdued. John R. Edwards of Harris County wrote to the governor that in the vicinity of Waverly Hall there were only four men available to ride patrol over 700 slaves. Women in Schley County petitioned the governor to hire a local man who kept a pack of "Negro dogs" to hunt escaped slaves. Julia A. Brooks gathered signatures for a petition to have her husband, B. F. Brooks, sent home from the army to organize slave patrols.[3]

In December 1863, a Burke County woman wrote to Brown about the lack of white men in her area, most of them forced away by the draft. She urged Brown to create a police force for the protection of Georgia's "planting interest." Green insisted that Brown must "see to it, that [the planter] class of citizens are protected & not left to meet a fate worse than death." The state assembly responded by reinforcing laws forbidding slaves to travel without a pass. It also canceled exemptions from patrol duty. Across the Confederacy, in frontline areas and larger towns, soldiers were diverted to augment slave patrols. In isolated rural regions, some slaveholders hired their own patrols.[4]

Nevertheless, patrols continued to lose their power of intimidation. Some slaves fought back. They tied ropes or vines neck-high across a dark stretch of road just before the patrollers passed by. These traps were guaranteed to unhorse at least one rider. When a group of patrollers broke in on a prayer meeting near Columbus, Georgia, one slave stuck a shovel in the fireplace and threw hot coals all over them. Instantly, the room "filled with smoke and the smell of burning clothes and white flesh." In the confusion, every slave got away.[5]

[2] John F. Andrews to Mrs. Clement Claiborne Clay [Virginia Tunstall Clay], July 10, 1863, Clay Papers, Duke University.

[3] Eubanks to Brown, July 18, 1864, Governor's Incoming Correspondence, Georgia Department of Archives and History; Edwards to Brown, January 8, 1864, ibid.; Petition from Ladies of the County of Schley to Brown, August [?] 1864, ibid.; Brooks to Brown, June 22, 1864, ibid.

[4] Mrs. John Green to Gov. Joseph E. Brown, December 11, 1863, Governor's Incoming Correspondence, Georgia Department of Archives and History; Bryan, *Confederate Georgia*, 126; Hadden, *Slave Patrols*, 186, 182.

[5] W. B. Allen, in Rawick et al., *American Slave*, supplement, series 1, vol. 3, *Georgia Narratives*, part 1, 7–8.

Try as they might, slaveholders had an increasingly difficult time controlling slaves. It was with good reason that, as a Texas slaveholder wrote, "a great many of the people are actually afraid to whip the negroes." In Choctaw County, Mississippi, slaves turned the tables on their owner's grown son, subjecting him to 500 lashes before shooting him to death. Texas bondsmen killed an overseer known for his "meanness over the slaves." In Virginia, slaves armed with shotguns killed two planters. After Mississippi slaveholder Jim Rankin returned from the army "meaner than before," as freedman Charlie Moses told it, a slave "sneaked up in the darkness an' shot him three times." Rankin lingered in agony the rest of the night before he died the next morning. "He never knowed who done it," Moses recalled. "I was glad they shot him down."[6]

Slaves sometimes devised or participated in elaborate plots to kill their owners. Occasionally, they even worked with whites to do it. Two slaves belonging to Columbus Holley of Dale County, Alabama, assisted John Ward, leader of a local deserter band, in doing away with their owner. Holley made a habit of turning in every deserter he could, and Ward hatched a plan to kill him for it. Holley's slaves were eager to cooperate. One evening, the slaves met Ward near Holley's plantation house and carried him on their shoulders to a bedroom window that Holley always left open at night. With one shot, Ward killed the planter as he slept. The slaves then carried Ward back to his horse, and he made a clean getaway. Because his feet never touched the ground, there was no scent for the bloodhounds to follow. The mystery of Holley's murder remained unsolved until years later when Ward finally confessed on his death bed.[7]

William Mansfield of Stewart County, Georgia, told Governor Brown that local planters were terrified of their slaves and feared that county militiamen were not "prepared to quell any riots that might begin." In Richmond, a black saloon waiter named Bob Richardson was thrown in Castle Thunder prison for plotting a slave uprising. Eighteen slaves in Hancock County, Georgia, were jailed for inciting insurrection. Sometimes authorities did not move quickly enough. Slaves in Yazoo City, Mississippi, did rise up, setting a fire that destroyed the courthouse and fourteen other

---

[6] Lizzie S. Neblett to William H. Neblett, August 13, 1863, in Murr, *Diary and Letters of Elizabeth Scott Neblett*, 135; *Greensboro (Miss.) Southern Motive* in *Richmond Sentinel*, June 2, 1864; Ida Henry, *Oklahoma Narratives*, 135; Bell Irvin Wiley, *Plain People of the Confederacy* (1943; reprint, with new introduction by Paul D. Escott, Columbia: University of South Carolina Press, 2000), 82; Charlie Moses, *Mississippi Narratives*, 115–16.

[7] Watson, *Winds of Sorrow*, 13–14.

buildings. A similar plot was discovered in North Carolina's Richmond and Montgomery Counties in which a number of whites were implicated.[8]

It was not uncommon to find whites involved with rebellious slaves. So strong was anti-Confederate sentiment among southern whites that some were perfectly willing to work with blacks in undermining the government. As early as July 1861, the *Columbus Daily Sun* reported that a vigilance committee in southwest Georgia's Mitchell County had uncovered plans for a slave uprising, naming seven local whites as conspirators. According to the *Sun*, they planned to supply the slaves "with as much ammunition as [they] possibly could to butcher the good citizens of the county." Five got the lash and were expelled from the county. Two escaped a whipping but were ordered never to set foot in Mitchell County again "under the penalty of death."[9]

In December 1861, the governor's office received news from north Georgia's Gordon County of local Unionists holding secret meetings and organizing a military force to protect themselves from Confederate authorities. They swore to aid the Federals in any way they could. Most alarmingly, they promised that "in case of an insurrection they will help the Negroes."[10]

The following spring, three white men in Georgia's Calhoun County planned to instigate such an uprising. Mindful of the previous year's failed attempt in Mitchell County, Harvell Scaggs, William Scaggs, and Giles Shoots, all citizens of Calhoun County, sought out federal help to back the venture. Traveling down to the Gulf Coast under pretense of making salt, the trio contacted Union blockaders. Soon they were running "superior new guns" to slaves in Calhoun County. The plot came to light in June, and the three men were sentenced "to receive a sound whipping, to be tarred all over, and then ordered to quit the State." Some thought the punishment too light. Georgia's *Early County News* editor asked, "Is it safe to the community to suffer such inhuman wretches, such dangerous animals, to go at large?" He suggested changing the sentence to life in prison or, better yet, execution.[11]

---

[8] Mansfield to Joseph E. Brown, May 26, 1864, Governor's Incoming Correspondence, Georgia Department of Archives and History; *Richmond Examiner*, June 13, 1864; *Milledgeville (Ga.) Southern Recorder*, October 6, 1863; *Richmond Sentinel*, June 2, 1864; *Wadesboro (N.C.) Argus* in *Milledgeville (Ga.) Southern Recorder*, December 27, 1864.

[9] *Columbus (Ga.) Daily Sun*, July 15, 1861.

[10] L. R. Ramsaur to Gov. Joseph E. Brown, December 14, 1861, Governor's Incoming Correspondence, Georgia Department of Archives and History.

[11] *Early County (Ga.) News* in *Augusta (Ga.) Constitutionalist*, June 24, 1862.

John Vickery and three slaves got just that when they tried to organize a slave uprising in south Georgia's Brooks County. Vickery was a local white man of modest means for whom no evidence can be found of prior trouble with the law. In fact, Vickery was listed on Brooks County jury rolls in 1863. However, he next appears in the records in August 1864 at the end of a hangman's rope. Details of events leading to his execution vary, but all sources agree that Vickery, with the assistance of local slaves, organized an insurrectionary force that intended to murder some of the county's wealthier planters.

After killing the planters and stealing whatever weapons they could find, the conspirators planned to set the county seat of Quitman afire and seize the rail depot. From there, they would head south toward Madison, Florida, then seize and burn that town. Hoping to be reinforced by deserters and Union troops on the Gulf Coast, the men would return to Quitman and take Brooks County for the Union. On the eve of the planned uprising, local authorities learned of its details from a slave arrested for theft. After forcing information out of other slaves, the Brooks County police patrol arrested Vickery and three of the leading slave coconspirators.

It is hardly surprising that Vickery's plan involved Confederate deserters and Union troops from Florida. As early as January 1863, Confederate officials were warned that Dead Man's Bay on the Gulf Coast could be a prime landing site for Union forces. Dead Man's Bay was in Taylor County, a stronghold of Unionists and deserters who were willing to help Union troops. The ground was firm, no natural obstructions blocked the roads between the bay and the interior, and there was a direct route from the bay to Madison, Florida. Just such a landing occurred one week prior to the planned Vickery uprising. Eight hundred Union troops disembarked at the mouth of the Aucilla River, with another 500 at Dead Man's Bay. It is possible that these were the men that Vickery and his allies were to meet at Madison and lead back into Georgia.

After Vickery's arrest, the Brooks County home guard determined to use the conspirators as warning examples against further plots. Although not authorized to do so, a home guard court quickly convened. Governor Brown had specified that either county inferior courts or state militia courts would try such cases, but, for that day at least, the home guard controlled Brooks County. Vickery and his three co-conspirators stood little chance of acquittal. After a mock trial, the guardsmen rendered their judgment: John Vickery – guilty of arson, inciting slaves to insurrection, and aiding slaves to flee to the Federals; Sam – guilty of insurrection and inducing slaves to insurrection; Nelson – guilty of insurrection; George – guilty of insurrection.

All were condemned to death by hanging. At six o'clock that evening, the sentence was carried out on the courthouse square.[12]

Despite the dangers, some white southerners continued to help blacks when they could. Some did so for pity's sake, others for profit, still others because they would take any chance to undermine planter rule. Robert Bezley of Atlanta was arrested in December 1862 for giving fraudulent passes to slaves. Lawmen in Shelby, North Carolina, hanged a white man for the same crime. A white stone cutter was found heading a slave insurrection plot in Columbia, South Carolina. Officials in Adams County, Mississippi, discovered a cache of guns that slaves had stored in preparation for a rebellion. At least one white man was implicated in the affair.[13]

White farmers sometimes gave escaped slaves safe haven in exchange for work. Others gave them cash for stolen plantation supplies. A white merchant in Plymouth, North Carolina, worked out a deal with local slaves to buy goods stolen from their owners. The deal fell through when word of it leaked out. Georgia's *Early County News* reported in April 1864 that blacks were selling stolen goods to whites "who bought them in the *dead hour of night*" [emphasis in original]. In some cases, blacks were such valuable trading partners that whites would take great risks to preserve the connections. In Granville County, North Carolina, two whites helped a free black named Archibald Kearsey break out of jail so he could maintain his extensive trade network.[14]

[12] Sarah Jones to Gov. Joseph E. Brown, August 22, 1864, Governor's Incoming Correspondence, Georgia Department of Archives and History; *Augusta (Ga.) Chronicle and Sentinel*, August 26, 1864; *Columbus (Ga.) Daily Sun*, August 27, 1864; *Augusta (Ga.) Constitutionalist*, August 26, 1864; *Macon (Ga.) Daily Telegraph*, August 26, 1864; Capt. Jos. John Williams to Gen. Howell Cobb [commanding, Middle District of Florida], January 11, 1863,*Official Records*, series 1, vol. 14, 752; *Augusta (Ga.) Constitutionalist*, August 24 and 31, 1864. See also Meyers, "'The Wretch Vickery' and the Brooks County Civil War Slave Conspiracy," 27–38; Williams et al., *Plain Folk in a Rich Man's War*, 144–50. In 2010, the Georgia Historical Society and the city of Quitman erected a marker in front of city hall commemorating the conspiracy.

[13] *Atlanta Southern Confederacy*, December 19, 1862; Mitchell, *Civil War Soldiers*, 4; Aptheker, *Slave Revolts*, 363–64, 365–66.

[14] J. B. Clements, *History of Irwin County* (1932; reprint, Spartanburg, S.C.: Reprint Co., 1997), 134–35; Clay County (Ga.) Superior Court, Minute Book, December Term, 1863; Lee County (Ga.) Superior Court, Minute Book C, September Term, 1863; William S. Kinsland, "The Civil War Comes to Lumpkin County," *North Georgia Journal* 1 (1984): 24; Spruill Memorandum, November 17, 1862, Pettigrew Papers, Southern Historical Collection, University of North Carolina at Chapel Hill, in Durrill, *War of Another Kind*, 132–33; John M. Hough to William S. Pettigrew, August 12, 1864, Pettigrew Papers, in ibid., 132–33; *Early County (Ga.) News*, April 6, 1864; Criminal Action Papers, Granville County, North Carolina Department of Archives and History, in

Illicit networks frequently involved deserter and draft-dodger gangs, some of them containing or cooperating with black fugitives. Elderly freedwoman Jane Lee recalled that in central North Carolina, "the woods was full of runaway slaves and Rebs who deserted the army." A number of black escapees hid out with Jeff Anderson's deserter band in the mountains around Dahlonega, Georgia. Farther south, the wiregrass region of southern Georgia, southern Alabama, and northern Florida was, as one Confederate official complained, "the common retreat of deserters from our army, tories, and runaway negroes."[15]

In August 1864, a band of 500 "Union men, deserters, and negroes" in central Florida was reported to be raiding toward Gainesville. Another Florida officer sent word to his superiors that deserters had gathered "in the swamps and fastnesses of Taylor, LaFayette, Levy and other counties, and have organized, with runaway negroes, bands for the purpose of committing depredations upon the plantations and crops of loyal citizens and running off their slaves." They had even threatened the cities of Madison, Marianna, and Tallahassee.[16]

Such cooperation, although not uncommon, was hardly the norm. Most white southerners never wanted secession and eventually turned against the war, but they remained largely committed to keeping the South a white man's country and to keeping blacks "in their place." That some whites were willing to help blacks usually said more about their attitudes toward slaveholders than slaves. Southern blacks were most often left to help each other or help themselves.

Nathaniel Evans, enslaved to an officer of the Sixth Alabama, forged a pass and made his way from Richmond to federal lines near Fredericksburg. Missouri slaves escaped to the neighboring free states of Iowa and Kansas throughout the war. For slaves in Texas, the route to freedom often led south to Mexico. Freedman Jacob Branch remembered that slave patrols constantly rode the Rio Grande during the war, but hundreds of refugees got through their lines and crossed the river.[17]

---

Victoria E. Bynum, *Unruly Women: The Politics of Social and Sexual Control in the Old South* (Chapel Hill: University of North Carolina Press, 1992), 123.

[15] Jane Lee, *North Carolina Narratives*, part 2, 52; *Atlanta Southern Confederacy*, October 4, 1862; Gov. John Gill Shorter of Alabama to Confederate Sec. of War James A. Seddon, January 14, 1863, *Official Records*, series 1, vol. 15, 947.

[16] Brig. Gen. John P. Hatch to Maj. Gen. J. G. Foster [commanding, Department of the South], August 4, 1864, *Official Records*, series 1, vol. 35, part 2, 215; Brig. Gen. John K. Jackson [Military District of Florida] to Gen. S. Cooper, August 12, 1864, ibid., 607.

[17] *Philadelphia Inquirer*, August 18, 1862; Berlin et al., *Remembering Slavery*, 227–28, 264–65; Jacob Branch, *Texas Narratives*, 141.

Slaves trapped farther east, in the heart of Dixie, had a much harder time making their way to free territory. That had always been true but was even more so during the war. With whites taking greater precautions, escaping slaves took greater risks. In South Carolina, William and Anne Summerson risked suffocation by having themselves packed in rice casks and driven out of Charleston. Then, in a small boat, they made their way past rebel sentries by night and made it to federal gunboats on the Stono River. In March 1864, several slaves struck out from Floyd County, Georgia, headed for the Federals in Tennessee. Slavecatchers cornered two of the fugitives just short of the state line. Both were suffering from exposure and frostbite. One later died from the ordeal.[18]

Fugitives often banded together for mutual support and protection. They sustained themselves by living off the land and making raids against local plantations – the very plantations on which they had labored without pay for years. In their view, it was time for back pay. S. S. Massey of Chattahoochee County, Georgia, complained to the governor that runaway slaves were "killing up the stock and stealing ever thing they can put their hands on." An April 1864 report from Blakely, Georgia, told of "more *stealing*, and *rascality generally*, going on ... for the past few months, than has ever been known ... negroes are doing a great deal of this stealing."[19]

For slaves in the tidewater regions of North Carolina and Virginia, the Great Dismal Swamp served as a refuge. In North Carolina's swamp counties of Camden and Currituck, a band of fugitives numbering between 500 and 600 made frequent raids on area plantations and Confederate supply depots. Swamps in South Carolina's Darlington District were home to refugees who, according to a petition signed by twenty-two slaveholders, lived by "under[min]ing meat houses, robbing hen houses, Killing Cattle Hogs &c and stealing everything the[y] can lay their hands on."[20]

Some of these refugee bands armed and organized themselves into militia companies. Near the mouth of Florida's Withlacoochee River, a detachment of Confederates fired on one company of escapees led by a "captain." The

[18] *National Anti-Slavery Standard*, December 27, 1862; Margaret Espey to Joseph S. Espey, March 21 and April 3, 1864, Joseph Espey Papers, Southern Historical Collection, in Clarence L. Mohr, *On the Threshold of Freedom: Masters and Slaves in Civil War Georgia* (Athens: University of Georgia Press, 1986), 87–88.

[19] Massey to Gov. Joseph E. Brown, March 9, 1865, Governor's Incoming Correspondence, Georgia Department of Archives and History; *Early County (Ga.) News*, April 6, 1864.

[20] *Richmond Daily Examiner*, January 14, 1864; Christopher Flinn et al. [South Carolina slaveholders] to Confederate Sec. of War James A. Seddon, March [?] 1864, in Berlin et al., *Destruction of Slavery*, 806–807.

blacks returned fire "very cool and deliberately." Near Baldwin, Florida, four blacks were hanged for trying to form a company. They had planned to take Baldwin and Lake City, then head for the Atlantic coast and enlist with the Federals at Fernandina.[21]

Those slaves who did not escape gave aid to those who did. They funneled food and supplies to their fugitive friends and relatives, passed information to them, and provided a much needed support network. It would have been difficult if not impossible for many fugitive bands to operate effectively without such support.

### READY TO HELP ANYBODY OPPOSED TO THE REBELS

Support from local slaves was crucial also for bands of white deserters, draft evaders, and their families. Like so many other enslaved blacks, Jeff Rayford did whatever he could to help deserters hiding in the bottomlands of Mississippi's Pearl River. As he told an interviewer years after the war, "I cooked and carried many a pan of food to these men." Another Mississippi freedman recalled carrying food to hideouts where deserters and their families had taken up residence. In Jones County, Rachel Knight, a slave of both white and black ancestry, was a key ally of the deserter gang led by Newton Knight, her owner's grandson. She supplied food and served as a spy in their operations against local Confederates.[22]

Slaves sometimes helped their owners avoid Confederate service. Riley Tirey, one of twelve slaves owned by Robert Guttery of Walker County, Alabama, carried blankets and other supplies to Guttery, who was hiding in the woods, "to help him keep out of the way of the rebel cavalry." Another Alabama slave, Benjamin Haynes, took provisions to his owner's son who was "hid out to prevent his being conscripted." Although slaves' motives for rendering such aid were often mixed, among them was the knowledge that every effort to help keep anyone out of Confederate service put them a step closer to freedom.[23]

Slaves also helped strangers trying to avoid Confederate service. Deserters traveling home through the plantation belt knew that slave cabins were their

---

[21] Capt. Samuel E. Hope [Confederate officer] to Capt. W. Call [Headquarters, Confederate District of Florida], September 8, 1863, in Berlin et al., *Destruction of Slavery*, 805–806; Statement of Washington Somerroy [Florida fugitive], November 26, 1864, in ibid., 142–43.

[22] Victoria E. Bynum, *The Free State of Jones: Mississippi's Longest Civil War* (Chapel Hill: University of North Carolina Press, 2001), 109–10.

[23] Margaret M. Storey, *Loyalty and Loss: Alabama's Unionists in the Civil War and Reconstruction* (Baton Rouge: Louisiana State University Press, 2004), 80.

safest bet for food, shelter, and support. One deserter killed Georgia planter William McDonald when the slaveholder discovered him hiding in his slave quarters. McDonald's slaves did not intervene. Nancy Johnson, enslaved on a Georgia plantation during the war, told how "some of the rebel soldiers deserted & came to our house & we fed them. They were opposed to the war & didn't own slaves & said they would die rather than fight. Those who were poor white people, who didn't own slaves were some of them Union people. I befriended them because they were on our side."[24]

Defining white Unionists as being on "our side" became easier for southern blacks as word of the Emancipation Proclamation spread. Increasingly, blacks came to identify with the Union cause, with white southern Unionists, and with Union soldiers. Taught from birth, however, to deal cautiously with whites, blacks did not always know what to make of their new allies' motives. Nor did they trust them entirely. Still, with freedom and Union joined together, blacks were ready to join with whites in whatever

FIGURE 4.1. Southern blacks constantly undermined the Confederate war effort. They worked with white anti-Confederates, supported fugitive slaves, and spied for the Union army. And they aided anyone headed for Union lines. As former Union prisoner of war Albert Richardson wrote, "They were always ready to help anybody opposed to the Rebels. Union refugees, Confederate deserters, escaped prisoners – all received from them the same prompt and invariable kindness." Image from Junius Henri Browne, *Four Years in Secessia* (1865).

---

[24] *Augusta (Ga.) Constitutionalist*, May 5, 1864; Testimony of Nancy Johnson, Southern Claims Commission, March 22, 1873, in Berlin et al., *Destruction of Slavery*, 151.

effort might serve the interests of both. As an escaping Union prisoner of war put it, "They were always ready to help anybody opposed to the Rebels. Union refugees, Confederate deserters, escaped prisoners – all received from them the same prompt and invariable kindness."[25]

Black women in Savannah took great risks in smuggling food to Union prisoners. Susie King Taylor, a Savannah native, wrote of the city's prison stockade as an awful place. "The Union soldiers were in it, worse than pigs, without any shelter from sun or storm, and the colored women would take food there at night and pass it to them through the holes in the fence. The soldiers were starving, and these women did all they could toward relieving those men, although they knew the penalty should they be caught giving them aid."[26]

Blacks sometimes helped imprisoned anti-Confederates escape. In December 1863, Robert Webster, a black barber in Atlanta, helped an aging Tennessee Unionist named William Clift break out of the city's military prison. Clift had served as a courier for the Federals in his home state until being arrested by his own son, a Confederate cavalry officer. Webster supplied the old man with a rope to use in making his escape. Along their routes of escape, people like Clift could expect safe haven and escorts among the slaves. Nancy Johnson later told of a federal fugitive who showed up at her doorstep one evening. After keeping him hidden through the next day, "my husband slipped him over to a man named Joel Hodges & he conveyed him off so that he got home."[27]

John Kellogg, a Union prisoner escaping through the Georgia mountains with the help of local blacks, was impressed by what he called their "telegraph line." They told Kellogg and his comrades of Union troop movements, some at a distance of 150 miles, between Chattanooga and Atlanta. The intelligence was essential to planning the safest route back to federal lines. Kellogg found his black associates "better informed of passing events" than most southern whites. Union captains Alured Larke and R. H. Day were similarly impressed with blacks in Charleston, South Carolina. After escaping from a Confederate prison, they hid out in the city for two months, sheltered by local blacks, before escaping to Union

---

[25] Richardson, *The Secret Service*, 445.

[26] Taylor, *Reminiscences*, 68.

[27] Thomas G. Dyer, *Secret Yankees: The Union Circle in Confederate Atlanta* (Baltimore: Johns Hopkins University Press, 1999), 88–89; Testimony of Nancy Johnson, Southern Claims Commission, March 22, 1873, in Berlin et al., *Destruction of Slavery*, 151.

lines. They described their saviors as "remarkably intelligent, thoroughly comprehending their own *Status* in the Rebellion."[28]

John Ennis, a captured Union officer, escaped with a small band of comrades from a South Carolina prison. Near Spartanburg, they happened upon an enslaved man who took them to the home of a white Unionist couple. There they were fed and sheltered. Next evening, their black friend escorted them to a river crossing and directed them north toward the Blue Ridge Mountains. Henry Estabrooks, a Union prisoner escaping through Virginia, recalled seeking shelter at "negro-cabins." He remembered one black couple who gave him "a small piece of miserable stuff they called bread, and some sour syrup, which I ate ravenously. The food was not fit for swine; but it was the best they had, and I was very thankful for it."[29]

Shortly after the war, Estabrooks made his gratitude public in a manuscript about his adventures. His publisher, Edmund Kirke, was eager to get it into print. Wrote Kirke of the book,

It tells what the North does not as yet fully realize, – the great fact that in the very heart of the South are four millions of people, – of strong, able-bodied, true-hearted people, – whose loyalty led them, while the heel of the "chivalry" was on their necks, and a halter was dangling before their eyes, to give their last crust, and their only suit of Sunday homespun, to the fleeing fugitive, simply because he wore the livery and fought the battles of the Union.[30]

Junius Henri Browne, a special correspondent for the *New York Tribune* who spent many months in Confederate prison camps, also gratefully remembered southern blacks as reliable allies.

"God bless the Negroes," say I, with earnest lips. During our entire captivity, and after our escape, they were ever our firm, brave, unflinching friends. We never made an appeal to them they did not answer. They never hesitated to do us a service at the risk even of life, and under the most trying circumstances revealed a devotion and a spirit of self-sacrifice that were heroic. . . . they always cherished a simple and a beautiful faith in the cause of the Union and its ultimate triumph, and never

---

[28] John Azor Kellogg, *Capture and Escape: A Narrative of Army and Prison Life* (n.p.: Wisconsin Historical Commission, 1908), 146–47, 149; Larke and Day to provost marshal general, Department of the South, December 7, 1864, in Berlin et al., *Destruction of Slavery*, 809–10.

[29] John W. Ennis, *Adventures in Rebeldom; or, Ten Months Experience of Prison Life* (New York: Business Mirror, 1863), 32–33; Henry L. Estabrooks, *Adrift in Dixie; or, A Yankee Officer Among the Rebels* (New York: Carleton, 1866), 74–78.

[30] Estabrooks, *Adrift in Dixie*, 11–12.

abandoned or turned away from a man who sought food or shelter on his way to freedom.[31]

Freedom was the driving force behind black aid to the Union cause. Alonzo Jackson repeatedly ferried escaped Union prisoners across Mingo Creek to federal outposts in South Carolina, knowing he would be killed if he were caught in the act. To Jackson, it was worth the risk. "I sympathized with the Union cause," he later testified. "I wanted to be free – and wanted my race to be free – I knew this could not be if the rebels had a government of their own."[32]

Blacks commonly helped Union forces whenever and however they could. In March 1863, seven escapees described as bright and intelligent arrived at Union lines in Mississippi with word of artillery positions around Vicksburg. A fugitive from the same area told of Confederate cavalry operations below Jackson. In Missouri, information from escaping slaves saved Union troops at Jefferson City from a surprise attack.[33]

On July 18, 1864, as a Union raiding party approached the outskirts of Auburn, Alabama, a group of blacks hurried out to warn its commander, Colonel William Hamilton, of Rebels hidden among the thickets ahead. In a charge that "could be better heard than seen," Hamilton and his men rushed the surprised Confederates, who, as Hamilton reported, "broke on our first fire and scattered in every direction." Toward the war's end, a slave named Percy from Troup County, Georgia, led a detachment of Union cavalry to a nearby swamp where his owner had hidden the family's fortune.[34]

"It is a matter of notoriety," lamented a Confederate official, "in the sections of the Confederacy where raids are frequent that the guides of the

---

[31] Junius Henri Browne, *Four Years in Secessia: Adventures within and beyond the Union Lines* (Hartford, Conn.: O. D. Case and Co., 1865), 368.

[32] Testimony of Alonzo Jackson, Southern Claims Commission, March 17, 1873, in Berlin et al., *Destruction of Slavery*, 813–18.

[33] Col. Charles H. Abbott [commanding an Iowa regiment] to Col. Jno. A. Rawlins [Headquarters, Department of Tennessee], March 26, 1863, in Berlin et al., *Destruction of Slavery*, 302–303; Affidavit of Jack [Mississippi fugitive], September 13, 1864, in ibid., 325; Col. Jno. C. Kelton [Headquarters, Second Brigade, Second Division, Army of the West] to assistant adjutant-general [Headquarters, Army of the West], October 6, 1861, *Official Records*, series 2, vol. 1, 772.

[34] Capt. Thomas H. Francis [Fourth Tennessee Infantry] to Brig. Gen. F. A. Shoup [chief of staff, Army of Tennessee], September 15, 1864, *Official Records*, series 1, vol. 38, part 3, 973–74; William Douglas Hamilton, *Recollections of a Cavalryman of the Civil War* (Columbus, Ohio: F. J. Heer Printing, 1915), 137; Celestia Avery, *Georgia Narratives*, part 1, 26.

enemy are nearly always free negroes and slaves." Jim Williams, an escaped former slave from Carroll Parish, Louisiana, led federal troops in an ambush of a small rebel force, during which he killed one Confederate and captured two more.[35] In North Carolina, Colonel S. H. Mix of the Third New York Cavalry expressed appreciation to his guide in the form of a certificate that read:

Samuel Williams, colored man, served the United States Government as guide to my Regiment on an expedition out of Newbern, N.C., in the direction of Trenton, on the morning of the 15th of May, and performed effectual service for us, at the imminent risk and peril of his life, guiding my men faithfully and truthfully, until his horse was shot down under him.[36]

North Carolina slaveowner Sarah Edmondston wrote in her journal in September 1863, "I wish sometimes that there was not a negro left in the country, for they keep the Federals informed of everything."[37]

Samuel Williams was but one of many North Carolina blacks who risked their all to help bring down the Confederacy and slavery with it. One grateful northerner reported that of those slaves who escaped to Newbern,

upwards of fifty volunteers of the best and most courageous, were kept constantly employed on the perilous but important duty of spies, scouts, and guides. In this work they were invaluable and almost indispensable. They frequently went from thirty to three hundred miles within the enemy's lines; visiting his principle camps and most important posts, and bringing us back important and reliable information. ... often on these errands barely escaping with their lives. They were pursued on several occasions by blood-hounds, two or three of them were taken prisoners; one of these was known to have been shot, and the fate of the others was not ascertained. ... They usually knelt in solemn prayer before they left, and on their return from these hazardous errands, as they considered the work as a religious duty.[38]

Harriet Tubman, famous for her antebellum service on the Underground Railroad, headed a ring of spies and scouts operating along the South Carolina coast. Mary Louveste, an employee at Virginia's Gosport Navy Yard where the Confederacy's ironclad warship *Virginia* was under construction, gathered plans and other documents related to the new secret

[35] P. H. Aylett [Confederate district attorney] to Brig. Gen. John Winder, March 15, 1865, *Official Records*, series 2, vol. 6, 1053; *Harper's Weekly* (New York), March 28, 1863.

[36] Vincent Colyer, *A Brief Report of Services Rendered by the Freed People to the United States Army in North Carolina in the Spring of 1862 after the Battle of Newbern* (New York: V. Colyer, 1864), 25.

[37] Crabtree and Patton, *Diary of Catherine Anne Devereaux Edmondston*, 463.

[38] Colyer, *Brief Report of the Services Rendered by the Freed People*, 9.

weapon. She smuggled the material to Washington, D.C., where she delivered it to Navy Secretary Gideon Welles. "Mrs. Louveste encountered no small risk in bringing this information," Welles recalled years later in support of her pension application. "I am aware of none more meritorious than this poor colored woman whose zeal and fidelity I remember and acknowledge with gratitude." There may even have been a black Union spy named Mary Bowser working as a maid in President Jefferson Davis's Richmond household.[39]

A black Virginia couple proved to be one of the most innovative spy teams of the war. In early 1863, as Union and Confederate armies eyed each other across the Rappahannock River, the refugees entered Union lines where the husband, known only as Dabney, found work as a cook and horse groomer. He became interested in the army's telegraph system and asked some of the soldiers how it worked. Soon after, his wife went back across the river and was put to work doing laundry for Confederate officers. Within a short time, Dabney began updating Union officers on movements of the three corps comprising Robert E. Lee's Army of Northern Virginia. The officers were astonished at how accurate the information was and asked Dabney how he knew such things. He took one of them to a hill overlooking the river and pointed across to Lee's encampment.

That clothes-line tells me in half an hour just what goes on at Lee's headquarters. You see my wife over there; she washes for the officers, and cooks, and waits around, and as soon as she hears about any movement or any thing going on, she comes down and moves the clothes on that line so I can understand it in a minute. That there gray shirt is Longstreet; and when she takes it off, it means he's gone down about Richmond. That white shirt means Hill; and when she moves it up to the west end of the line, Hill's corps has moved upstream. That red one is Stonewall. He's down on the right now, and if he moves, she will move that red shirt.

During the weeks leading up to the Battle of Chancellorsville, Confederates could not make a move without the Federals knowing about it thanks to the "clothes-line telegraph."[40]

---

[39] Poole, *South Carolina's Civil War*, 104; Ervin L. Jordan Jr., *Black Confederates and Afro-Yankees in Civil War Virginia* (Charlottesville: University of Virginia Press, 1995), 284; Elizabeth R. Varon, *Southern Lady, Yankee Spy: The True Story of Elizabeth Van Lew, A Union Agent in the Heart of the Confederacy* (New York: Oxford University Press, 2003), 165–68; William Gilmore Beymer, "Miss Van Lew," *Harper's Monthly* (June 1911), 90. See also Lois Leveen, "A Black Spy in the Confederate White House," *New York Times*, June 21, 2012.

[40] John Truesdale, *The Blue Coats and How They Lived, Fought, and Died for the Union* (Philadelphia: Jones Brothers and Co., 1867), 132–34.

Southern blacks so effectively helped undermine the Confederacy that some white southerners began to imagine what had once seemed unimaginable – freeing the slaves and arming them. By mid-1863, half the army's men were absent with or without leave. None were coming to take their places. If a way could not be found to fill the ranks, the war would be lost. In September 1863, the *Montgomery Weekly Mail* insisted that although making soldiers of blacks would mean "practical equalization of the races," it had to be done "for the sake of preserving our very existence." Any means to defeat the Yankees had to be used, and "one of these, and the only one which will checkmate him, is the employment of negroes in the military service of the Confederacy."[41]

Irish-born General Patrick Cleburne, commanding a division in the Army of Tennessee, was the first high-ranking Confederate to urge filling depleted ranks with black troops. In January 1864, Cleburne and several fellow officers pointed out that "for many years, ever since the agitation of the subject of slavery commenced, the negro has been dreaming of freedom. . . . To attain it he will tempt dangers and difficulties not exceeded by the bravest soldier in the field." Already blacks were fighting for their freedom in the Union army. Why not give blacks freedom at home and use them to Confederate advantage?[42]

Southern whites were generally reluctant to place weapons in the hands of blacks. Military service, especially in local militias, had long been a mark of citizenship. Proslavery doctrine held that only white men could be citizens because only white men possessed the qualities of duty and fortitude necessary to stand in battle. General Howell Cobb of Georgia warned that "if slaves will make good soldiers our whole theory of slavery is wrong." Tens of thousands of black men had already proven Cobb wrong, and more were eager for the chance. An enslaved man named Tom told a federal lieutenant, "Just put the guns into our hands and you'll soon see that we not only know *how* to shoot but *who* to shoot. *My* master wouldn't be worth much if I was a soldier."[43]

---

[41] *Montgomery Weekly Mail*, September 2, 1863, in Robert F. Durden, *The Gray and the Black: The Confederate Debate on Emancipation* (Baton Rouge: Louisiana State University Press, 1972), 32–34.

[42] Cleburne et al. to Gen. Joseph E. Johnston [commanding, Army of Tennessee], January 2, 1864, *Official Records*, series 1, vol. 52, part 2, 586–92. Quote found on page 590.

[43] Cobb to Confederate Sec. of War James A. Seddon, January 8, 1865, *Official Records*, series 4, vol. 3, 1009–10; George H. Hepworth, *The Whip, Hoe, and Sword: or, The Gulf-Department in '63* (Boston: Walker, Wise, and Co., 1864), 187.

Although slaveholders rightly feared arming blacks, by the fall of 1864 they were running out of options. More than a quarter-million Confederate soldiers were already dead and two-thirds had deserted. In January 1865 General Robert E. Lee wrote to a friend that although he considered "the relation of master and slave ... the best that can exist between the white and black races while intermingled as at present in this country," blacks were being used to crush the Confederacy. Might the Confederacy not use them in its own defense? He urged the Confederate Congress to authorize black enlistments and to adopt "at once" a plan for "gradual and general emancipation."[44]

Lee's men had mixed views on the matter. A month after their commanding general penned his sentiments, a North Carolina sergeant wrote that men in his company were deserting rapidly over talk of freeing blacks and putting them in the army. He too was considering it. "I did not volunteer my services to fight for a free negroes country." But a Louisiana sergeant took a more practical view. "If we continue to lose ground as we have for the last 12 months, we will soon be defeated, and then slavery will be gone any way, and I think we should give up slavery and gain our independence."[45]

In February 1865, the Eighteenth Virginia Infantry, entrenched at Petersburg, passed a resolution supporting Lee's move to arm blacks. Of the 325 officers and men present, only fourteen dissented. The four regiments of Thomas's Georgia Brigade declared their support as well. General John B. Gordon polled his entire corps and found its officers and men overwhelmingly favored enlisting blacks. General Howell Cobb suspected that the men favored black enlistment mainly because they thought it might better their chances of getting a furlough or discharge.[46]

Still there were those would not support making blacks soldiers for any reason, although they were no less eager to get home. Confederate soldier Grant Taylor wrote to his wife, "To think we have been fighting four years

---

[44] Lee to Hon. Andrew Hunter [Virginia state senator], January 11, 1865, *Official Records*, series 4, vol. 3, 1012–13.

[45] Joseph F. Maides to mother, February 18, 1865, Maides Papers, Duke University, in McPherson, *What They Fought For*, 55.

[46] Resolutions of the Eighteenth Virginia Infantry, February 20, 1865, in Berlin et al., *Black Military Experience*, 297–98; Resolutions of Thomas's Brigade, February 10, 1865, Telamon Cuyler Collection, University of Georgia, Athens, in Mohr, *On the Threshold of Freedom*, 278; Maj. Gen. John B. Gordon to Col. W. H. Taylor [assistant adjutant-general, Army of Northern Virginia], February 18, 1865, *Official Records*, series 1, vol. 51, part 2, 1063; Edward Porter Alexander to wife, February 21, 1865, Edward Porter Alexander Papers, Southern Historical Collection, University of North Carolina at Chapel Hill, in Mohr, *On the Threshold of Freedom*, 278.

to prevent the slaves from being freed, now to turn round and free them to enable us to carry on the war. The thing is outrageous. . . . I say if the worst comes to the worst let it come and stop the war at once and let us come home."[47] One way or another – with or without black enlistment, with or without victory – soldiers simply wanted the war to end.

On March 13, 1865, at the urging of General Lee and President Davis, the Confederate Congress by a one-vote margin finally authorized recruitment of up to 300,000 blacks. The act made no mention of freedom for those who agreed to serve, insisting that both the states and slaveholders must consent to any alteration in the legal standing of slave-soldiers. But in his General Orders No. 14 implementing the program, Davis went a step further, stating that "no slave will be accepted as a recruit unless with his own consent and with the approbation of his master by a written instrument conferring, as far as he may, the rights of a freedman." It was hardly an Emancipation Proclamation. But it was a startling admission that blacks had long since become, as an editorial from Columbus, Georgia, put it, "a sort of balance power in this contest, and that the side which succeeds in enlisting the feelings and in securing the active operation and services of the four millions of blacks, must ultimately triumph."[48]

That observation had merit enough, but the Confederacy came to realize it far too late. No more than a few dozen blacks were ever enlisted under its banner. On very rare occasions throughout the war, blacks had been unofficially pressed into combat service with guns at their backs and their families held hostage in slavery. But no blacks ever saw combat as congressionally authorized Confederate soldiers. By contrast, roughly 200,000 blacks had joined Union land and naval forces by March 1865 to fight for freedom. Hundreds of thousands more were already free. They needed no favors from a near-dead Confederacy to secure that freedom. They were taking full measure of it themselves, especially black Union soldiers. James Jones of the Fourteenth Rhode Island Heavy Artillery wrote with pride to the *Christian Recorder* that "for once in his life, your humble correspondent walked fearlessly and boldly through the streets of a southern city! And he

---

[47] Ann K. Blomquist and Robert A. Taylor, eds., *This Cruel War: The Civil War Letters of Grant and Malinda Taylor, 1861–1865* (Macon, Ga.: Mercer University Press, 2000), 322–23.

[48] General Orders No. 14, Adjutant and Inspector General's Office, Richmond, March 23, 1865, *Official Records*, series 4, vol. 3, 1161–62; *Columbus (Ga.) Daily Sun*, March 22, 1865. For the most recent and complete treatment of the subject see Bruce Levine, *Confederate Emancipation: Southern Plans to Free and Arm Slaves during the Civil War* (New York: Oxford University Press, 2006).

did this without being required to take off his cap at every step, or to give all the side-walks to those lordly princes of the sunny south, the planters' sons!"[49]

Another point of pride that former slaves generally shared was the opportunity to become literate. "Children love the school as white children love a holiday," wrote one teacher at Port Royal, South Carolina. Older blacks loved the school too. One of its pupils was a 105-year-old man who had once served Revolutionary War General Nathanael Greene. An elderly black woman was asked why she took the trouble to learn to read at her advanced age. She replied, "Because I want to read the Word of the Lord."[50]

Charlotte Forten saw that passion up close. The daughter of escaped slaves who had fled to Philadelphia years before, Forten volunteered as a teacher for the Philadelphia Port Royal Relief Association. It was one of dozens of refugee aid societies, many run by blacks themselves, that funneled money, supplies, and teachers to the South. Soon after Forten arrived at Port Royal, she wrote to *The Liberator*, "I wish some of those persons at the North, who say the race is hopelessly and naturally inferior, could see the readiness with which these children, so long oppressed and deprived of every privilege, learn and understand." It was all part of a rapid transformation that had taken place in Union-occupied areas of the South. Colonel Robert Gould Shaw, who knew Forten while at Port Royal, remarked in a letter home, "Can you imagine anything more wonderful than a coloured-Abolitionist meeting on a South Carolina plantation? . . . two years ago, their masters were still here, the lords of the soil & of them. Now they all own a little themselves, go to school, to church, and work for wages. It is the most extraordinary change."[51]

### WE HAS A RIGHT TO THE LAND

Although Shaw may have assumed too little about antebellum worship practices among Sea Island blacks, to attend school and be paid wages was certainly a new thing for them. So was owning land. Unfortunately, Shaw's observation did not reflect the experience of most southern blacks.

[49] *Christian Recorder*, May 28, 1864.

[50] *North American Review* (Boston: Ticknor and Fields, 1865), 101: 4; *Weekly Vincennes (Ind.) Western Sun*, January 3, 1863; *Liberator*, July 25, 1862.

[51] *Liberator*, December 12, 1862; Shaw to mother, July 4, 1863, in Duncan, *Blue-Eyed Child of Fortune*, 373. For a treatment of what the first few years of freedom meant to the former slaves at Port Royal see Willie Lee Rose, *Rehearsal for Reconstruction: The Port Royal Experiment* (New York: Vintage Books, 1964).

Planters often did run off as the Federals closed in. When that happened, slaves commonly assumed that the land on which their families had lived and died, sometimes for generations, was theirs. After planter Charles Pettigrew fled his estate in North Carolina, resident blacks divided the land and livestock among themselves and kept on farming. So did former slaves on nearby Somerset plantation. When Union troops showed up at the Mississippi plantations of Jefferson Davis and his brother Joseph, the overseer had long since been driven off and former slaves were running the property as their own.[52]

They were doing a good job of it too, as were so many other blacks who now considered themselves freeholding farmers as well as free people. "The dogma of the 'Lords of the Lash,'" as one report put it, that blacks were "unable to take care of themselves is now exploded." That dogma was held by many white northerners as well. When a northern philanthropist expressed such views to Moses Battle of Tennessee, the freedman seemed puzzled. "Don't know what for, sir, anybody think that. The colored folks [are] what been a keepin' up the country. When they had to work all day for the masters, they work all night and Sundays to make a little somethin' for themselves. Now when its all day to themselves, don't know what for they lie down and starve."[53]

"The Freedmen do best for themselves as independent cultivators of small farms" reported Superintendent of Contrabands John Eaton. "Those who worked for themselves, have raised on the average the most cotton per acre." Just as impressed was a Union soldier stationed at Plymouth, North Carolina, who went "among the negroes" to see for himself how they were getting along. "They were very intelligent," he recalled, "although they could neither read nor write." They were certainly not, as he had otherwise so often heard, lacking in good sense. His visit dispelled other myths as well. "There is no use in repeating that they are not capable of taking care

<hr />

[52]  Wilson A. Norman to Josiah Collins, June 28, 1863, George Spruill to Collins, May 16, 1863, Girard W. Phelps to Collins, March 14, 1863, Joseph W. Murphy to Collins, May 30, 1863, Josiah Collins Papers, North Carolina Division of Archives and History, in Durrill, *War of Another Kind*, 141; Joseph E. Davis to Jefferson Davis, May 22, 1862, in Crist et al., *Papers of Jefferson Davis*, 8: 196–97; William Porterfield to Jefferson Davis, June 5, 1862, in ibid., 227; Charles J. Mitchell to Jefferson Davis, June 7, 1862, in ibid., 231–33.

[53]  Capt. Chas. B. Wilder [superintendent of Negro Affairs, First District of the Department of Virginia and North Carolina] to Maj. George J. Carney [general superintendent of Negro Affairs in the department], December 30, 1864, in Berlin et al., *Upper South*, 217; Cimprich, *Slavery's End in Tennessee*, 71.

of themselves and that they do not desire their freedom, for it is wholly false."[54]

Unfortunately for former slaves, the notion that they held title to their land was just as false. As far as the Lincoln administration was concerned, plantations held by formerly enslaved people were "abandoned" lands subject to federal confiscation. Although the Second Confiscation Act entitled the government to take rebel property, Lincoln's December 1863 Proclamation of Amnesty and Reconstruction promised to restore that property to its former owners as soon as they took an oath of allegiance to the Union. In the meantime, under the Direct Tax Act of 1862, abandoned

FIGURE 4.2. Former slaves, such as those seen here working an "abandoned" South Carolina plantation in Union-held territory, claimed the land as hard-earned compensation for years of unpaid labor. But Lincoln's reconstruction plan returned both land and political power to slaveholders. Federal troops enforced labor contracts that practically reenslaved southern blacks. Dr. James McCune Smith, the first African American to earn a medical degree, denounced Lincoln's plan as an effort to preserve "all the wrongs of slavery, without its name." Photo courtesy of the Library of Congress.

---

[54] Eaton [general superintendent of freedmen, Department of Mississippi and State of Arkansas] to Sec. of the Treasury W. P. Fessenden, January 31, 1865, in Berlin et al., *Lower South*, 871–72; George F. Weston to sir, February 2, 1863, New Bern Occupation Papers, Southern Historical Collection, University of North Carolina at Chapel Hill, in Durrill, *War of Another Kind*, 144.

plantations were to be leased, sold, or operated by the government itself. In any case, there would be no land grants for former slaves. A few congressmen proposed such grants, but most doggedly opposed distributing land to former slaves.[55]

Blacks protested vigorously at the injustice of such a policy. If they owned no land, how could they make a living? How could they truly be free? They had worked the land all their lives. The land, they insisted, was theirs by right.

We has a right to the land where we are located. For why? I tell you. Our wives, our children, our husbands has been sold over and over again to purchase the lands we now locates upon; for that reason we have a divine right to the land. . . . And then didn't we clear the land, and raise the crops of corn, of cotton, of tobacco, of rice, of sugar, of everything. And then didn't them large cities in the North grow up on the cotton and the sugars and the rice that we made? Yes! . . . they has grown rich and my people is poor.[56]

Such was the heart-felt reasoning of Virginia freedman Bayley Wyat, who reflected a sentiment so often repeated as Union forces pushed south. But the government was not listening to ex-slaves. In 1862, federal authorities began selling and leasing abandoned plantations, usually to favored clients. Most wound up in the hands of northern investors and cotton textile companies. Many went to army officers and government officials. What little was left sometimes went to those few freedmen who could afford to buy small plots. In South Carolina's Sea Islands auctions, the smallest parcels went to groups of blacks who pooled their scarce funds for the purchases.[57]

"The disappointment to them is almost unbearable," wrote one northern minister after a land sale, mostly to northern speculators, in the South Carolina tidewater. "They see neither justice nor wisdom in such treatment." What former slaves did see, what they had seen all their lives, was that "the white man loves power & money, and is sharp enough to grasp

---

[55] *Statutes at Large*, 13: 737–39; *Statutes at Large*, 12: 422–26; Syrett, *Confiscation Acts*, 123–24, 137.

[56] *A Freedman's Speech* (Philadelphia: Friends Association, n.d. [1866?]), Printed Ephemera Collection, Portfolio 159, Folder 14b, Rare Book and Special Collections Division, Library of Congress.

[57] Eric Foner, *Reconstruction: America's Unfinished Revolution, 1863–1877* (New York: Harper and Row, 1988), 52–53; Berlin et al., *Lower South*, 103. The best treatment of northern speculation in southern plantations is Lawrence N. Powell, *New Masters: Northern Planters during the Civil War and Reconstruction* (New Haven, Conn.: Yale University Press, 1980).

both, when he can." General Rufus Saxton told the Lincoln administration that the South Carolina sales were putting blacks "at the mercy of men devoid of principle." Wrote another officer in Louisiana of the new land-lords, "Cotton closes their eyes to justice just as it did in the case of the former slave masters." Francis Bird, a white abolitionist who toured government farms in tidewater Virginia, insisted that "truly loyal and prosperous" communities would inevitably spring up if only "the men and women who have watered the soil with their tears and blood should be allowed to own it."[58]

Blacks often adopted a "squatter sovereignty" plan, refusing to give up their land or recognize anyone else's right to it. At Beaufort and Hilton Head in South Carolina, they threatened violence against white specula-tors to deter them from leasing or purchasing lands. Some blacks made good on their threats when speculators tried to occupy their claims. In such cases, the army intervened on behalf of the speculators.[59]

Blacks employed on government-run or leased plantations often lived in thrown-together structures or old out-buildings that hardly kept out the rain or cold. At Downey Plantation in Virginia, former slaves occupied a tobacco barn that was, wrote an army inspector, "wholly unfit for human beings to occupy." Such living conditions, he felt, were "a disgrace to the 'peculiar institution' in its better days."[60]

Residents on government lands worked with a promise of wages to be distributed when the crop was sold. Frequently, however, they saw no income at all. One official reported that blacks on government plantations in southern Louisiana "were generally cheated out of their pay." Another wrote that black employees in South Carolina, although they had been promised twenty-five cents a day, had not been paid for some time. As of June 1863, blacks on St. Helena Island had gone six months without pay.

[58] M. French to Hon. Mr. Lewis [commissioner of internal revenue], February 23, 1864, in Berlin et al., *Lower South*, 291–92; Saxton to Edwin M. Stanton, December 7, 1862, in ibid., 220; Gen. John P. Hawkins [commanding, District of Northeastern Louisiana] to Hon. Gerritt Smith, October 21, 1863, in ibid., 743; Testimony of Hon. F. W. Bird, American Freedmen's Inquiry Commission, December 24, 1863, in Berlin et al., *Upper South*, 180–81.

[59] Wm. Henry Brisbane [direct tax commissioner] to Joseph J. Lewis [commissioner of internal revenue], December 12, 1863, in Berlin et al., *Lower South*, 276; Lt. Col. Ed. W. Smith [Headquarters, Department of the South] to Messrs. Brisbane, Wording, and Smith [direct-tax commissioners for South Carolina], February 25, 1864, in ibid., 293–94; E. P. Hutchinson [northern businessman] to Hon J. B. Alley [Massachusetts congressman], March 2, 1864, in ibid., 307.

[60] A. A. [acting assistant] Surgeon L. D. Seymour to Lt. Col. J. B. Kinsman, May 18, 1864, in Berlin et al., *Upper South*, 105–106.

For more than a year there had been "a very general complaint among the hands on these estates that they have received no compensation."[61]

One group of Louisiana freedmen wrote to the army's Department of the Gulf complaining that a Union officer had "told us to go on and cultivate the land on the Plantation, and do something for ourselves, until the Government could do something for us." Shortly after, with no consideration for the former slaves, government agents leased out their lands. "Now a Mr Wright comes on the plantation with Authority from the Government to work it and claims the results of our labor – We have had a hard struggle to get along and we feel it hard now that we have succeeded in making ourselves in a measure independent, to have to [turn] it all over to someone else." The freedmen received no reply.[62]

Most plantations in Union territory remained in the hands of planters who quickly disavowed any Confederate loyalties when the Federals arrived. Those who had the opportunity to do so before January 1, 1863, when the Emancipation Proclamation went into effect, kept title to their land *and* their slaves. In areas reclaimed for the Union after that date, slaves were technically free. But in fact – whether plantations were government-run, leased out, or privately owned – to black folk, the new freedom seemed much like the old slavery. Government lands were supervised by appointed overseers, most of them local whites who drove blacks with the whip and club. Leased plantations hired the same type of men. "They treat the Negroes brutally," wrote one federal officer, "and chastise them worse than their former masters did." Harsh treatment, along with infrequent or nonexistent pay, led many blacks to seek other options. In late 1863, one northern observer in the Mississippi Valley wrote that blacks were engaged in a "general stampede" away from the plantations.[63]

To counter that stampede and keep much-needed labor on the land, planters often negotiated with their workers, sometimes giving in even to the demands of those still technically enslaved. Blacks "know their rights," wrote one observer, "and, knowing, dare maintain." The result saw whites

---

[61] George S. Denison [collector of internal revenue] to Sec. of the Treasury Salmon P. Chase, October 23, 1863, in Berlin et al., *Lower South*, 471–73; General Orders No. 12, Department of the South, December 20, 1862, in ibid., 223; Testimony of Capt. E. W. Hooper, American Freedmen's Inquiry Commission, June 1863, in ibid., 239; Richard Soule Jr. to Edward L. Pierce, March 29, 1862, in ibid., 179.

[62] Henry Norvall et al. [Louisiana freedmen] to Brig. Gen. James Bowen [provost marshal general, Department of the Gulf], April 5, 1863, in Berlin et al., *Lower South*, 438–39.

[63] Berlin et al., *Upper South*, 96; Berlin et al., *Lower South*, 645; Adm. David D. Porter [commanding, Mississippi Squadron] to Gen. Lorenzo Thomas, October 21, 1863, in ibid., 747; William Burnet to W. P. Mellen, January [?] 1864, in ibid., 639.

making "extraordinary efforts" to keep blacks on the land, often with the help of government-authorized labor contracts. Under these contracts, landowners promised not to engage in physical abuse. They offered shorter working hours and Saturdays as well as Sundays off. They granted larger garden plots on which blacks could raise their own produce and livestock, making them less dependent on wages. And they offered crop shares in lieu of wages, which often went unpaid in any case.[64]

To the dismay of blacks, white landowners quickly turned the share-cropping system against them. Resistant as whites were to keeping blacks at work through bargaining, perhaps debt might accomplish the same end. Labor contracts normally called for landowners to provide housing, shoes, clothing, and tools as part of the deal, but such stipulations were easily ignored. Basic supplies, as well as the "luxuries" of tobacco and coffee, were doled out from plantation stores to penniless blacks on credit, always with profit margins and interest rates controlled by planters. Those markups, which ranged as high as 200 percent, were designed to total more than any income black workers could earn through crop shares. Inevitably, when crops were harvested and sold, workers' profit share rarely covered their debt. At one northern-leased plantation in Louisiana, former slaves ended their first year of freedom with debts ranging from four cents to more than twelve dollars. One of the families showed earnings of $184. Their debt at the plantation store was $190.[65]

Thus it was that black folk became trapped in debt slavery, sometimes called the "new slavery," and it was backed by federal force. Government-sanctioned contracts made it illegal for workers to leave the plantations without their employers' permission. Military provost marshals rounded up "vagrant" blacks under orders that forbade them to "wander . . . without employment." And officials were authorized to discipline blacks who resisted the new labor arrangement. One federal officer wrote that the freedman had been reduced to a "more servile and pitiable condition than when a slave." Another blamed the situation on "our over-careful President" who

---

[64] Hepworth, *Whip, Hoe, and Sword*, 30; Berlin et al., *Upper South*, 560; Berlin et al., *Destruction of Slavery*, 412; Berlin et al., *Lower South*, 105, 623.

[65] Berlin et al., *Lower South*, 369; A. A. Surgeon John F. Tallon to Hon. B. Flanders [supervising agent of the Treasury Department, Fifth Agency], January 9, 1864, in ibid., 511; Capt. Jas. White to Capt. Sterns, August 24, 1864, in ibid., 544; Gen. John P. Hawkins to Hon. Gerritt Smith, October 21, 1863, in ibid., 742–43; Powell, *New Masters*, 90–91.

"was desirous to conciliate" former slaveholders. A petition from New Orleans blacks called Lincoln's new system "disguised bondage."[66]

Despite lack of federal support and threats of punishment, blacks continued fighting for their rights as free people. One federal officer wrote that former slaves could hardly be restrained from demonstrating "a spirit of independence – a feeling that they are no longer slaves, but hired laborers; and demand to be treated as such." When that feeling was ignored, the result was "trouble, immediately – and the negroes band together, and lay down their own rules, as to when, and how long they will work." Workers sometimes drove off their overseers and demanded more humane supervisors. In a few cases, they refused supervision of any kind. If their demands were not met, they simply walked away and resisted any attempt to force them back. One former slave told a federal officer, "you may shoot me before I will return to the old plantation." Blacks on one Louisiana plantation laid down their tools and "left in a body." When blacks on another Louisiana plantation complained about a newly hired overseer who "was in the habit of wielding the whip pretty freely," the planter refused to fire him. So the blacks packed their bundles and started down the road. They had not gone far before the planter ran after them, saying they could have "any overseer they wanted."[67]

The main problem blacks faced when considering whether to leave was where to go. The most immediate opportunities for employment lay with the army, but blacks were often as likely to be turned away as taken in. Even when they did find government employment, wages were low by design. General Benjamin Butler, commanding the Department of Virginia and North Carolina, issued orders that the government not compete with itself by paying black refugees more than the $10 a month it paid black

---

[66] George C. Strong [assistant adjutant-general and chief of staff, Department of the Gulf] to Gen. G. Weitzel [commanding, District of the Teche], November 2, 1862, *Official Records*, series 1, vol. 15, 162–63; Berlin et al., *Lower South*, 355; Gen. James Bowen to Capt. Kilburn [provost marshal of Orleans Parish, Louisiana], March 5, 14, and 18, 1863, in ibid., 431; Maj. Julian E. Bryant [inspecting officer, District of Northeastern Louisiana] to [Headquarters, District of Northeastern Louisiana], October 10, 1863, in ibid., 729; Hepworth, *Whip, Hoe, and Sword*, 27; James H. Ingraham and Dr. A. W. Lewis et al. to Gen. S. A. Hurlbut [commanding, Department of the Gulf], March 21, 1865, in ibid., 595.

[67] Capt. John W. Ela [provost marshal, Jefferson Parish, Louisiana] to Gen. James Bowen [provost marshal general, Department of the Gulf], June 11, 1863, in Berlin et al., *Lower South*, 455–56; Testimony of Col. George H. Hanks, American Freedmen's Inquiry Commission, February 6, 1864, in ibid., 518; Unsigned, undated to Gen. Nathaniel P. Banks [February 1863?], in Louis S. Gerteis, *From Contraband to Freedman: Federal Policy toward Southern Blacks, 1861–1865* (Westport, Conn.: Greenwood Press, 1973), 90; Hepworth, *Whip, Hoe, and Sword*, 29–30.

soldiers. Often, blacks could not even get the $10 rate. One report from Arkansas told of blacks "in numerous instances" receiving counterfeit money for their services or no pay at all. Virginia freedman Abraham Cannaday, after working at a government sawmill for more than a year, complained to the Lincoln administration that he had never "recevd a cent of money and my famley is aseffring for the sorport of my labor for I Can not by inney thing without money."[68]

Lack of pay was hardly the only worry blacks had in government work camps. At Kenner, Louisiana, former slaves assigned to labor on the levees "worked from sunrise till dark, Sundays included." The majority had no shoes, and their clothing was in "the most ragged state." They were forced to live in an old barn, shacks made from old fences, or tents that had been declared unfit for soldiers. A report from nearby Bonnet Carre reflected similar conditions. Wrote the inspecting officer, "My cattle at home are better cared for than these unfortunate persons."[69]

Worse still, physical abuse was common in government work camps. Lewis Johnson, a freedman at one Virginia facility, complained that Danforth Nichols, the superintendent, frequently beat and kicked blacks under his supervision. "I speak from my heart before the Lord when I say that the conduct of Mr Nichols was worse than the general treatment of slave owners." Freedmen on Roanoke Island in North Carolina wrote a petition to Lincoln informing him that their white bosses "have done every thing to us that our masters have done except b[u]y and Sell us." One refugee at a Washington refugee camp, disgusted with mistreatment of every kind, declared, "I am going back to my old master – I never saw hard times till since I called myself a freeman."[70]

[68] General Orders No. 46, Headquarters, Department of Virginia and North Carolina, December 5, 1863, in Berlin et al., *Black Military Experience*, 135–36; Chaplain Samuel Sawyer [superintendent of contrabands, District of Eastern Arkansas] to Gen. Samuel R. Curtis [commanding, Department of the Missouri], January 26, 1863, enclosing Samuel Sawyer et al. [committee of chaplains and surgeons] to Gen. Curtis, December 29, 1862, in Berlin et al., *Lower South*, 675; Cannaday to [Sec. of State William Seward], May 3, 1865, in Berlin et al., *Upper South*, 239.

[69] Lt. Charles L. Stevens [guard commander, Kenner, Louisiana] to Lt. J. H. Metcalf [Headquarters, Third Brigade, Second Division, Department of the Gulf], January 27, 1863, enclosed in Col. F. S. Nickerson [commanding a brigade] to Capt. A. Badeau [Headquarters, Defenses of New Orleans], January 28, 1863, in Berlin et al., *Lower South*, 410–14.

[70] Testimony of Lewis Johnson, January [?], 1864, in Berlin et al., *Upper South*, 295–96; Freedmen of Roanoke Island, N.C., to Mr. President, March 9, 1865, and Freedmen of Roanoke Island to [Edwin M. Stanton], March 9, 1865, in ibid., 231–35; Testimony of Mrs. Louisa Jane Barker [Union chaplain's wife], January [?], 1864, in ibid., 312.

Few refugees ever willingly returned to their former owners. When they did, it was usually under threat of arrest and forced labor. Under federally sanctioned vagrancy and impressment policies, former slaves not working on private plantations could be rounded up and made to work on government projects. In January 1863, at Murfreesboro, Tennessee, General William Rosecrans ordered his subordinates to "procure and employ negroes ... found free and roaming at large." That same month in New Orleans, General Nathaniel Banks ordered that blacks "without visible occupation ... be arrested as vagrants, and put to labor upon the public works or the Quartermaster's plantations."[71]

That summer in Washington, quartermasters encouraged the use of "forcible persuasion" to obtain the services of some 2,000 "idle negroes." In Memphis, Tennessee, Federals ordered that blacks "without lawful occupation ... be arrested and confined at hard labor." November found 3,000 blacks being impressed at Nashville for work on fortifications without pay. And in Natchez, Mississippi, General J. M. Tuttle expelled all blacks from the city who were not employed "by some *responsible white person*." Those not so employed were impressed – hauled off to labor in a government work camp.[72]

The labor status of blacks, whether self-employed or not, mattered little to officers charged with carrying out impressment. In March 1863, under orders from General James Bowen, provost marshal-general of the Department of the Gulf, soldiers swept through New Orleans detaining blacks "with no regular habitation or Employment." Dozens of self-supporting men and women were picked up in the rush and marched off to forced labor. In Baton Rouge, black businessmen who had been free all their lives were herded out of the city along with former slaves, some of them their employees. When Federals at Virginia's Fortress Monroe received orders from Washington for "contraband" labor, they trolled the streets of nearby Norfolk taking black men at will. At a local African

---

[71] General Orders No. 6, Headquarters, Department of the Cumberland, January 27, 1863, in Berlin et al., *Upper South*, 390–91; Circular, Headquarters, Department of the Gulf, February 6, 1863, in Berlin et al., *Lower South*, 419.

[72] Capt. Chas. B. Wagner [aide of the chief quartermaster] to Brig. Gen. Rufus Ingalls [chief quartermaster], June 15, 1863, in Berlin et al., *Upper South*, 154–55; General Orders No. 75, Headquarters, District of Memphis, July 17, 1863, in Berlin et al., *Lower South*, 714–15; Testimony of Maj. George L. Stearns, American Freedmen's Inquiry Commission, November 23, 1863, in Berlin et al., *Upper South*, 416; Order, Health Office, March 19, 1864, in Berlin et al., *Lower South*, 814–15.

Methodist Church, just as the sermon was ending, soldiers burst through the door and began hauling men away.[73]

Neither age nor infirmity seemed to matter to impressing officers. One impressed man from Norfolk was later declared too old for heavy labor. Another had a "rupture," probably a hernia, which rendered him unfit. Blacks at Roanoke complained to General Benjamin Butler that Union soldiers had combed the island, taking up "every man that could be found indiscriminately[,] young and old[,] sick and well." One Roanoke man later wrote that "they treated us mean a[s] our owners ever did they taken us just like we had been dum beast."[74]

FIGURE 4.3. Blacks who refused to work for their former owners could be arrested under federally sanctioned vagrancy laws and sent to government plantations or work camps to labor without wages. When Virginia blacks, such as those seen here, refused to work, protesting inadequate food and lack of pay, officials had them jailed or whipped. In a letter to President Lincoln, a North Carolina freedman complained that federal agents "treated us mean as our owners ever did." Photo courtesy of the National Archives.

[73] Bowen to Capt. C. W. Killborn [provost marshal, Orleans Parish], March 5, 1863, in Berlin et al., *Lower South*, 431; S. W. Ringgold et al. [Louisiana free blacks] to the generals commanding the District and Department of the Gulf, December 1864, in ibid., 570–71; Rev. Asa Prescott [northern minister] to Edwin M. Stanton, July 11, 1863, in Berlin et al., *Upper South*, 157.

[74] Rev. Asa Prescott to Edwin M. Stanton, July 11, 1863, in Berlin et al., *Upper South*, 157; Ned Baxter et al. [North Carolina freedmen] to Maj. Gen. Butler, September 1864,

Protests through official channels did little good and could sometimes result in physical abuse. When Virginia blacks held in service by the Union army refused to work over lack of pay and inadequate food, officials had them jailed or whipped. Some were "knocked down senseless with shovels and clubs." Little wonder that blacks frequently tried to escape from federal forced labor just as they had from slavery. To them, there seemed little difference between the two. Some hired themselves as servants and cooks to officers and soldiers. Pay for such service often went lacking, but it shielded blacks from harsher unpaid labor. Others ran off to cities near or far, hoping to find work and avoid any sort of government labor.[75]

Deserting black labor hampered work on essential military projects, as Lieutenant George Burroughs discovered while directing construction at Nashville's fortifications. He asked the city's chief of police to help impress more black men, but the only place left to get them was from local plantations. The chief was hesitant to work against planter interests. Clearly, harsh treatment and nonpayment of black workers had taken their toll. Hoping to improve the army's reputation in middle Tennessee and draw black workers, General Rosecrans asked his superiors to authorize immediate wage payments, pointing out that "from want, say, nine-tenths have deserted, and I think justly."[76]

## SOUTHERN NEGROES MUST STAY WHERE THEY ARE

As a mark of freedom, the right to be paid for their work was one that blacks struggled for constantly. The need for their labor, coupled with their own persistence, sometimes brought success. The fall of 1863 saw workers in Washington, black and white, demanding higher wages to keep up with rampant inflation. Threatening a strike that might throw the war effort into "utter confusion," black workers at the Quartermaster Department received a 20 percent salary increase.[77]

---

in ibid., 202–203; Roanoke Island [freedmen] to Mr. President, March 9, 1865, in ibid., 231–32.

[75] Rev. Lewis C. Lockwood [northern minister] to U.S. Senator Henry Wilson of Mass., January 29, 1862, in Berlin et al., *Upper South*, 112–13; Affidavit of Suthey Parker, September 2, 1865, in ibid., 110–11.

[76] Berlin et al., *Upper South*, 275; Col. Wm. Treudail [chief of police, Nashville] to Maj. Gen. Rosecrans [commanding, Department of the Cumberland], March 7, 1863, in Berlin et al., *Destruction of Slavery*, 301; Rosecrans endorsement of Gen. J. St. C. Morton to Maj. J. D. Kurtz, April 29, 1863, *Official Records*, series 1, vol. 23, part 2, 290–91.

[77] Berlin et al., *Upper South*, 255–56.

In Beaufort, South Carolina, a "poor old lame colored man" named Charles Gelston made a living by collecting discarded army clothes and blankets from trash heaps, then cleaning and selling them as rags. In March 1864, Treasury Department officials confiscated the rags, calling them government property. Gelston, with the help of an army surgeon, complained by letter to Austin Smith, the Treasury agent at Beaufort. Smith was sympathetic, but refused to take responsibility. He forwarded the letter to Washington for a final decision with his endorsement. "This is a small matter, but it is one which may be distorted. . . . I should be sorry to have the government represented as competing with the negroes in the rag picking business." A response finally arrived in October from Treasury Secretary William Fessenden saying that Gelston could keep his rags. This "small matter" had taken seven months to resolve.[78]

Economic justice could take much longer, when it arrived at all. Samuel Larkin, a refugee from Alabama, fled to Nashville and used his small savings to buy two wagons, a dray, a mule, and four horses, one of them blind. With these, he started an express service, hauling goods for merchants in the Nashville area. In August 1863, Union troops under orders to confiscate "all serviceable stock" took Larkin's whole inventory. After complaining of the seizure, Larkin had his wagons and blind horse returned as unserviceable. He was promised pay for the rest, but no money came, at least not right away. Nine years later, in 1872, the Southern Claims Commission, a U.S. agency set up to compensate loyal southerners for property lost during the war, paid Larkin $350 for his mule and three horses.[79]

Despite the many obstacles, thousands of blacks in federally occupied towns like Nashville, Memphis, Natchez, New Orleans, Beaufort, Plymouth, and Norfolk made a decent living for themselves. From Helena, Arkansas, an army chaplain wrote of local blacks that "the town contains many, who, by their industry, economy and good judgment, have made and saved money. They are traders, mechanics and laborers, and if let alone, will compete successfully with any people in the same walks of life."[80]

The truth of that statement had much to do with economic obstacles thrown in the path of former slaves. Whites wanted no competition from

---

[78] A. A. Surgeon W. J. Randolph to Hon. Austin Smith, April 28, 1864, enclosed in Austin Smith to Hon. S. P. Chase, May 14, 1864, in Berlin et al., *Lower South*, 312–13; W. P. Fessenden to Albert G. Browne, Esq., October 19, 1864, in ibid., 313.

[79] Testimony of Samuel Larkin, Southern Claims Commission, February 9, 1872, in Berlin et al., *Upper South*, 403–404.

[80] Chaplain J. I. Herrick to Brig. Gen. N. B. Buford [commanding, District of Eastern Arkansas], November 30, 1864, in Berlin et al., *Lower South*, 861–63.

blacks, and the Federals wanted no trouble with local whites. Toward that end, except for the issues of Union and, to a lesser extent, chattel slavery, federal policy from top to bottom worked to appease southern whites at the expense of southern blacks. Debt slavery, vagrancy decrees, impressment orders, and "forcible persuasion" all sought to limit any economic gains blacks might achieve.

When former slaves fled farther north to escape such policies, they often ran into similar difficulties. Border state towns used many of the same tactics to suppress blacks. Sometimes they tried to exclude blacks entirely. Sedalia, Missouri, passed an ordinance expelling blacks from the town. In other Missouri communities, bands of "regulators" made nightly visits to "certain Citizens who had free negros hired, and with force and threats drove off the negros." In St. Louis, there were systematic efforts to expel free black laborers not only from the city but also from the state. "Bushwhackers" in Columbia lynched a black man after giving notice that all blacks were to leave within ten days or be killed.[81]

Refugees fleeing through the border states, where slavery was still legal, risked not only violence but also reenslavement. Kentucky passed a law forbidding blacks freed by the Emancipation Proclamation from entering the state under threat of being "arrested, dealt with, and disposed of as runaways." It was a common thing for Kentucky lawmen to seize free blacks and sell them at auction to the highest bidder. By February 1863, Louisville's jail was filled to capacity with "runaway slaves." When it could hold no more, they were turned over to private slavecatchers.[82]

Lincoln's administration tried just as hard to keep black refugees from penetrating into the free states. That effort, in large part, lay behind the army's effort to keep former slaves employed in, or otherwise confined to, the South. Doing so, Secretary of War Stanton assured Lincoln, would

[81]  G. R. Smith [civil official, Sedalia, Missouri] to Gen. E. B. Brown [commanding, District of Central Missouri], March 16, 1864, in Berlin et al., *Upper South*, 590–91; Col. Samuel M. Wirt [Missouri militia officer] to Brig. Gen. Clinton B. Fisk [commanding, District of North Missouri], April 20, 1864, in ibid., 604; Samuel Sawyer [superintendent of contrabands at St. Louis] to Maj. Gen. Curtis, April 18, 1863, in ibid., 568–69; F. T. Russell [resident of Columbia, Missouri] to [commanding general, District of North Missouri], February 21, 1865, in ibid., 616.

[82]  An Act to prevent certain negroes and mulattoes from migrating to or remaining in this State, March 2, 1863, *Acts of Kentucky, 1861–1863*, in Berlin et al., *Destruction of Slavery*, 504; An Act concerning runaway slaves, March 2, 1863, *Acts of Kentucky, 1861–1863*, in ibid., 504–505; Mittimus by a Jefferson County justice of the peace, February 17, 1863, and excerpt from Bullitt County Court records of sale of slaves, April 13 and May 18, 1863, in ibid., 568–70.

avoid "all possibility of competition from negro labor in the North" and the political complications it would bring.[83]

Stung by public backlash against the Emancipation Proclamation, in his December 1862 message to Congress, Lincoln sought to calm white fears by asking "Why should emancipation south, send the free people north? People, of any color, seldom run, unless there be something to run from. *Heretofore*, colored people, to some extent, have fled north from bondage; and *now*, perhaps, from both bondage and destitution." Urging the border states to end slavery on their own, Lincoln insisted that "if gradual emancipation and deportation be adopted, they will have neither to flee from. Their old masters will give them wages . . . till new homes can be found for them in congenial climes, and with people of their own blood and race." But, insisted Lincoln, whether these measures discouraged blacks from trying to migrate north was immaterial. "Cannot the north decide for itself, whether to receive them?"[84]

Lincoln's comments made clear that colonizing blacks out of the country remained a large part of his plan to maintain postwar peace. Although he cancelled an agreement with swindler Bernard Kock to employ black timber cutters on Ile a Vache near Haiti in January 1863, he approved a contract in April with New York financiers allied with Kock. Five hundred blacks of a projected 5,000 were sent to the island, but the effort proved disastrous. Kock and his associates stole colonists' money, gave them inadequate housing, and left them in a state of near starvation. After smallpox swept through the settlement and killed nearly a hundred people, Lincoln gave up on the venture. In 1864, he recalled the survivors.[85]

Although Lincoln abandoned the Ile a Vache scheme, he continued to worry about what the presence of blacks would mean for the nation's future. As late as 1865, shortly before his assassination, Lincoln pressed the issue with General Benjamin Butler. "But what shall we do with the negroes after they are free?" Lincoln worried that a "race war" might break out in the South, or, worse yet, another civil war might occur. "I can hardly believe that the South and North can live in peace," Lincoln reportedly told

---

[83] *Congressional Globe*, Thirty-Seventh Congress, Third Session (1862), Appendix, 32.

[84] Annual Message to Congress, December 1, 1862, in Basler et al., *Collected Works of Abraham Lincoln*, 5: 535–36.

[85] *National Anti-Slavery Standard*, March 19, 1864; A. Lincoln to William H. Seward, January 6, 1863, in Basler et al., *Collected Works of Abraham Lincoln*, 6: 41–42. See also Warren A. Beck, "Lincoln and Negro Colonization in Central America," *Abraham Lincoln Quarterly* 6 (September 1950): 162–83; Paul J. Scheips, "Lincoln and the Chirqui Colonization Project," *Journal of Negro History* 36 (1952): 418–53.

Butler, "unless we can get rid of the negroes. .... I believe that it would be better to export them all."[86]

The more immediate concern for most white northerners was keeping blacks out of their communities. Well before the president's December 1862 congressional message, efforts were under way to establish or strengthen already existing state laws limiting black migration. By the spring of 1862, petitions bearing the names of up to 40,000 citizens flooded the Ohio legislature demanding that blacks be kept out of the state. "Ohio," declared a Columbus editor, "shall never become the depot for the runaway and freed negroes of the South." Illinois voters, by a majority of more than 100,000 votes, reaffirmed their support for a ban on black immigration.[87] The editor of Indiana's *Vincennes Western Sun* was sure that

the rest of the States of the North feel on the subject of negro immigration as Illinois does. They are all set like flint against the thing. This fact was brought out very distinctly in the debates of the last session of Congress. Not one of the Northern States will consent to the admittance of Negroes in any considerable number. Not one. The abolitionists themselves will not consent to it. .... the Southern negroes as a body must stay where they are.[88]

The next year, when Indiana passed a law barring blacks from entering the state, Sojourner Truth defied the act with a speaking tour. Authorities arrested her several times, but she kept to her mission. After a crowd at Angola threatened to burn down the hall in which she was scheduled to speak, she pointedly responded, "Then I will speak upon the ashes."[89]

Threats of violence aimed at blacks were hardly uncommon. In Iowa's Wapello and Johnson Counties, whites declared their intention to "resist the introduction of free negroes into Iowa; first by lawful means, and when that fails, we will drive them, together with such whites as may be engaged in bringing them in, out of the State or afford them 'hospitable graves.'" Farmers in Page County who had hired "colored girls" as house servants were warned "that they must send those 'niggers' back" or see their farms

---

[86] Benjamin F. Butler, *Autobiography and Personal Reminiscences* (Boston: A. M. Thayer and Co., 1892), 903. Some scholars have expressed doubt that these were Lincoln's words. Nevertheless, the passage certainly reflects fears that he had previously voiced. The most insightful analysis of Lincoln's probable thoughts on colonization at the time of his meeting with Butler is found in Magness and Page, *Colonization after Emancipation*, 109–16.

[87] *Columbus (Ohio) Crisis*, April 30 and October 29, 1862; *Springfield Illinois Daily State Journal*, August 16, 1862.

[88] *Weekly Vincennes (Ind.) Western Sun*, October 25, 1862.

[89] *Narrative of Sojourner Truth; A Bondswoman of Olden Time* (1878; reprint, New York: Oxford University Press, 1991), 139–40. Truth's most complete biography is Nell Irvin Painter, *Sojourner Truth: A Life, a Symbol* (New York: W. W. Norton, 1996).

FIGURE 4.4. Fear of black immigration led several northern states to erect legal barriers. Illinois amended its constitution to forbid black settlement. Indiana barred blacks from entering the state at all. Ever defiant, Sojourner Truth set out for an Indiana speaking tour. Authorities arrested her several times, but she kept to her mission. After a crowd at Angola threatened to burn down the hall in which she was scheduled to speak, she proclaimed, "Then I will speak upon the ashes." Photo courtesy of the Library of Congress.

burned to the ground. In Muscatine County, twenty whites visited a local farmer who had hired a former slave. "By threats of personal violence," they intended to convince the farmer of his error.[90]

In April 1863, a gang of whites drove at least forty black workers off a farm in Union County, Illinois. A month later, two armed Illinois whites halted three black fugitives from Missouri, shot one, and sent the other two back the way they came. In Ottawa, Illinois, gangs of vigilantes assaulted any blacks they could find. According to one witness, "these ruffians combine in squads, and hit every wooly head that presents itself." March of 1863 found a white mob in Detroit, Michigan, trying to drive blacks out of the city. Dozens were beaten and about thirty-five had their homes

[90] Leslie A. Schwalm, "'Overrun with Free Negroes': Emancipation and Wartime Migration in the Upper Midwest," *Civil War History* 50 (2004): 166.

burned before federal troops intervened. An untold number of blacks fled to Canada after the riot. Two months later, white workers and local authorities in St. Paul, Minnesota, tried to expel black refugees.[91]

## IT IS ENOUGH TO FREE THEM

That spring, Republican Representative George Julian visited Lincoln and found him despondent over the violent reactions to emancipation. "My proclamation was to stir the country; but it has done about as much harm as good." The comment disturbed Julian, a firm emancipation supporter. Julian later wrote with regret that such comments "were characteristic, and showed how reluctant [Lincoln] was to turn away from the conservative counsels he had so long heeded."[92]

Lincoln did little to reassure those who questioned his commitment to slavery's effective end when, in December 1863, he issued his "Proclamation of Amnesty and Reconstruction." Under the Constitution's authority granting him power to issue "reprieves and pardons for offences against the United States," Lincoln declared that any Confederate state would be allowed to reestablish a federally recognized government when a number of its citizens totaling at least 10 percent of those who had voted in the 1860 presidential election took an oath of loyalty to the United States and promised to abide by congressional acts and presidential edicts regarding slavery. Any newly formed government applying for recognition must have no provision in its constitution "contravening said oath."[93]

Lincoln's Ten Percent Plan, as it came to be called, did not quite settle the issue of slavery's future in the secessionist states once they were readmitted. As Lincoln stated in his amnesty proclamation, all acts and edicts of the federal government in reference to slavery were war measures subject to being "repealed, modified or held void by Congress, or by decision of the Supreme Court." Nor did Lincoln's plan ensure any legal protection for blacks. Wendell Phillips, a long time Boston abolitionist, complained that Lincoln's plan restored "all power into the hands of the unchanged white race." Phillips pointed to the newly reconstructed government in Louisiana where, with Lincoln's backing, General Nathaniel Banks was forcing blacks

---

[91] Brig. Gen. N. B. Buford to Edwin M. Stanton, April 25, 1863, *Official Records*, series 2, vol. 5, 521; Voegeli, *Free But Not Equal*, 89–90.

[92] George W. Julian, *Political Recollections, 1840 to 1872* (Chicago: Jansen, McClurg, and Co., 1884), 230.

[93] Proclamation of Amnesty and Reconstruction, December 8, 1863, in Basler et al., *Collected Works of Abraham Lincoln*, 7: 53–56.

into labor contracts and debt slavery at the point of federal bayonets. "Such reconstruction," wrote Phillips, "makes freedom of the negro a sham, and perpetuates Slavery under a softer name."[94]

Blacks in Louisiana had hoped for better. During the constitutional convention of April–July 1864, they held rallies and signed petitions calling for equal rights, including the right to vote. The black newspaper *L'Union* insisted that they deserved nothing less than "universal equality before the law." Lincoln wrote a private letter to Governor Michael Hahn suggesting that the franchise might be extended to some few blacks, perhaps the "very intelligent," a reference to New Orleans Creoles, and those who had "fought gallantly in our ranks." But that was as far a Lincoln was willing to go. When the convention issued its constitution, with no mention of black voting rights or of any protection for blacks beyond the elimination of chattel slavery, Lincoln pronounced the document "an excellent new constitution."[95]

Creoles and other African Americans in Louisiana were bitterly disappointed in Lincoln, Banks, and federally appointed officials who followed their lead. The *New Orleans Tribune*, a public voice for free blacks in Louisiana since before the war, lamented that "deep-rooted prejudice against this people still remains in all its pristine strength and vigor, in the North quite as much as at the South." The *Tribune* castigated Banks, whose allies held sway at the convention, for allowing the new constitution to be framed by men motivated by "hatred of their fellows of African descent." Some New Orleans blacks, including the *Tribune* editor, were so upset that they advocated a mass migration to Mexico.[96]

Congress had concerns as well, although of a different sort. To require that only 10 percent of any southern state's voters swear loyalty to the United States might restore secessionists to power. It might even invite future rebellion. Certainly it would provide no fertile field for the Republican Party to develop and flourish. To counter that threat, Congress passed the Wade-Davis Bill, requiring 50 percent of the number voting in 1860 to take a loyalty oath before governments could be reorganized in former Confederate

[94] Proclamation of Amnesty and Reconstruction, December 8, 1863, in Basler et al., *Collected Works of Abraham Lincoln*, 7: 54; McPherson, *Political History of the United States of America, during the Great Rebellion*, 412.

[95] *New Orleans L'Union*, April 9, 1864; A. Lincoln to Michael Hahn, March 13, 1864, in Basler et al., *Collected Works of Abraham Lincoln*, 7: 243; A. Lincoln to Stephen A. Hurlbut, November 14, 1864, in ibid., 8: 107.

[96] *New Orleans Tribune*, August 11 and 13, 1864; P. M. Tourne to John F. Collins, August 12, 1864, and Thomas W. Conway to Dr. J. B. Foudenez, August 19, 1864, Nathaniel P. Banks Papers, Library of Congress, in Ripley, *Slaves and Freedmen in Civil War Louisiana*, 175.

states. Furthermore, any delegates to state constitutional conventions would be required to swear that they had never taken up arms against the United States. Chattel slavery could not be reinstated by state constitutions under Wade-Davis, but there was no reference to black voting rights. Not wanting to repudiate his new Louisiana government reconstructed under the Ten Percent Plan, Lincoln refused to sign the Wade-Davis Bill and let it die by pocket veto.

The bill's supporters were outraged. They charged Lincoln with endangering the nation by restoring power to the very men who had torn it apart. But there was little Congress could do about it. Lacking enough votes to override Lincoln's veto, Wade-Davis supporters responded with a "manifesto" printed in newspapers throughout the country criticizing the president for "dictatorial usurpation."[97]

Black leaders were even more upset with Lincoln. Frederick Douglass blasted the Ten Percent Plan as "an entire contradiction of the constitutional idea of Republican Government." After promising freedom for blacks and asking them to fight for the Union, Lincoln was now prepared to hand former slaves back to their old owners, with little or no legal power to shield themselves "from the vindictive spirit sure to be roused against the whole colored race." Douglass called Lincoln's claim of abolishing slavery a "swindle." The president was, in fact, "practically re-establishing that hateful system." James McCune Smith fully agreed. In a letter to the *Anglo-African*, Smith railed against efforts to appease southern whites at the expense of southern blacks. To Smith, Lincoln's reconstruction plan preserved "all the wrongs of slavery, without its name."[98]

Despite his opposition to slavery, Lincoln stressed that the Emancipation Proclamation was a war measure that might end with the war. Once the Union was restored, whatever the courts might rule on emancipation, or however Congress might modify it, the matter was out of his hands. In a letter to General John McClernand, an old acquaintance from Illinois, Lincoln went so far as to suggest that even if emancipation stood, slaveholders "need not be hurt by it. Let them adopt systems of apprenticeship for the colored people." In exchanging slaves for apprentices, former slaveholders would "be nearly as well off, in this respect, as if the present trouble

---

[97] Foner, *Reconstruction*, 60–61. See also Michael Vorenberg, *Final Freedom: The Civil War, the Abolition of Slavery, and the Thirteenth Amendment* (Cambridge: Cambridge University Press, 2003), 143–44, 150–51.

[98] *Liberator*, September 16, 1864; *Anglo-African*, August 20, 1864. Smith simply signed the initial "S" in his letters to the *Anglo-African*.

had not occurred." Lincoln asked McClernand to keep the letter confidential but assured him that he would stand by his remarks.[99]

Lincoln surely knew that it would be a practical impossibility to reverse chattel slavery's demise. After all, the Second Confiscation Act and resulting Emancipation Proclamation had done little more than recognize the freedom that blacks had largely taken for themselves. But Lincoln's efforts to distance himself politically from abolitionists and to highlight the limits of his own Proclamation left blacks, and many of their white allies, worried about the direction of Lincoln's postwar plans.

That concern drove Frederick Douglass, along with white abolitionists such as Wendell Phillips and Elizabeth Cady Stanton, to break with Republicans and support the newly formed Radical Democratic Party. In May 1864, party delegates met in Cleveland and nominated John C. Frémont for president. The convention's platform called for equality under the law regardless of race, protection of civil liberties, congressional rather than presidential control of reconstruction, abolition of the electoral college and election of the president by direct popular vote, distribution of confiscated southern plantations to former slaves, and a constitutional amendment abolishing slavery.[100]

Few party members had any real hope that Frémont could win in November. The more politically astute hoped only that the threat of a radical splinter party might force Republicans either to dump Lincoln at their upcoming convention or at least make their party platform more friendly to blacks. It did neither. To enhance their chances at the polls, Republicans allied themselves with war-supporting Democrats to form the Union Party. It met in convention at Baltimore and nominated Lincoln for president. His vice presidential running mate was former slaveholder Andrew Johnson, a Democrat from Tennessee and the only U.S. senator from a seceded state not to have resigned his seat. As for the Union Party's platform, the only plank it had in common with the Radical Party was its call for ending slavery by constitutional amendment.[101]

[99] Lincoln to McClernand, January 8, 1863, in Basler et al., *Collected Works of Abraham Lincoln*, 6: 48–49. For an early reference by Lincoln to apprenticeship see "Drafts of a Bill for Compensated Emancipation in Delaware," November [26?], 1861, in ibid., 5: 29–31.

[100] *New York Tribune*, June 1, 1864.

[101] T. Harry Williams, *Lincoln and the Radicals* (Madison: University of Wisconsin Press, 1941), 315–16. As early as the mid-term elections of 1862, many Republicans and War Democrats, especially in the Midwest and Border states, ran as Unionists. See Adam I. P. Smith, *No Party Now: Politics in the Civil War North* (New York: Oxford University Press, 2006), 57–63, 90–92, 101–23, 135–53.

Republicans had long been moving toward support for such an amendment in any case. Some were surely moved at least in part by altruism, but racism and practical politics were prime motives as well. Large numbers of slaves flooding into Union lines convinced some in Congress that ending slavery was the only way to keep blacks in the South. Constitutional emancipation as one element of a racial containment policy was beginning to sway War Democrats as well. Certainly racial containment was viewed as a palatable way to sell northern voters on the idea of an emancipation amendment. So was the threat of another civil war. If slavery did not end finally and forever, might not the old difficulties of fugitive slaves, slavery's expansion, and perhaps a future war follow? Still, most congressmen so feared being branded "nigger worshipers" that few were willing to lead a public charge toward abolishing slavery once and for all. The main push would come from below.

Organized efforts toward statutory abolition began in the spring of 1863 when Elizabeth Cady Stanton and Susan B. Anthony established the Women's Loyal National League and led it in a petition drive aimed at pressuring Congress for a universal emancipation act. Aside from their own abolitionist motives, women like Stanton and Anthony hoped that rights for blacks might lead to rights for women as well, perhaps even the right to vote. Relying, ironically, on a vein of white racism, women's rights supporters reasoned that the nation could hardly count black men as voting citizens while denying that distinction to white women. For their part, black leaders viewed women's righters as useful allies who might help bridge the gap between themselves and resistant whites.[102]

The Women's Loyal National League sent out speakers, circulated petitions, and organized League affiliates across the North. The American Anti-Slavery Society soon joined the petition effort, sending speakers of their own far and wide. One of their lecturers was William Andrew Jackson, a former slave once held by Jefferson Davis.[103]

---

[102] For involvement of white women in the wartime abolitionist movement see Wendy Hamand Venet, *Neither Ballots nor Bullets: Women Abolitionists and the Civil War* (Charlottesville: University of Virginia Press, 1991).

[103] McPherson, *Struggle for Equality*, 125–26; Vorenberg, *Final Freedom*, 80–81. There were some abolitionists, blacks among them, who thought that pushing for an emancipation amendment might be wasted effort. Some feared reviving old arguments about whether the Constitution was a proslavery document. Others felt that slavery was already dead in any case and that efforts should be focused on obtaining black equality. See *Speeches and Letters of Gerrit Smith* (New York: American News Co., 1865), 2: 5; Ripley et al., *Black Abolitionist Papers*, 5: 268–71.

Although abolitionists at first called only for a congressional emancipation act, they shifted their focus after Lincoln announced in December 1863 that his Emancipation Proclamation might end with the war. Even an emancipation act could be overturned by the courts. The only way to head off that possibility was with a Constitutional amendment abolishing slavery. Within a few weeks, Stanton and Anthony were ready to send Senator Charles Sumner of Massachusetts 100,000 signatures calling for action. It was far short of their original goal of 1 million, but impressive nonetheless.

On February 9, 1864, in a gesture both solemn and symbolic, two black men carried the petitions into the U.S. Senate chamber and laid them on Sumner's desk. Sumner then addressed the Senate. "This petition is signed by one hundred thousand men and women, who unite in this unparalleled number to support its prayer," he told his colleagues. "They are from all parts of the country and from every condition of life. . . . Here they are, a mighty army, one hundred thousand strong, without arms or banners, the advance guard of a yet larger army." [104]

Over the next few weeks, the Senate discussed pros and cons of an emancipation amendment, breaking largely along party lines. Republicans stressed slavery's danger to the Union; Democrats stressed antislavery's danger to white supremacy. A turning point came when Reverdy Johnson, a Maryland Democrat who had long defended slaveholding interests, rose to repudiate slavery. "Let the institution be abolished, and the subject is taken from the political controversies of the day on which and in relation to which alone the southern people can be excited to madness by the traitors who may come into existence from time to time." Johnson called the doctrine of state sovereignty a "political heresy" that would pose little danger to the Union once slavery was dead. Besides, Johnson said, slavery had already been "fatally wounded," in large part by "those Africans, whom we are now calling around our standard." It was time to recognize that fact and put the issue to rest. [105]

Johnson's speech was stunning. Such remarks coming from a slave-state senator and member of a party that had opposed emancipation for so long were unheard of. Perhaps most astonishing was the credit Johnson gave blacks for their role in fatally wounding slavery. Wrote the editors of the *Chicago Tribune*, "We doubt if the rebel cause has got a harder blow since Vicksburg was taken than it got in the Senate when Reverdy Johnson laid his blows." On April 8, three days after Johnson's address, the Senate

---

[104] *Congressional Globe*, Thirty-Eighth Congress, First Session (1864), 536.
[105] *Congressional Globe*, Thirty-Eighth Congress, First Session (1864), 1422, 1424.

passed what would eventually become the Thirteenth Amendment and sent it to the House of Representatives.[106]

Signatures from the "larger army" of which Sumner spoke poured into House offices during the next few months. By July, the list of names totaled nearly 400,000. Clearly, the alliance of long time abolitionists and newly minted emancipationists, who feared continuing conflict over slavery, was becoming stronger by the day. Lincoln himself, expressing Union Party policy, gave the amendment his support. Although conservative on granting the rights of full citizenship to blacks, Lincoln knew that he would need the help of Radicals to win reelection. And he would need the help of blacks to win the war. "Any different policy in regard to the colored man," Lincoln admitted, "deprives us of his help, and this is more than we can bear. . . . Keep it and you can save the Union. Throw it away, and the Union goes with it."[107]

Despite backing from Lincoln, his Union Party, and the Radicals, the amendment's sponsors could not muster the two-thirds majority in the House necessary to get it passed and sent to the states for ratification. There was too much trepidation among House Democrats. Many of them had been elected in 1862 on an anti-abolition platform. Now another election year was upon them, and "abolitionist" was still a dirty word among large segments of the northern electorate – so much so that even some of the amendment's backers called themselves "emancipationists" as a signal that they supported little more than nominal freedom for former slaves.[108]

Such attitudes, held as they were even by antislavery allies, had worried black leaders for years. As much resistance as there was to emancipation among northern whites, there was much more toward social and political equality for blacks. Even among white abolitionists, there was often apathy if not hostility to anything more than ending chattel slavery. That William Lloyd Garrison, feeling that its work was effectively done, sought to disband the American Anti-Slavery Society in the war's later years showed how wide the gulf was between what abolitionism meant to blacks and what it meant to whites. The attitude of most white abolitionists,

---

[106] *Chicago Tribune*, April 10, 1864; *Congressional Globe*, Thirty-Eighth Congress, First Session (1864), 1490.

[107] A. Lincoln to Isaac M. Schermerhorn, September 12, 1864, in Basler et al., *Collected Works of Abraham Lincoln*, 8: 1–2.

[108] *Congressional Globe*, Thirty-Eighth Congress, First Session (1864), 2977–95.

wrote the editors of the *New Orleans Tribune*, seemed to be that "it is enough to free them ... let them be free as the beasts in the fields."[109]

## A PARTIAL EMANCIPATION UNWORTHY OF THE NAME

In May 1864, in a speech before a black artillery regiment, John Rock was plain and direct about what blacks wanted. "We ... are contending for and shall not be satisfied until we get equal rights for all." Black soldiers themselves were making the same point. "Give me my rights," insisted a black soldier in South Carolina, "the rights this Government owes me, the same rights as the white man has." J. H. Hall of the Fifty-Fourth Massachusetts agreed. "All we ask is the proper enjoyment of the rights of citizenship." Foremost among those rights, the one that symbolized citizenship like no other, was the right to vote. As Pennsylvania soldier Zack Burden boldly wrote to President Lincoln, it was the height of hypocrisy to "make A man go and fite and Wont let him vote."[110]

As the campaign for an emancipation amendment got under way in 1863, Robert Hamilton, like so many others, pointed out that simply ending slavery would not be enough. In an *Anglo-African* editorial, he warned that freedom without the franchise would be "a partial emancipation unworthy of the name." In Michigan, leading blacks demanded equal rights, including the right to vote. They asked legislators to remove the word "white" from Michigan's racially restrictive constitution and called for the repeal of all laws making reference to skin color. Blacks in Indiana petitioned the legislature to repeal the most onerous of the state's Black Laws and to appropriate money for "colored" schools. Chicago blacks went even further, demanding repeal of all Illinois's Black Laws and an end to segregation in public schools.[111]

[109] Ripley et al., *Black Abolitionist Papers*, 5: 321; Jean-Charles Houzeau, *My Passage at the New Orleans Tribune: A Memoir of the Civil War Era*, ed. David C. Rankin (Baton Rouge: Louisiana State University Press, 1984), 92.

[110] Rock to the Soldiers of the Fifth Regiment, United States Colored Heavy Artillery, May 30, 1864, George Ruffin Papers, Howard University, Washington, D.C., in Ripley et al., *Black Abolitionist Papers*, 5: 274; *Christian Recorder*, June 11 and August 27, 1864; Burden to Abraham Lincoln, February 2, 1865, in Berlin et al., *Black Military Experience*, 647–48. Like so many blacks who had the nerve to do such a thing, Burden wrote his letter to Lincoln with some trepidation. Near his conclusion, he asked Lincoln not to "get mad with what I say for I Don't mene any harme." Still, as a soldier with his life on the line, he felt he deserved an answer. Burden asked the president to "rite soon if you pleze and let me know how you feel." There was no reply.

[111] *Anglo-African*, September 26 and March 7, 1863; Voegeli, *Free But Not Equal*, 165.

In October 1864, 150 black leaders from seventeen states, North and South, and the District of Columbia met at Syracuse, New York, for "the most truly national black convention" that had ever assembled. In his speech before the gathering, John Rock summed up the purpose of this National Convention of Colored Men. "All we ask is equal opportunities and equal rights. This is what our brave men are fighting for. They have not gone to the battle-field for the sake of killing and being killed; but they are fighting for liberty and equality. We ask the same for the black man that is asked for the white man; nothing more and nothing less." In a "Bill of Wrongs and Rights," the convention denounced colonization, called for immediate and universal emancipation, maintained the former slaves' right to land, and demanded full citizenship for blacks throughout the country. Before adjourning, delegates set up the National Equal Rights League as an umbrella organization to fight for equality throughout the nation.[112]

Auxiliaries of the National Equal Rights League formed all across the country. In Tennessee, which sent several delegates to the Syracuse meeting, Memphis and Nashville became focal points of demands for equality. January 1865 found sixty-two "colored citizens of Nashville" petitioning the state's white Unionist constitutional convention "to abolish the last vestige of slavery" by reinstating the right of "free colored men" to vote, a right that had existed in Tennessee until 1835. Blacks in New Orleans called for the formation of a local Equal Rights League to combat the injustices that "are daily practiced on our people."[113]

Blacks had some success in gaining admission to schools, churches, streetcars, and other facilities from which they had long been barred. Segregation on New York City streetcars was lifted by court order after Ellen Anderson, a war widow, refused to leave a streetcar reserved for whites. Such successes were limited and local, and they did not include voting rights beyond those few that already existed. Indeed, it would have been political suicide for any politician to support extending the franchise to blacks. Lincoln himself mentioned the idea of limited black voting rights only twice – once in a private letter to Louisiana's governor, the other

---

[112] *Proceedings of the National Convention of Colored Men, Held in the City of Syracuse, N.Y., October 4, 5, 6, and 7, 1864; with the Bill of Wrongs and Rights, and the Address to the American People* (Boston: George C. Rand and Avery, 1864). John Rock's speech appears on pages 23–25.

[113] "Petition of the Colored Citizens of Nashville," January 9, 1865, in Berlin et al., *Black Military Experience*, 811–16; *New Orleans Tribune*, January 3, 1865.

during his last speech on April 11, 1865, to a crowd outside the White House.[114]

Although Lincoln hinted at supporting the right to vote for at least some blacks, it was never a priority. His only commitment regarding blacks was to emancipation, and even that seemed precarious at times. Adding to the confusion was a widely published speech by Secretary of State William Seward. Echoing Lincoln's own earlier statements, in the summer of 1864, Seward publicly pronounced that "when the insurgents shall have disbanded their armies ... all the war measures then existing, including those which affect slavery, will cease also." Despite black hopes that he might do so, Lincoln refused to contradict Seward. It was an election year, and many northerners already viewed Lincoln as too "soft" on the "negro question."[115]

With Lincoln ever waffling on slavery, many blacks and some sympathetic whites threw their support to John C. Frémont for president. His platform, with its call for "absolute equality," was a far cry from that of Lincoln. A black soldier signing himself "Africano" wrote to the *Anglo-African*:

Mr. Lincoln's policy ... has always been one of a fickle-minded man – one who, holding anti-slavery principles in one hand and colonization in the other, always gave concessions to slavery when the *Union* could be preserved without touching the peculiar institution. Such a man is not again worthy [of] the votes of the voting portion of the colored race, when the intrepid Frémont ... the well-known freedom-cherishing, negro-equalizing patriot, is the competitor.[116]

But Frémont was not the only other candidate in the race. Uncertain as blacks were on Lincoln's position, there was no question about the Democrats' policy. At their August 1864 convention, Democrats refused to support the emancipation amendment, which had already been blocked twice by Democrats in the House of Representatives. Even their support for maintaining the Union was considerably vague. They adopted a platform promising to halt the fighting, call a convention of all the states, and restore the Union. But the question of whether any Confederate state would send delegates to such a convention was left entirely aside. So was the question of slavery, although the Democratic nominee, George McClellan, did say

[114] Iver Bernstein, "Securing Freedom: The Challenges of Black Life in Civil War New York," in Ira Berlin and Leslie M. Harris, eds., *Slavery in New York* (New York: New Press, 2005), 319–20; Basler et al., *Collected Works of Abraham Lincoln*, 8: 403.

[115] Escott, *What Shall We Do with the Negro?*, 131–32; A. Lincoln to Charles D. Robinson, August 17, 1864, in Basler et al., *Collected Works of Abraham Lincoln*, 7: 499–501. Basler suggests that Lincoln's letter may not have been sent.

[116] *Anglo-African*, August 6, 1864.

that any state returning to the Union would receive a full guarantee of its constitutional rights. McClellan's message to slaveholders was clear. Under his administration, their claim on slaves would be upheld.[117]

It was too much for many of the Radicals. Some began encouraging Frémont to drop out of the race. Even "Africano" wrote of Lincoln that "though we abhor him when we consider the many injustices he has allowed to be practiced on colored men, we cannot but think him a better object than George B. McClellan."[118] As weak as Lincoln was on anything but nominal freedom for blacks, his platform was at least committed on that point. McClellan, on the other hand, seemed determined to preserve slavery as a constitutional right. That was the last thing Frémont and the Radicals wanted.

Lincoln's reelection chances improved with the fall of Atlanta on September 2, 1864. But fear remained that Frémont might draw enough Radical votes to give McClellan the presidency. After meeting twice in mid-September with a delegation from the White House asking him to withdraw, Frémont suspended his bid for the presidency and threw his support to Lincoln. "It became evident," Frémont later explained, "that Mr. Lincoln could not be elected if I remained in the field." And he may have been right. After one of the most racist campaigns in U.S. history – with Democrats charging that Lincoln wanted equality for blacks, and Republicans denying the accusation at every turn – Lincoln won the popular vote in November by no more than a questionable 10 percent margin.[119]

Although they had succeeded in keeping McClellan out of the White House, Radicals were hardly enthusiastic about giving Lincoln a second term. "When there was any shadow of a hope," wrote Frederick Douglass in October 1864, "that a man of a more decided anti-slavery conviction and policy could be elected, I was not for Mr. Lincoln." Still, Lincoln did stand by the party platform, pushing the House to approve the Senate's antislavery amendment. Taking the election's outcome as a referendum, House members finally passed the measure in a lame duck session on January 31,

---

[117] Smith, *No Party Now*, 117–20; Stephen W. Sears, *George B. McClellan: The Young Napoleon* (New York: Da Capo Press, 1999), 376.

[118] *Anglo-African*, September 24, 1864.

[119] Allan Nevins, *War for the Union*, vol. 4, *The Organized War to Victory* (New York: Charles Scribner's Sons, 1971), 105–106; Shankman, *Pennsylvania Antiwar Movement*, 201–202; Adam I. P. Smith, "Beyond Politics: Patriotism and Partisanship on the Northern Home Front," in Paul A. Cimbala and Randall M. Miller, eds., *An Uncommon Time: The Civil War and the Northern Home Front* (New York: Fordham University Press, 2002), 151–52; William B. Hesseltine, *Lincoln's Plan of Reconstruction* (Chicago: Quadrangle Books, 1967), 30.

FIGURE 4.5. Lincoln's apparent willingness to backtrack on emancipation and his refusal to support equal rights led Frederick Douglass and other "radicals" to endorse John C. Frémont's third-party presidential run in 1864. By September, when it appeared that his candidacy might throw the election to proslavery Democrat George McClellan, Frémont dropped out of the race. "When there was any shadow of a hope," Douglass wrote in October, "that a man of a more decided anti-slavery conviction and policy could be elected, I was not for Mr. Lincoln." Photo courtesy of the National Archives.

1865. With fifteen Democrats voting yea, resulting in two votes more than the two-thirds needed, the proposed Thirteenth Amendment went out to the states for ratification with Lincoln's blessing. But that was as far as he was willing to go. He feared the consequences of publicly pressing any further. So he held to a lenient Reconstruction policy, including his Ten Percent Plan, and left the political and economic fate of southern blacks in the hands of their former owners.[120]

Lincoln's ambiguous attitude toward blacks mirrored that of most northern whites. How former slaves, and blacks generally, might fare in the war's aftermath was not an overriding concern for them. Whatever liberties black folk might carve out for themselves in the postwar period would be, for the most part, of their own making.

---

[120] Douglass to Theodore Tilton, October 15, 1864, in Foner, *Life and Writings of Frederick Douglass*, 3: 424; Annual Message to Congress, December 6, 1864, in Basler et al., *Collected Works of Abraham Lincoln*, 149; *Congressional Globe*, Thirty-Eighth Congress, Second Session (1865), 523–31.

# 5

## "All We Ask Is Justice"

### Continuing Struggles for Freedom

DEMANDING ABSOLUTE LEGAL EQUALITY

In post–Civil War America, the struggle for freedom went on much as it always had among people of African descent. Chattel slavery was gone, but its trappings remained in the form of black codes, convict labor, tenancy, segregation, political suppression, and violence. Black resistance had helped bring on the Civil War and had made it a war against slavery. Now, largely by their own efforts, blacks were at least nominally free. But freedom was not simply the absence of slavery, as northern blacks had known for years. The freedom war would continue long after the Union war was won.

Seizing what momentum they could, black folk quickly took the offensive. The Reverend Henry Highland Garnet, himself born in slavery, helped set the tone. In celebration of the House of Representatives passing the Thirteenth Amendment and sending it to the states for ratification, the House chaplain invited Garnet to deliver a commemorative sermon. He would be the first African American to speak in the halls of Congress.

On Sunday morning, February 12, 1865, in the House chamber, Garnet quoted scripture, saying "Whoso stealeth a man, and selleth him ... he shall surely be put to death." Garnet gave the nation's leaders credit for having "bowed with reverence to the Devine edict." He stressed, however, that ending slavery was not enough. "It is often asked when and where will the demands of the reformers of this and coming ages end?" Garnet answered, "When emancipation shall be followed by enfranchisement, and all men holding allegiance to the government shall enjoy every right

FIGURE 5.1. On Sunday, February 12, 1865, Henry Highland Garnet – former slave, long time freedom activist, and pastor of Washington's Liberty (Fifteenth) Street Presbyterian Church – delivered the first address ever given by an African American in the halls of Congress. Although few congressmen attended Garnet's sermon, he made it plain that the freedom struggle would not end until blacks enjoyed "every right of American citizenship." Image from Henry Highland Garnet, *A Memorial Discourse* (1865).

of American citizenship. . . . When there shall be no more class-legislation, and no more trouble concerning the black man and his rights."[1]

Although few congressmen attended the sermon, it was a bold statement to make before a chamber that had passed the Thirteenth Amendment with only two votes to spare. Ratification was hardly certain. Enfranchisement was out of the question. Only seven of twenty-five Union states recognized black voting rights to any degree. Fear of a future civil war did push enough of those states to ratify the Thirteenth Amendment, but efforts to extend the franchise that year failed miserably. Supporters succeeded only in placing the issue before voters in Minnesota, Connecticut, and Wisconsin. Reminding Connecticut that until 1818 it had allowed them to vote, black men assembled in New London and called on their fellow citizens "for your

[1] Henry Highland Garnet, *A Memorial Discourse; Delivered in the Hall of the House of Representatives, Washington City, D.C., on Sabbath, February 12, 1865* (Philadelphia: Joseph M. Wilson, 1865), 65, 82, 85–86.

aid in restoring us to a long lost right." Similar appeals were issued in Wisconsin and Minnesota. Although blacks made up only a tiny percentage of their populations, voters soundly rejected universal male suffrage in all three states.[2]

Blacks were disappointed but not dissuaded. In the fall of 1865, John Mercer Langston, president of the National Equal Rights League, delivered a rousing speech at the Indiana state convention. "The colored man is not content when given simple emancipation," Langston told the crowd. "That is certainly his due, at once and without condition, but he demands much more than that: he demands absolute legal equality. . . . the free and untrammeled use of the ballot." At a Davenport meeting attended by 700 soldiers of Iowa's Sixtieth Regiment, USCT, a resolution passed proclaiming that "He who is worthy to be trusted with the musket can and ought to be trusted with the ballot." In December, Washington blacks petitioned Congress for voting rights in the District of Columbia. The document bore 2,500 signatures.[3]

Southern blacks were pressing for their rights as well. On May 9, 1865, black leaders in Richmond, Virginia, organized the Colored Men's Equal Rights League, resolving to fight for "recognition of the rights of the colored people of the Nation as American citizens." Blacks in Petersburg and Norfolk followed suit with resolutions demanding the franchise and full equality.[4]

Similar meetings took place all across the South in the summer and fall of 1865. Blacks in Vicksburg called on Congress to act since Mississippi refused to "enfranchise her loyal colored citizens." At the Tennessee freedmen's convention in Nashville, Reverend James Lynch spoke of the gathering's intent "to impress upon the white men of Tennessee, of the United States, and of the world that we are part and parcel of the American

---

[2] *Congressional Globe*, Thirty-Eighth Congress, Second Session (1865), 531; Forrest G. Wood, *Black Scare: The Racist Response to Emancipation and Reconstruction* (Berkeley: University of California Press, 1968), 85; Escott, *What Shall We Do with the Negro?*, 228–38.

[3] John Mercer Langston, *Freedom and Citizenship: Selected Lectures and Addresses* (Washington, D.C.: Rufus H. Darby, 1883), 99–100; *Muscatine (Iowa) Journal* in *Christian Recorder*, November 18, 1865; John Francis Cook et al. to Honorable Senators and Members of the House of Representatives in Congress Assembled, December 1865, in Berlin et al., *Black Military Experience*, 817–18.

[4] *Anglo-African*, June 24, 1865; *Petersburg (Va.) News* in *New York Tribune*, June 15, 1865; *Equal Suffrage. Address from the Colored Citizens of Norfolk, Va., to the People of the United States. Also an Account of the Agitation among the Colored People of Virginia for Equal Rights* (New Bedford, Mass.: E. Anthony and Sons, 1865).

Republic." At a meeting in Edgecomb County, North Carolina, to select state convention delegates, freedmen insisted that "representation and taxation should go hand in hand." They resented being taxed "for the support and expense of the Government" while being refused the right of representation.[5]

Southern blacks insisted on religious liberty too. Avoiding the slavery-supporting churches that so many had been forced to attend in earlier days, they formed their own congregations. For Jermain Wesley Loguen, the effort was especially poignant. An African Methodist Episcopal Zion minister from Syracuse, New York, who had been active on the Underground Railroad, Loguen headed for Tennessee in the late spring of 1865. He located the plantation from which he had escaped thirty-two years earlier, found his mother, and set about organizing dozens of area churches. On a return visit to Syracuse, where he encouraged others to follow his lead, Loguen rejoiced that "God in His goodness has opened wide the door for the school-teacher and missionary." He appealed for a sense of urgency lest the opportunity for progress be lost. "We must work while it is day. If the military is withdrawn ere the colored man has his God-given rights granted and guaranteed to him, it will be a dark day for the friends of freedom all over the land. The black man *must* have equal rights before the law, or I fear this is a ruined Nation after all that has been done." By "the military" Loguen meant "colored soldiers. ... Wherever they are, there is safety for the colored people."[6]

Loguen was hardly alone in connecting the work of ministers and teachers to the cause of equality. Former slaves saw education as a necessary springboard for social and economic advancement, and the church was central to the effort. Most black schools were established at black folk's expense, with local preachers taking a leading role. Soon after slavery was abolished in Washington in 1862, the city's black churches turned their basements into free schools. Within weeks of Sherman taking Savannah in December 1864, there were 500 black children attending schools supported by blacks. In Tallahassee, black ministers established five schools and served as the first teachers. Soon after the war, there were nearly 2,000 black Texas students enrolled in self-sustaining schools. In

---

[5] *New York Tribune*, July 11, 1865; *Nashville Daily Press and Times*, August 8, 1865; *Raleigh (N.C.) Journal of Freedom*, October 28, 1865.

[6] *Anglo-African*, August 5, 1865. In contrast with "colored soldiers," Loguen wrote that "many of the white soldiers were drunken, and loafing about abusing colored people. ... Quite different with the black soldiers; they all *acted*, as well as *looked like men*."

Missouri, Madison Frederick Ross, a literate freedman and former Union soldier, set up a rural school near Commerce. His students included "grown folks ... some of them fifty and sixty year old." Little Rock blacks established the Freedmen's School Society. It set up the first free schools for Arkansas's children, black and white. Most poor whites being functionally illiterate, it was efforts such as these that spurred the move toward free public education in the South.[7]

Northern blacks, along with white allies, also aided the education movement. The New England Freedmen's Aid Society and the National Freedmen's Relief Association were among the dozens of organizations that raised money for schools and sent volunteer teachers south. In March 1865, the federal government finally joined the effort with its creation of the Freedmen's Bureau. By year's end, the Bureau had constructed 740 buildings for 1,314 teachers and 90,589 students. Together, the Freedmen's Bureau, northern abolitionists, and southern blacks established a system of public education that was unparalleled, even in the North. Daily attendance at New York state's public schools averaged 43 percent in 1865. At black schools in Alabama, the attendance rate was 79 percent. It was 82 percent in Virginia. One Freedmen's Bureau inspector wrote that no people on earth had ever displayed "such a passion for education" as southern blacks.[8]

It would be hard to overstate the importance of education to people who had for so long been forbidden by law to read or write. Some wanted to read the Bible for themselves. For others, their children's future was a driving force. "I don't care how hard I has to work," said one North Carolina mother, "if I can only send Sallie and the boys to school looking respectable."[9] All these motives wrapped into blacks' view of literacy as a hallmark of freedom and a personal repudiation of their former status as slaves. Sidney Andrews, a northern journalist, saw that clearly as he traveled through the South just after the war.

---

[7] Mary Jane Wilson, *Virginia Narratives*, 55; Madison Frederick Ross, *Missouri Narratives*, 300; Quarles, *Negro in the Civil War*, 293–94.

[8] Williams, *Self-Taught*, 42, 90–91, 105, 129; Quarles, *Negro in the Civil War*, 294. See also Henry Lee Swint, *The Northern Teacher in the South, 1862–1870* (New York: Octagon Books, 1967); Robert C. Morris, *Reading, 'Riting, and Reconstruction: The Education of Freedmen in the South, 1861–1870* (Chicago: University of Chicago Press, 1981); Jacqueline Jones, *Soldiers of Light and Love: Northern Teachers and Georgia Blacks, 1865–1873* (Chapel Hill: University of North Carolina Press, 1980); Ronald E. Butchart, *Schooling the Freed People: Teaching, Learning, and the Struggle for Black Freedom, 1861–1876* (Chapel Hill: University of North Carolina Press, 2010).

[9] *The American Freedman* 3 (April 1869): 8.

Many of the negroes . . . common plantation negroes, and day laborers in the towns and villages, were supporting little schools themselves. Everywhere, I found among them a disposition to get their children into schools if possible. I had occasion very frequently to notice that porters in stores and laboring men about cotton ware-houses, and cart drivers on the streets, had spelling books with them, and were studying them during the time they were not occupied with their work. Go into the outskirts of any large town, and walk among the negro habitations, and you will see children, and in many instances grown negroes, sitting in the sun alongside their cabins studying.[10]

Decades after the war, Georgia freedwoman Hannah Austin proudly spoke of her old blue-back speller, which she still possessed as a treasured token of freedom.[11]

### THE OLD SLAVE LAWS REMAIN UNREPEALED

Through education, political action, and missionary work, blacks moved quickly to secure their hard-won freedom. But everywhere they faced stubborn resistance from former slaveholders who hardly seemed willing to acknowledge that the war and slavery were over. Not long after he passed through the Deep South in the late spring of 1865, Union General Benjamin Grierson recorded this impression of attitudes among southern whites.

The poor people, including the returned Confederate private soldiers, are, as a general thing, now loyal; but the far greater portion of the wealthy classes are still very bitter in their sentiments against the Government, and clutch on to slavery with a lingering hope to save at least a relic of their favorite yet barbarous institution for the future.[12]

During a tour through southwest Georgia, one federal officer frequently heard members of the old slaveocracy comment that "if we cannot whip the Negro, they and I cannot live in the same country." In Chattahoochee County, Freedmen's Bureau agent James McNeil ordered J. H. Wilkinson to release a young girl named Hannah. McNeil warned Wilkinson that soldiers would be arriving shortly to enforce all such orders if necessary. A white woman in Opelika, Alabama, demanded that occupying Federals

---

[10] U.S. Congress, *Report of the Joint Committee on Reconstruction*, Thirty-Ninth Congress, First Session (Washington, D.C.: Government Printing Office, 1866), part 3, 174.

[11] Hannah Austin, *Georgia Narratives*, part 1, 21.

[12] Grierson [commanding cavalry forces] to Lt. Col. C. T. Christensen [assistant adjutant-general, Headquarters, Cavalry Forces, Military Division of West Mississippi], June 4, 1865, *Official Records*, series 1, vol. 49, part 1, 301.

return a young girl who had fled to their camp. When told that the girl was now free and could work for wages if she wished, the enraged woman replied, "I will not pay her a cent. I will work my hands to the bone first. She belongs to me."[13]

Some slaveholders were more fearful of having to do physical labor themselves. "I'm no book-keeper," said one planter just after the war. "I never learned a trade; I have no profession. I own these lands, and, if the niggers can be made to work, they'll support me; but there's nothing else I know anything about, except managing a plantation." A woman of Alabama's old slaveholding class said she could not bear the thought of her daughters working in the fields like common folk. Ann Browder of Eufaula, Alabama, wrote in her diary, "I begin to realize poverty now – last week our cook left." John Horry Dent confided to his journal in the summer of 1865, "Had an ominous dream last night – pulling fodder."[14]

Underlying planters' lack of a work ethic was the social stigma that labor represented. The prevailing attitude among them was, as a northern visitor recalled, "Work is for 'niggers' – not for white men," at least not for white men of the old slaveocracy.[15] The slaveocracy's white women were just as determined to maintain their social standing in relation to blacks. The Reverend Henry McNeal Turner, a black chaplain with the First Regiment, USCT, bore witness to that in Smithville, North Carolina, when his regiment occupied the town.[16] During a visit to one of Smithville's leading black women, Turner saw a party of white females enter the yard and try to take some wood. Turner's hostess stepped to the door and asked what they were doing with her wood. The intruders promptly accused her of having stolen it. When she protested that she had gotten it from Federal troops, the

[13] Col. Horace N. Howard [commanding a cavalry detachment] to Capt. Inhoff [acting assistant adjutant-general, Second Division, Cavalry Corps, Military Division of the Mississippi], *Official Records*, series 1, vol. 49, part 2, 1041–42; McNeil to Wilkinson, n.d., folder 3, Wilkinson Family Papers, Georgia Department of Archives and History; Alexander Nunn, ed., *Lee County and Her Forebears* (Montgomery, Ala.: Herff Jones, 1983), 255.

[14] Whitelaw Reid, *After the War: A Southern Tour* (New York: Moore, Wilstach, and Baldwin, 1866), 151; Mary Love Edwards Fleming, "Dale County and Its People during the Civil War," *Alabama Historical Quarterly* 19 (1957): 80; Dorothy Stugis Pruett, ed., *Diary of Ann Browder* (Macon, Ga.: Pruett, 1984), 51; Ray Mathis, *John Horry Dent: South Carolina Aristocrat on the Alabama Frontier* (Tuscaloosa: University of Alabama Press, 1979), 213.

[15] Reid, *After the War*, 151.

[16] Smithville, located in Brunswick County at the mouth of the Cape Fear River, changed its name to Southport in 1886.

whites called her a liar. "I am no more a liar than you are," the woman replied. Turner recalled what happened next.

This expression, from a negro wench, as they called her, was so intolerable, that the white women grabbed up several clubs, and leaped in the door, using the most filthy language in the vocabulary of indecency. They had not yet observed me as being on the premises. But at this juncture, I rose up, met them at the door and cried out, "Halt!" Said they, "Who are you?" "A United States Officer," was my reply. "Well, are you going to allow that negro to give us impudence?" "You gave her impudence first," was my reply. "What, we give a negro impudence! We want you to know we are white, and are your superiors. You are our inferior, much less she." "Well," said I, "All of you put together would not make the equal of my wife, and I have yet to hear her claim superiority over me." After that, I don't know what was said, for that remark was received as such an aggravated insult, that I can only compare the noise that followed, to a gang of fice dogs, holding at bay a large cur dog, with a bow-wow-wow-wow.

Turner shortly became "tired of their annoying music" and threatened to arrest the whole gang if they did not leave. The women marched to regimental headquarters and insisted that Turner be arrested. The colonel refused and dismissed the women. "I afterwards learned," Turner wrote, "that they were some of the Southern aristocracy."[17]

Slaveholders who held to their old attitudes had a firm friend in the White House. Andrew Johnson, who ascended to the presidency in April 1865 after Lincoln's assassination, was a former slaveholder from Tennessee who was no more committed to civil rights for former slaves than Lincoln had been. Adhering to Lincoln's Ten Percent Plan, Johnson's only condition for a Confederate state's readmission to the Union was a loyalty oath from 10 percent of adult white males and ratification of the Thirteenth Amendment. Aside from that, Johnson was content to leave southern state governments in the hands of ex-Confederates. They took full advantage of the opportunity. Delegates to the 1865 Georgia constitutional convention reluctantly ratified the Thirteenth Amendment but defended slavery as "consistent with the dictates of humanity and the strictest principles of morality and religion." And their new constitution, like its 1861 predecessor, gave control of the General Assembly largely to Black Belt planters.[18]

Alabama also ratified the Thirteenth Amendment but added that in no way did the action "confer upon Congress the power to legislate upon the political status of freedmen in this State." All the former slave states

---

[17] *Christian Recorder*, February 25, 1865.
[18] *Journal of the Proceedings of the Convention of the People of Georgia* (Milledgeville: R. M. Orme and Son, 1865), 191.

reserved that power for themselves. Said Alabama politician Henry Clayton of the black man, "We are the only people in the world who understand his character, and hence, the only people in the world capable of managing him." And there was only one way to manage blacks, according to Clayton. "Teach them their places, and how to keep them."[19]

One of the first steps in teaching blacks their place came with a series of state laws called black codes. Under these laws, many of which mirrored the old slave codes, freedom for former slaves was almost nonexistent. Blacks could not serve on juries, hold public office, or leave employment without their employer's permission. In some states, they could not own firearms. Nor could they testify against whites in court. Responding to the threat, South Carolina blacks from all over the state met at Charleston's Zion Church in November 1865. This "Colored People's Convention" called on the state legislature to reject its black codes and asked Congress to outlaw them if the state would not. The freedmen also demanded that "the same laws which govern white men shall direct black men." They wanted unfettered access to the courts, schools for their children, homesteads for themselves, and "equality and justice."[20] Despite the convention's protest, and many others like it, the black codes remained in place.

William Wells Brown, a former slave who authored the first history of African Americans during Civil War era, observed bitterly that, backed by President Johnson, former slaveholders were "determined to reduce the blacks to a state of serfdom if they cannot have them as slaves." Samuel Childress wrote to the *Anglo-African* that under Johnson, it seemed "a greater crime to be black than to be a rebel." Tennessee blacks complained to a Freedmen's Bureau agent of "the old slave laws of the State remaining unrepealed." Richmond blacks lamented in a public declaration, "all that is needed to restore slavery in full is the auction block."[21]

---

[19] *The American Annual Cyclopedia and Register of Important Events of the Year 1865* (New York: D. Appleton and Co., 1869), 5: 19; Victoria V. Clayton, *White and Black under the Old Regime* (Milwaukee, Wisc.: Young Churchman Co., 1899), 162.

[20] *Proceedings of the Colored People's Convention of the State of South Carolina, Held in Zion Church, Charleston, November 1865* (Charleston: South Carolina Leader Office, 1865), 25; *American Annual Cyclopedia, 1865*, 5: 766.

[21] Brown, *Negro in the American Rebellion*, 345; *Anglo-African*, December 16, 1865; Rev. Lewis Bright et al. to Gen. Clinton B. Fisk [Freedmen's Bureau assistant commissioner for Kentucky, Tennessee, and northern Alabama], July 27, 1865, in Steven Hahn et al., eds., *Freedom: A Documentary History of Emancipation, 1861–1867*, series 3, vol. 1: *Land and Labor, 1865* (Chapel Hill: University of North Carolina Press, 2008), 262–63 (hereafter cited as *Land and Labor*); *Alexandria (Va.) Gazette*, June 13, 1865.

The auction block was in fact restored under what were perhaps the most oppressive of the black codes, the vagrancy laws. These acts mandated that officials arrest blacks found "wandering or strolling about in idleness, who are able to work, and who have no property to support them." Authorities then auctioned them off, usually to large landholders, for the price of their fine. "Vagrants" were supposed to do forced labor only until their fines were worked out. But with the costs of food, clothing, and shelter added to their debt, blacks convicted of vagrancy could remain in bondage for years. Since few blacks owned real estate of any kind, most were in grave danger of being reenslaved under the vagrancy laws. Freedmen in Claiborne County, Mississippi, wrote to their governor insisting that such laws were entirely unnecessary. "We are willing to worke for our former masters or eny Stranger that will treate us well and pay us what we earn all we ask is justice and to be treated like humane beings."[22]

To be paid what they earned was often difficult for former slaves. From Columbus, Georgia, a Freedmen's Bureau agent reported that employers commonly swindled former slaves out of their wages and crop shares. Fifty miles farther south, an agent in Cuthbert complained that most of his time was spent trying to secure wages due to black folk. Recalling a typical occurrence that played out all over the postwar South, Emma Knight of Missouri told an interviewer in the 1930s, "The master told mother not to go away, that if she stayed a while he would give her a couple hundred dollars. We stayed a while but she never got no money."[23]

That Knight was able to leave when her mother did made her more fortunate than many. Even before the war ended, former slave states began passing apprentice laws allowing whites to hold black children. Maryland ended slavery in 1864, but kept blacks under twenty-one years of age enslaved with its apprentice law. The act was supposed to apply only to children whose parents could not support them, but that provision was generally ignored. One witness in New Town reported that whites were "laying hold, by violence, of Coloured peoples Children ... and having

---

[22] Henry Jackson, comp., *Reports of Cases in Law and Equity, Argued and Determined in the Supreme Court of Georgia* (Macon, Ga.: J. W. Burke and Co., 1875), 51: 267; We the Colorede [sic] people to the governor of Mississippi, December 3, 1865, in Hahn et al., *Land and Labor*, 856–57.

[23] Maj. John Leonard [Freedmen's Bureau agent] to Col. J. R. Lewis, August 26, 1868, in LaWanda Cox and John H. Cox, eds., *Reconstruction, the Negro, and the New South* (Columbia: University of South Carolina Press, 1973), 266–67; George R. Ballou [Freedmen's Bureau agent] to Maj. O. H. Howard, September 1, 1868, in ibid., 274–75; G. Ballou to Maj. O. H. Howard, October 31, 1868, in ibid., 276; Emma Knight, *Missouri Narratives*, 220.

them bound to themselves in Spite of all remonstrance upon the part of Parents." A Tennessee slaveholder continued to hold one couple's four children despite written testimony from the father's white employer that he and their mother were "fully competent to properly care for them." One anguished mother wrote to a federal officer, "God help us, our condition is bettered but little; free ourselves, but deprived of our children. . . . It was on their account we desired to be free."[24]

Blacks often took matters into their own hands. Jane Kamper secreted her children out of Talbot County, Maryland, and headed for Baltimore. Susan Rhodes of Missouri, a girl who was being held with a younger sibling, had an older sister who "stole us away." After a series of whippings, Carter Holmes stole himself away from a Maryland plantation and fled to Washington in search of his parents. He was only twelve years old.[25]

Others turned to the Federals for help, and sometimes got it. Harriet Clemens, with assistance from a provost marshal, got her children released from a Mississippi plantation. As often as not, however, blacks could expect little if any government support. In Savannah, the provost marshal refused to aid former slaves in obtaining their children. The local post commander was no help either. He was, according to Savannah minister J. M. Simms, actually "in Sympathy with those who have lately Been Masters over us." Looking for relief, Simms wrote to a Washington friend in May 1865 asking if and when the Freedmen's Bureau would be coming to Georgia.[26]

It came soon after but provided little relief, staffed as it was by local whites whose main purpose, according to one account, was to impose "crouching servility." J. C. DeGraffenried, the Bureau agent in Miller County, forced blacks into the fields to grow cotton. Joseph Taylor did the same in

---

[24] Capt. Andrew Stafford [provost marshal, First District of Maryland] to Brig. Gen. Henry H. Lockwood [commanding, Third Separate Brigade, Eighth Army Corps], November 4, 1864, in Berlin et al., *Upper South*, 510; Brig. Gen. Henry. H. Lockwood to Lt. Col. S. B. Lawrence [Headquarters, Middle Department and Eighth Corps], December 15, 1864, in ibid., 532; James Murray [postmaster, New Town, Maryland] to Maj. Gen. Lew Wallace, [commanding, Middle Department and Eighth Army Corps], December 5, 1864, in ibid., 524; Urbain Ozanne [Tennessee brewer] to Gov. William G. Brownlow, April 10, 1865, in ibid., 462–63; Lucy Lee to Lt. Col. W. E. W. Ross [Freedmen's Bureau officer], January 10, 1865, in ibid., 498 n. 36.

[25] Statement of Jane Kamper, November 14, 1864, in Berlin et al., *Upper South*, 519; Susan Rhodes, *Missouri Narratives*, 285; Holmes to Lt. Col. William M. Beebe [Freedmen's Bureau, Washington, D.C.], April 22, 1867, in Berlin et al., *Upper South*, 346–47.

[26] Anna Baker, *Mississippi Narratives*, 15; Simms to John McC. Perkins, May 25, 1865, in Hahn et al., *Land and Labor*, 199–200. Perkins forwarded Simms's letter, along with a positive endorsement, to the Freedmen's Bureau.

Randolph County, where his large-landholding relatives especially benefitted. In Memphis, Tennessee, Bureau agents detained black men, causing them to lose whatever jobs they had, then used their unemployment as a pretext to arrest them for vagrancy and sell them as laborers to area planters. The agents pocketed the proceeds.[27]

Such corruption came as no surprise to William Wells Brown, who predicted as much just after the war's end when he wrote, "But little aid can be expected for the freedmen from the Freedmen's Bureau; for its officers, if not Southern men, will soon become upon intimate terms with the former slave-holders, and the Bureau will be converted into a power of oppression, instead of a protection."[28]

Brown's prediction was based on sound evidence. In June 1865, blacks in Charleston, South Carolina, informed Secretary of War Stanton, under whose authority the Freedmen's Bureau fell, that its administration was characterized by "unfairness and imposition." They begged Stanton not to use whites as agents. The Bureau would never be any help to blacks, they insisted, "without the appointment of competent colored men to aid in directing the Freedmen's Affairs." Stanton ignored the request. He did not take criticism well. Nor did the Freedmen's Bureau. Aaron Bradley, a former South Carolina slave, discovered that first-hand. Bradley had escaped to Boston in the 1830s, where he studied and practiced law. He returned in early 1865 and became a leading advocate for black suffrage and land distribution along the Georgia–South Carolina coast. When Bradley encouraged blacks not to vacate lands being reclaimed by long-absent planters, the Bureau had him arrested. When Bradley made a speech criticizing Lincoln and Stanton, the Bureau had him expelled.[29]

---

[27] Susan Eva O'Donovan, *Becoming Free in the Cotton South* (Cambridge: Harvard University Press, 2007), 221–22; Warner Madison [black resident of Memphis] to General C. B. Fisk [Freedmen's Bureau assistant commissioner for Kentucky, Tennessee, and northern Alabama], September 13, 1865, in Hahn et al., *Land and Labor*, 269–70.

[28] Brown, *Negro in the American Rebellion*, 359. Ways in which the Freedmen's Bureau often hampered as much as helped the formerly enslaved are explored in Claude F. Oubre, *Forty Acres and a Mule: The Freedmen's Bureau and Black Land Ownership*, with a new foreword by Katherine C. Mooney (Baton Rouge: Louisiana State University Press, 2012).

[29] Samuel Bing and William G. Pinkney [president and secretary respectively of an organization representing the freedmen of Charleston] to Edwin M. Stanton, June 15, 1865, in Hahn et al., *Land and Labor*, 222–23; Paul A. Cimbala, *Under the Guardianship of the Nation: The Freedmen's Bureau and the Reconstruction of Georgia, 1865–1870* (Athens: University of Georgia Press, 1997), 174; Foner, *Reconstruction*, 163–64; Eric Foner, "'The Tocsin of Freedom': The Black Leadership of Radical Reconstruction," in Boritt and Hancock, *Slavery, Resistance, Freedom*, 125. See also Joseph P. Reidy, "Aaron A. Bradley: Voice of

Bradley might have suffered much worse, as so many southern blacks did. Tennessee's Clinton Hamilton received 200 blows to his back with a white oak stick for being too sick to work. When Willis Crump of North Carolina had the nerve to ask for wages, he was tied up by the thumbs and whipped. John White recalled that his former Texas owner just laughed when his slaves claimed their freedom. After being threatened with a whipping, White escaped to Arkansas.[30]

That blacks were no longer slaves induced a murderous fury in some former slaveholders. Blacks in Lafayette County, Missouri, were threatened by their former owners "with the merciless vengeance of the Bushwhacker, if they should presume to leave them or exercise the simplest rights of freemen." Many blacks were "killed after freedom," recalled Texas freedwoman Susan Merritt. "Their owners had them bushwhacked," shot down while they were trying to leave. "They [would] catch them swimming across Sabine River and shoot them." The murderers hung bodies from trees lining the river as a warning to other blacks. Such killings were rarely prosecuted. "Nigger life's cheap now," said one white Tennessean. "Nobody likes 'em enough to have any affair of the sort investigated; and when a white man feels aggrieved at anything a nigger's done, he just shoots him and puts an end to it." It was a clear message to blacks that the war had not changed their place in the social order. It was also clear that the Federals would not intervene.[31]

The Johnson administration's policy of allowing ex-Confederates political free rein also jeopardized the lives and livelihoods of white southern Unionists. As a measure of self-protection, they formed Union Leagues, which in some places evolved out of the old antiwar, anti-Confederate peace societies. But the war's end brought little peace for these men. Attacks against them became so frequent and violent in north Alabama that the war hardly seemed to have ended. One Union League activist in the region wrote that they "could no longer do without troops unless you allow the loyal men to kill the traitors out."[32]

Black Labor in the Georgia Lowcountry," in Howard N. Rabinowitz, ed., *Southern Black Leaders of the Reconstruction Era* (Urbana: University of Illinois Press, 1982), 281–308. Bradley later returned to Georgia and served as a delegate to the state constitutional convention of 1867–68 and as a state senator.

[30] Affidavit of Clinton Hamilton, Memphis, Tennessee, July 31, 1865, in Berlin et al., *Lower South*, 819; Elias Thomas, *North Carolina Narratives*, part 2, 345–46; John White, *Oklahoma Narratives*, 327–28.

[31] General Orders No. 7, Headquarters, Fourth Subdistrict, District of Central Missouri, April 25, 1865, in Berlin et al., *Upper South*, 622; Susan Merritt, *Texas Narratives*, part 3, 78; Reid, *After the War*, 352.

[32] William C. Garrison to John B. Callis [subassistant commissioner, Freedmen's Bureau, Huntsville, Alabama], April 18, 1866, in Michael W. Fitzgerald, *The Union League*

To strengthen their position, many Union Leaguers became strong Republicans and allied themselves with blacks in the cause of universal male suffrage. In Tennessee, the state government under its new Republican governor, long time Unionist William Brownlow, enacted black male suffrage and became the first ex-Confederate state readmitted to the Union. The effort, however, was not without bloodshed. One of the most violent outbreaks, the Memphis riot of May 1866, saw nearly fifty blacks murdered. The killers looted and burned dozens of homes, schools, and churches.[33]

In July, when Louisiana's staunchly Unionist Republican Governor James Madison Wells called a constitutional convention in New Orleans to enfranchise blacks, a white mob attacked the assembly. Before federal troops could stop the massacre, three white delegates and thirty-four blacks were dead. More than a hundred were injured. Local police, most of them ex-Confederates, had joined in the killing. President Johnson had been warned of the impending attack but did nothing to stop it. On the contrary, Johnson bypassed Governor Wells and sent word to the ex-Confederate mayor of New Orleans that a request to prevent the convention from meeting was approved. It was a license to kill.[34]

If Johnson cared nothing for Republican voting rights, Congress's Republican majority certainly did. Some, such as Senator Charles Sumner of Massachusetts, often called "Radicals" for their unwavering support of black voting rights, railed against the "brutality and cruelty" suffered by the South's "Unionists ... and the poor freedmen." Sumner called the government's obligation to protect them a "sacred duty."[35] Others feared that the violence might signal a second civil war. After refusing to seat ex-Confederates, congressional Republicans took steps to shore up their base in the South with a series of Reconstruction Acts. Beginning in 1867, over Johnson's veto, Congress divided most of the former Confederacy into

*Movement in the Deep South: Politics and Agricultural Change during Reconstruction* (Baton Rouge: Louisiana State University Press, 1989), 21.

[33] See James G. Ryan, "The Memphis Riot of 1866: Terror in a Black Community During Reconstruction," *Journal of Negro History* 62 (1977): 243–57; Bobby L. Lovett, "Memphis Riots: White Reaction to Blacks in Memphis, May 1865-July 1866," *Tennessee Historical Quarterly* 38 (1979): 9–33.

[34] Ted Tunnell, *Crucible of Reconstruction: War, Radicalism, and Race in Louisiana, 1862–1877* (Baton Rouge: Louisiana State University Press, 1984), 103–107. See also James G. Hollandsworth, *An Absolute Massacre: The New Orleans Race Riot of July 30, 1866* (Baton Rouge: Louisiana State University Press, 2004); Gilles Vandal, *The New Orleans Riot of 1866: Anatomy of a Tragedy* (Lafayette, La.: Center for Louisiana Studies, University of Southwest Louisiana, 1983).

[35] Charles Sumner to John Bright, November 5, 1865, in Beverly Wilson Palmer, ed., *The Selected Letters of Charles Sumner* (Boston: Northeastern University Press, 1990), 2: 341–42.

five military districts, put military governors in place, and charged them with guaranteeing Republican voting rights, black and white. The next year saw ratification of the Fourteenth Amendment granting citizenship to "all persons born or naturalized in the United States" and promising them "equal protection of the laws." Finally, with the Fifteenth Amendment, the Constitution guaranteed voting rights to all citizens regardless "of race, color, or previous condition of servitude."

Despite all appearances, the Reconstruction Acts and their accompanying amendments were nearly worthless. They reflected more political posturing than any commitment to the principles they proclaimed. At the time of the Fifteenth Amendment's ratification in 1870, half the states that had remained loyal during the Civil War still denied blacks the vote. Several Radical congressmen, such as Charles Sumner, committed as they were to black enfranchisement, refused to support the amendment because they knew it lacked teeth. It failed to ban explicitly state laws that could restrict or even eliminate black suffrage.[36] Sumner's fears and those of his few like-minded colleagues proved to be prophetic.


### EVERY MAN WHO VOTED WAS WATCHED

The Reconstruction Acts did succeed for a time in extending the franchise, mainly through the efforts of blacks who took Congressional Reconstruction far more seriously than Congress did. By the fall of 1867, voter registration drives had signed up more than 90 percent of the eligible black men in every state except Mississippi, where the rate was 83 percent. Although denied the vote themselves, women were crucial to the voting campaign's success. Preachers exhorted the women in their flock to encourage their men to vote. At election time, women accompanied men to the polls, providing additional protection from threats of ambush. So serious were such threats that few blacks dared to vote alone. In 1868, 100 blacks in Columbia County, Georgia, armed themselves and assembled twelve miles from the county seat before setting out to vote. Black legislator Abram Colby of Greene County organized local blacks into armed companies, marched them to the polls, and carried local elections for the Republicans.[37]

---

[36] Wood, *Black Scare*, 85–86; William Gillette, *The Right to Vote: Politics and the Passage of the Fifteenth Amendment* (Baltimore: Johns Hopkins University Press, 1969), 75–76.

[37] Hahn, *A Nation under Our Feet*, 198; Julie Saville, *The Work of Reconstruction: From Slave to Wage Labor in South Carolina, 1860–1870* (Cambridge: Cambridge University Press, 1996), 169–170; Tera Hunter, *To 'Joy My Freedom: Southern Black Women's Lives*

FIGURE 5.2. Leading up to the 1868 elections, black voter registration drives signed up more than 90 percent of eligible black men in every state except Mississippi, where the rate was 83 percent. Threats of ambush by white vigilantes were so serious that few blacks dared vote alone. Many formed militias for self-protection. In this scene, armed Georgia freedmen wade a creek on their way to vote in Appling, the seat of Columbia County. Image from Charles Stearns, *The Black Man of the South, and the Rebels* (1872).

Before the end of Reconstruction, about 2,000 blacks would hold public office at the federal, state, and local levels. Two of them, Hiram Revels and Blanche Bruce of Mississippi, won seats in the United States Senate. Fourteen others sat in the House of Representatives. On the whole, black officeholders were not the illiterate field hands that popular misconception long held them to be. Eighty-three percent could read and write. Sixty-four had attended institutions of higher learning. There were 237 ministers and 172 teachers. Nearly 40 percent held real estate and personal property worth up to $1,000. Another 40 percent had more than $1,000 in property, which was quite a sum considering that most urban laborers averaged less than $500 annually, and southern farm workers earned between $10 and $15 a month.[38]

*and Labors after the Civil War* (Cambridge: Harvard University Press, 1997), 32; Mack Taylor, *South Carolina Narratives*, part 4, 159; Charles Stearns, *The Black Man of the South, and the Rebels; or, The Characteristics of the Former and the Recent Outrages of the Latter* (New York: American News Co., 1872), 208; Jonathan M. Bryant, *How Curious a Land: Conflict and Change in Greene County, Georgia, 1850–1885* (Chapel Hill: University of North Carolina Press, 1996), 127.

[38] Foner, "Tocsin of Freedom," 131, 132, 128–29. For a complete listing see Eric Foner, *Freedom's Lawmakers: A Directory of Black Officeholders during Reconstruction* (Baton Rouge: Louisiana State University Press, 1996).

Despite widespread political activism among blacks, Reconstruction was hardly an era of black political dominance in the South. In no state did blacks control government operations, and nowhere were they represented in proportion to their numbers. Ironically, this was by design of white Republicans who actively courted the white vote at the expense of blacks. So eager were Republican leaders to attract white support that they drew up state constitutions with legislative apportionment favoring white-majority counties. Republican rule, they promised, would be no threat to white supremacy.

A black South Carolinian wrote bitterly of white Republicans who made "loud and big promises to the freedmen till they got elected to office, then did not one single thing. ... Those men have meanly deceived and cheated our race." Matthew Gaines, a black Republican state senator in Texas, accused white party leaders of playing "BIG GODS of the negroes. ... They treat us as bad as we could ever expect the worst Democrats, and yet they call themselves our friends. ... these leaders will soon kill the Republican party."[39]

As Gaines predicted, white Republicans' betrayal of southern blacks was a self-defeating prospect. They could not hope to remain competitive without the firm support of black allies, especially where Democrats held the reins of economic power. In plantation districts, it was often difficult for black men to make a living if they voted Republican. In South Carolina, those who voted for Democrats were issued "certificates of democracy." Without these certificates, blacks could not find employment, rent houses or lands, and were subject to losing what livelihood they had. One Clarendon County planter wrote to a friend, "I have given those on my places to understand if they vote the Radical ticket again that [I] will not keep them on my places." It was no idle threat. A landholder expelled tenants from his plantation in Greene County, Georgia, after they refused to support his bid for a seat in the legislature. Such intimidation led one Mississippi planter to boast that his tenants would "vote side by side with me always. ... They are dependent upon me for every morsel they eat."[40]

It was not difficult to know who voted for whom in an era before the secret ballot was in common use. Tickets were normally deposited in

[39] Kush, *The Political Battle Axe for the Use of the Colored Men of the State of South Carolina in the Year 1872. With Constitution of the Progressive Association* (Charleston, S.C.: n.p., 1872), 3–4; *Austin (Tex.) Reformer*, October 14, 1871.

[40] Saville, *Work of Reconstruction*, 180; Isiah Green, *Georgia Narratives*, part 2, 55–56; U.S. Congress, *Report of the Select Committee to Inquire into the Mississippi Election of 1875* (Washington, D.C.: Government Printing Office, 1876), 1: 210.

separate boxes for each party, and anyone present could see which box a voter selected. In some areas, the "oral ballot" was standard. Democrats easily targeted voters, black or white, who supported Republican candidates. John Cobb of Sumter County, Georgia, a planter and Democratic legislator, wrote in 1868 that "every man who voted the Radical ticket in this county was watched & his ticket marked & all are now known & they will never cease to regret it as long as they live." Various terrorist organizations, nearly all eventually falling under the umbrella of the Ku Klux Klan, would see to that.[41]

Operating as paramilitary arms of the Democratic Party, bands of robed and hooded night riders terrorized both blacks and whites who openly supported Republicans. They broke up prayer meetings; burned homes, churches, and schools; and beat or killed their unfortunate victims. One particularly vicious Klansman, John Lyons of Lee County, Alabama, was widely known for his habit of cutting off body parts. The Reverend Wade Owens, a former Lee County slave, recalled that Lyons would not hesitate to "cut off a woman's breast and a man's ear or thumb." No one can know how many southern blacks were murdered during the Reconstruction era, but estimates range as high as 40,000, roughly 1 percent of the South's black population.[42]

Klan riders were often driven by motives beyond politics, including contempt and simple theft. They plundered homes, stole livestock, and robbed blacks of whatever cash they had. "Where we lived," said Georgia freedman Charlie Hudson, "Ku Kluxers was called 'night thiefs.'" They took $50 in gold that Hudson's deceased parents had left for him and his brother. Said former Texas slave Pierce Harper, if the occasional freedman "made good money and had a good farm, the Klu Klux would come and murder 'em." Two Alabama brothers were shot and killed for no other reason than local Klansmen "didn't want 'em to have anything."[43]

---

[41] John A. Cobb to wife, April 26, 1868, Howell Cobb Papers, in Edmund L. Drago, *Black Politicians and Reconstruction in Georgia: A Splendid Failure* (Athens: University of Georgia Press, 1992), 148. Various local and regional terrorists went by such names as Black Horse Cavalry, Pale Faces, White Brotherhood, Invisible Empire, Knights of the Black Cross, Knights of the Rising Sun, Ku Klux Rangers, and Knights of the White Camellia. See Cimbala, *Under the Guardianship of the Nation*, 210; Hahn, *A Nation under Our Feet*, 267; Kwando Mbiassi Kinshasa, *Black Resistance to the Ku Klux Klan in the Wake of the Civil War* (Jefferson, N.C.: McFarland, 2006), 64–65.

[42] Wade Owens, *Alabama Narratives*, 308; Page Smith, *Trial by Fire: A People's History of the Civil War and Reconstruction* (New York: McGraw-Hill, 1982), 855.

[43] Charlie Hudson, *Georgia Narratives*, part 2, 231; Pierce Harper, *Texas Narratives*, part 2, 112; Oliver Bell, *Alabama Narratives*, 29. For other examples see Charlie Hudson, *Georgia*

Although politics was not the only motive for violence, it was the main justification. Republicans posed little threat to white supremacy, but Democrats effectively painted them as such for supporting even limited black suffrage. In contrast, Democrats presented themselves, and by extension the Klan, as guardians of white men's honor and white women's virtue. They repeatedly warned of "nigger rapists" and the need to keep them subdued. They called blacks at the polls an affront to white honor and promised to keep them away. Before election day, Democrats posted signs reading "No niggers to come out to the polls tomorrow." Blacks who tried to vote took a death-defying risk. As Texas freedman Tom Holland recalled, "If a Negro wanted to vote, the Klu Kluxes was right there. . . . They'd ride up by a Negro and shoot him just like a wild hog and never a word said or done about it."[44]

Black office holders became special Klan targets. Nearly three dozen died violently during Reconstruction. Dozens more were attacked and injured. Forty Klansmen broke into the home of Alfred Richardson, a black member of the Georgia legislature, and shot him nearly to death. Another black Georgia legislator, Abram Colby, was given 1,000 lashes after turning down a bribe to cease his political activity. Klansmen assassinated Benjamin Randolph, black chairman of South Carolina's Republican executive committee, for his party-organizing efforts.[45]

White Republicans died as well. In Camilla, Georgia, blacks and some of their white allies were massacred during a Republican rally in September 1868. The next month in New Orleans, Democratic vigilantes murdered dozens of Republicans, whites as well as blacks. George Ashburn, a white Georgian and Republican politician, was killed during a visit to Columbus. Between one and two o'clock in the morning, roughly a dozen Klansmen broke into Ashburn's boarding house room and shot him dead. Despite eyewitness testimony, civil authorities concluded that persons unknown killed Ashburn. The local military commander intervened and arrested several suspects, some of them leading Columbus Democrats. But when Congress readmitted Georgia to the Union, the accused men were handed over to city officials who let the matter drop.[46]

---

Narratives, part 2, 226; James D. Johnson, *Texas Narratives*, part 2, 217; Anderson Bates, *South Carolina Narratives*, part 1, 44; Frank Wise, *Arkansas Narratives*, part 7, 220.

[44] Samuel S. Taylor, *Arkansas Narratives*, part 1, 277; Tom Holland, *Texas Narratives*, part 2, 147.

[45] Foner, "Tocsin of Freedom," 137; Drago, *Black Politicians and Reconstruction in Georgia*, 146–47; Foner, *Reconstruction*, 351, 548.

[46] Lee W. Formwalt, "The Camilla Massacre of 1868: Racial Violence as Political Propaganda," *Georgia Historical Quarterly* 71 (1987): 399–426; Melinda Meek Hennessey, "Race and

On the rare occasion that violence against Republicans resulted in a trial, and even more rarely a conviction, the sentence was usually light. After a former South Carolina slaveholder plead guilty to beating "a Radical nigger," the judge sentenced him to "hard labor for a period of ten years ... or pay a fine of one dollar!" Whites in the courtroom cheered the judge as he rose to take a bow.[47]

Without effective protection from either the legal system or Reconstruction governments, blacks were most often left to defend themselves. As early as 1865, they formed armed militias for self-protection. That year black activist Tunis Campbell organized local governments and unofficial militias along the Georgia coast. These black militias, sometimes connected with local Union Leagues, made no secret of their military preparedness. Freedmen in southwest Georgia drilled nightly on the outskirts of Bainbridge and Albany in full view of whites. In Stewart County, they fought off night riders, killing three, and forced the release of a prisoner in the Lumpkin jail by threatening to set the town on fire.[48]

After one battle in North Carolina, blacks learned the identity of a number of local Klansmen "'cause a lot of 'em was kilt." When the Klan tried to burn a black church in South Carolina, armed freedmen killed the would-be arsonists, carried their bodies to the nearby white Pilgrim's Church, and set the place alight. "It burnt everything up to the very bones of the white folks," recalled one freedman. "Ever since then, that spot has been known as 'Burnt Pilgrim.'" In Hancock County, Georgia, blacks ambushed Klan riders as they crossed a bridge. Firing from both ends, they forced the Klansmen to jump into the river. For the time being at least, that ended Klan activity in Hancock County.[49]

Although temporarily effective, black militias had no backing from Reconstruction governments. Nor did they hold any force in law. That placed them on legal ground every bit as shaky as that of the Klan but without the accompanying political protection. It meant open season

Violence in Reconstruction New Orleans: The 1868 Riot," in Donald G. Nieman, ed., *Black Freedom/White Violence, 1865–1900* (New York: Garland, 1994), 171–85; Elizabeth Otto Daniell, "The Ashburn Murder Case in Georgia Reconstruction, 1868," *Georgia Historical Quarterly* 59 (1975): 296–312.

[47] Jesse Williams, *South Carolina Narratives*, part 4, 204.

[48] Russell Duncan, *Freedom's Shore: Tunis Campbell and the Georgia Freedmen* (Athens: University of Georgia Press, 1986), 25, 30; O'Donovan, *Becoming Free in the Cotton South*, 230, 223–24; Cimbala, *Under the Guardianship of the Nation*, 210; Bryant Huff, *Georgia Narratives*, part 2, 242.

[49] Pierce Harper, *Texas Narratives*, part 2, 112; Unnamed former slave, *South Carolina Narratives*, part 2, 121; Claiborne Moss, *Arkansas Narratives*, part 5, 164.

on blacks whenever whites were inclined to engage in the hunt. A clear example of that came on Easter Sunday 1873 when rampaging whites slaughtered a black militia company at Colfax, Louisiana. Between sixty and a hundred or more blacks lost their lives. Dozens were killed after they surrendered. It was the bloodiest single killing spree of the Reconstruction era. The Colfax Massacre sent shockwaves of terror across the black South. So gruesome were the murders that James Beckwith, U.S. Attorney in New Orleans, tried to bring at least a few of the killers to justice. Despite his tireless efforts and the testimony of 300 witnesses, the Supreme Court overturned a lower court's conviction of eight conspirators.[50]

The Court's decision reflected a rapidly waning commitment among northern Republicans to securing the vote for southern Republicans, especially blacks. Congress itself allowed nearly all ex-Confederates to vote and hold elective office again with the 1872 Amnesty Act. Black allies could provide votes, but southern landholders could provide northern elites with something much more important – the very thing they had gone to war for in the first place – access to cheap southern resources, especially cotton. All northerners had to do was give their former adversaries a free hand in dealing with southern blacks, and easy riches in the form of lumber, oil, tobacco, and cotton would flow north. This economic alliance with the South's landed gentry was much more valuable to northern industrialists than any political alliance they could ever have with southern blacks. As historian James McPherson notes, the North's conversion to "emancipation and equal rights" had been "primarily a conversion of expediency rather than one of conviction." By the early 1870s, it had become "expedient for northern political and business interests to conciliate southern whites, and an end to federal enforcement of Negro equality in the South was the price of that conciliation." W. E. B. Du Bois put it even more bluntly. "The North was not Abolitionist. It was overwhelmingly in favor of Negro slavery so long as this did not interfere with Northern moneymaking."[51]

---

[50] The actual number of blacks killed remains unclear. Estimates range from the low sixties to more than 150, although authors LeeAnna Keith and Charles Lane, the best authorities on Colfax, view the higher figures as probable exaggerations. See LeeAnna Keith, *The Colfax Massacre: The Untold Story of Black Power, White Terror, and the Death of Reconstruction* (New York: Oxford University Press, 2008); Charles Lane, *The Day Freedom Died: The Colfax Massacre, the Supreme Court, and the Betrayal of Reconstruction* (New York: Henry Holt and Co., 2008).

[51] McPherson, *Struggle for Equality*, 430–31; Du Bois, *Black Reconstruction*, 83. McPherson added that "the mass of northern people had never loved the Negro, were tired of the 'everlasting negro question,' and were glad to see the end of it" (431). Some Republicans continued to call for black voting rights, although with little success. Their efforts are

FIGURE 5.3. Whites, North and South, trample a black veteran underfoot, the ballot box just beyond his reach. In the background, a black school and orphanage burn while lynch victims hang from a lamp post and tree. This illustration came to symbolize how northern capital, the Lost Cause, and white supremacy all combined to betray Reconstruction's promise. Never enthusiastic about a freedom war, much less the prospect of black equality, northern whites had little difficulty abandoning commitments to southern blacks, even those commitments enshrined in the Constitution. Image from *Harper's Weekly*, September 5, 1868.

Never enthusiastic about a war for emancipation, much less civil rights for blacks, white northerners found the new arrangement comfortable. Throughout the early to mid-1870s, they disbanded their largely noncommittal Reconstruction governments and left blacks to fend for themselves.

## REBEL RULE IS NOW NEARLY COMPLETE

With planters back in control politically and economically, they moved to shore up the old order. Southern state governments passed a series of segregation laws, patterned after those of the North, firmly establishing the

explored in Xi Wang, *Trial of Democracy: Black Suffrage and Northern Republicans, 1860–1910* (Athens: University of Georgia Press, 1997).

"Jim Crow" system that would last for generations.[52] Blacks were barred from mingling with whites in restaurants, theaters, hotels, and other businesses. They had separate schools, public transportation, and even drinking fountains.

In the North, although most segregation statutes were off the books by the turn of the century, local ordinances and social norms kept blacks at a distance. Some school administrators assigned blacks and whites to separate classrooms. Others consigned black children to an annex, excluding them from the whites-only main building. Still others ignored the law altogether and maintained a system of entirely separate schools.[53]

That segregation of all kinds continued in the North is hardly surprising when even those considered to be among blacks' warmest friends openly expressed their white supremacist convictions. Ben Butler – former Union general, postwar Republican congressmen, and supporter of universal male suffrage – said of the black man at an 1865 Massachusetts Republican convention, "my 'pride of race' teaches me that my race is superior to his." Abolitionist congressman Schuyler Colfax, who as Speaker of the House had shepherded the Thirteenth Amendment through that chamber, spoke of white supremacy as divinely ordained. "I never believed in negro equality," Colfax told a white audience in 1866. "God made us, for his own wise purposes, a superior race."[54]

Despite "equal protection of the laws" promised by the Fourteenth Amendment and a Civil Rights Act to back it up, federal courts, including the Supreme Court, consistently refused to declare segregation unconstitutional. It was most disheartening to people like Frederick Douglass as they watched the promise of freedom evaporate. "He is a wiser man than I am," Douglass wrote in 1894, "who can tell how low the moral sentiment of this

---

[52] The phrase came from an antebellum minstrel song-and-dance routine in which a white performer named Thomas "Daddy" Rice blackened his face and mocked African Americans as the fictional "Jim Crow." Abolitionists in Massachusetts first applied the phrase to the state's segregated railroad cars. Over time, segregation laws generally came to be referred to as Jim Crow. An excellent essay on early resistance to segregation, North and South, is Mary Block, "African American Responses to Early Jim Crow," in Haggard, *African Americans in the Nineteenth Century*," 111–32.

[53] Davison M. Douglas, *Jim Crow Moves North: The Battle over Northern School Segregation, 1865–1954* (Cambridge: Cambridge University Press, 2005), 2–3. See also Hugh Davis, "*We Will Be Satisfied with Nothing Less*": *The African American Struggle for Equal Rights in the North during Reconstruction* (Ithaca, N.Y.: Cornell University Press, 2011).

[54] State Central Committee, Democratic Party of Pennsylvania, *The Issues of the Hour: Negro Suffrage and Negro Equality* (Philadelphia: n.p., 1865), 9; *Boston Daily Evening Transcript*, November 8, 1866. See also Leslie H. Fishel Jr., "Northern Prejudice and Negro Suffrage, 1865–1870," *Journal of Negro History* 39 (1954): 8–26.

republic may yet fall. ... The Supreme Court has surrendered. State sovereignty has been restored. It has destroyed the civil rights Bill, and converted the Republican party into a party of money rather than a party of morals." Douglass summed up, with obvious despair:

The pit of hell is said to bottomless. Principles which we all thought to have been firmly and permanently settled by the late war, have been boldly assaulted and overturned by the defeated party. Rebel rule is now nearly complete in many States and it is gradually capturing the nation's Congress. The cause lost in the war, is the cause regained in peace, and the cause gained in war, is the cause lost in peace.[55]

As early as 1866, Douglass had allowed himself to wonder whether the Civil War might "pass into history a miserable failure, barren of permanent results ... a strife for empire ... of no value to liberty or civilization."[56] He hardly lived to see the worst of it, in a judicial sense at least.

In 1896, a year after Douglass died, the Supreme Court constitutionally canonized Jim Crow by establishing the "separate but equal" doctrine with its *Plessy v. Ferguson* decision. Segregation was entirely constitutional so long as facilities provided for blacks were equal to those of whites. The justices well knew that "separate but equal" was a fiction, but only one had the integrity to say it. Justice John Marshall Harlan, ironically a former slaveholder, admitted that facilities for blacks were and never would be equal to those of whites if segregation were constitutionally sanctioned. The very act of legislated separation, he argued, imposed state-sanctioned inequality, an inequality made unconstitutional by the Fourteenth Amendment's equal protection clause. It would be another fifty-eight years before blacks, constantly pushing and prodding for judicial justice, would see the "separate but equal" doctrine overturned in 1954 with *Brown v. Board of Education*. Even that case would have been impotent without blacks pressing for enforcement.[57]

The intervening decades were a horrific time for African Americans. They suffered through segregation, discrimination, and the threat of arbitrary arrest in ongoing white efforts to keep blacks "in their place." For many whites, that place was still slavery, and they developed a convict lease system to help reinstate it. Blacks could be arrested on any trumped-up

---

[55] Frederick Douglass, *Lessons of the Hour* (Baltimore: Thomas and Evans, 1894), 23–24.
[56] Frederick Douglass, "Reconstruction," *Atlantic Monthly* 18 (December 1866): 761.
[57] *Plessy v. Ferguson*, 163 U.S. 520 (1896). See also Charles A. Lofgren, *The Plessy Case: A Legal-Historical Interpretation* (New York: Oxford University Press, 1987). Justice David Brewer, who later dissented in *Giles v. Harris*, was absent due to his daughter's illness during the *Plessy* argument and did not render an opinion in the case.

charge, then leased to plantations, lumber yards, coal mines, or nearly any other business concern requiring hard labor. The system depressed wages for whites and ensured that many blacks received no wages at all. Although sentences under convict lease necessarily stopped short of the death penalty, convicts frequently died all the same from neglect, abuse, or outright murder. Besides, they were cheap, plentiful, and easily replaced. The common labor management practice in firms using convict labor was summed up with the phrase "one dies, get another."[58]

Murder was just as arbitrary as arrest and used to instill the same message of fear. It hardly mattered who the victim was. "When there is a row, we feel like killing a nigger whether he has done anything or not," admitted a young white southerner. He was not exaggerating. In 1890, a black man in Augusta, Georgia, was shot repeatedly and left to die in the street. A city resident questioned one of the men whom he suspected of being involved. "Pat, who killed that nigger?" "Oh, some of the boys," replied Pat with a grin. "What did they do it for?" he asked. Pat said simply, "Because he was a nigger." To stress how casual the killing had been, Pat added, "And he was the best nigger in town. Why, he would even take his hat off to me."[59]

Blacks sometimes succeeded in warding off white vigilantes and saving lives. In 1899, armed blacks in Darien, Georgia, surrounded the jail to turn back vigilantes trying to lynch a black man accused of raping a white woman. A jury later found the man not guilty. But such success was by far the exception. White mobs shot, burned, and lynched blacks with impunity, certain that the law would not touch them. In many cases, the terrorists themselves were law officers and law makers. Lynchings were often organized by the Ku Klux Klan, which counted sheriffs, state legislators, and congressmen among its members. Between 1882 and 1968, there were close to 5,000 recorded lynchings, almost one a week. Many more blacks, untold thousands, were the victims of sham trials, legal lynchings, and

[58] Among the best works on the convict lease system are Matthew J. Mancini, *One Dies, Get Another: Convict Leasing in the American South, 1866–1928* (Columbia: University of South Carolina Press, 1996); Douglas A. Blackmon, *Slavery by Another Name: The Re-Enslavement of Black Americans from the Civil War to World War II* (New York: Doubleday, 2008); David M. Oshinski, *Worse than Slavery: Parchman Farm and the Ordeal of Jim Crow Justice* (New York: Free Press, 1996).

[59] Albert Bushnell Hart, "Outcome of the Southern Race Question," *North American Review* 188 (July 1908): 56; Frederick Alexander Durham, *The Lone-Star of Liberia: Being the Outcome of Reflections on Our Own People* (London: Elliot Stock, 1892), 5. Amy Louis Wood explores the meaning and impact of racial violence in *Lynching and Spectacle: Witnessing Racial Violence in America, 1890–1940* (Chapel Hill: University of North Carolina Press, 2009).

"nigger hunts." Some blacks simply disappeared – carried off and disposed of by "persons unknown."[60]

Few white clergymen ever criticized lynching for fear of losing church members. When the Reverend Whitely Langston of Bulloch County, Georgia, expelled several of his flock for participating in a lynch mob, two dozen more resigned. White ministers with Langston's integrity were few and far between. Some ministers themselves were members of the Klan. "Our American Christians," observed black editor and antilynching activist Ida B. Wells, "are too busy saving the souls of white Christians from burning in hell-fire to save the lives of black ones from present burning in fires kindled by white Christians."[61]

Mary Turner was the victim of one especially gruesome burning. She was twenty-one years old and eight months pregnant when her husband was caught up in a Georgia lynching rampage that spanned Brooks and Lowndes Counties. After Mary threatened to bring charges against the killers, a mob lynched her. They bound her ankles, hoisted her upside down, doused her with gasoline, and set her on fire. With the flames dying down and Mary still clinging to life, someone sliced her belly open. Her baby fell to the ground and cried for a moment before having its head crushed under a vigilante's heel. The mob then riddled Mary's mutilated body with hundreds of bullets, nearly tearing it to pieces.[62]

At the turn of the century, Susie King Taylor, a Georgia woman who had survived slavery and its aftermath, read that the United Daughters of the Confederacy (UDC) had petitioned theaters to ban stage performances of

---

[60] W. Fitzhugh Brundage, *Lynching in the New South: Georgia and Virginia, 1880–1930* (Urbana: University of Illinois Press, 1993), 133–35; Leon F. Litwack, "Hellhounds," in James Allen et al., *Without Sanctuary: Lynching Photography in America* (Sante Fe, N.M.: Twin Palms Publishers, 2000), 21. For more on the Darien incident see W. Fitzhugh Brundage, "The Darien 'Insurrection' of 1899: Black Protest during the Nadir of Race Relations," *Georgia Historical Quarterly* 74 (1990): 234–53.

[61] Leon F. Litwack, *Trouble in Mind: Black Southerners in the Age of Jim Crow* (New York: Knopf, 1998), 297; Ida B. Wells, *Crusade for Justice: The Autobiography of Ida B. Wells*, ed. Alfreda M. Duster (Chicago: University of Chicago Press, 1970), 154–55. For an overview of Klan activities in the early twentieth century see Nancy MacLean, *Behind the Mask of Chivalry: The Making of the Second Ku Klux Klan* (New York: Oxford University Press, 1994).

[62] Walter F. White, "The Work of a Mob," *The Crisis* 16 (1918): 222. See also Christopher C. Meyers, "'Killing Them by the Wholesale': A Lynching Rampage in South Georgia," *Georgia Historical Quarterly* 90 (2006): 214–35; Julie Buckner Armstrong, *Mary Turner and the Memory of Lynching* (Athens: University of Georgia Press, 2011). At the urging of Valdosta State University's Mary Turner Project, in 2010, the Georgia Historical Society dedicated a marker where Mary died at Folsom Bridge on the Brooks/Lowndes County line. Relatives of Mary Turner attended the ceremony.

*Uncle Tom's Cabin*. Its portrayal of the slaves' ill treatment, they claimed, was exaggerated, and it "would have a very bad effect on the children who might see the drama." Taylor wondered why the UDC never circulated petitions to "prohibit the atrocious lynchings and wholesale murdering and torture of the negro? Do you ever hear of them fearing this would have a bad effect on the children?"

Taylor had seen the Civil War as a fugitive from slavery and in camp with black soldiers. For years she had seen men struggle and die, and she had struggled herself, to make freedom real. Now, as a new century dawned, it seemed to promise little better than the old.

I sometimes ask, "Was the war in vain? Has it brought freedom, in the full sense of the word? ... In this "land of the free" we are burned, tortured, and denied a fair

FIGURE 5.4. With blacks disenfranchised, forcibly segregated, held in tenancy, and lynched with impunity, Susie King Taylor asked, "Was the war in vain? Has it brought freedom?" Taylor had experienced the war first as a slave, then a fugitive, and finally as a nurse and teacher among black soldiers. She had seen them struggle and die, and she had struggled herself, to make freedom real. It was clear to Taylor, and black folk generally, that the postwar era would be one of continuing self-emancipation. Photo from Taylor, *Reminiscences of My Life in Camp* (1902).

trial, murdered for any imaginary wrong conceived in the brain of the negro-hating white man. There is no redress for us from a government which promised to protect all under its flag. It seems a mystery to me.[63]

African Americans of Taylor's day could see little reason to hope for much better. They could hardly fight back politically, barred as they were by various state laws from voting. As Charles Sumner had foreseen, state laws made a mockery of the Fifteenth Amendment. Poll taxes deprived poor blacks of the franchise. Those who paid the tax often faced the barrier of a literacy test, although by the turn of the century many southern blacks were functionally literate. Even so, they were usually judged to have failed the test regardless of their ability to read. If they passed, they might still be disenfranchised by a grandfather clause under which one's grandfather must have been eligible to vote in order for an applicant to register. As late as the 1950s, blacks trying to register to vote were sometimes presented with foreign-language newspapers as a test of literacy. When a black Savannah school teacher tried to register, the clerk handed him a Chinese newspaper and asked him if he knew what it said. The teacher replied that he knew perfectly well what it said – that no black man would be registering to vote in Savannah that day.[64]

There were constant challenges from blacks who tried to get the Fifteenth Amendment enforced. The Supreme Court finally weighed in with *Giles v. Harris* in 1903. Jackson W. Giles, president of the Colored Men's Suffrage Association of Alabama, petitioned the Court to force Montgomery's Board of Registrars to register black voters. Justice Oliver Wendell Holmes, a former Union army officer, spoke for the Court's majority in denying the request. As in the *Plessy* case, John Marshall Harlan refused to join the majority. Also dissenting were David Brewer and Henry Brown. Ironically, Brown had authored the majority opinion in *Plessy*.[65]

Blacks across the country were bitterly disappointed. *The Guardian*, a black-owned newspaper in Boston, ran a front page headline calling Holmes a "Second Roger Taney." Under the Holmes Court, it was clear that blacks still had no rights that whites were bound to respect. If they did, wrote the

---

[63] Taylor, *Reminiscences*, 61–62, 65–66.

[64] By 1900, literacy among blacks in North Carolina reached 53 percent. In early twentieth-century Georgia, the rate was 70 percent. See Sharon Ann Holt, *Making Freedom Pay: North Carolina Freedpeople Working for Themselves, 1865–1900* (Athens: University of Georgia Press, 2000), 132; Cimbala, *Under the Guardianship of the Nation*, 220. The Savannah incident was related to me many years ago by the school teacher who tried to register. I wish I could recall his first name. I knew the old gentleman only as Mister Boyd.

[65] *Giles v. Harris*, 189 U.S. 475 (1903); *Plessy v. Ferguson*, 163 U.S. 520 (1896).

editor of *The Colored American Magazine*, then Holmes and most of his colleagues were "afraid to make [whites] respect them." It seemed to the editor that the Court had "not progressed in humanity, and certainly not in courage" since the days of *Dred Scott*.[66]

Less than two years before his death, in a speech at the Chicago World's Fair, Frederick Douglass had angrily dismissed talk of what white America called "the Negro problem." "There is no Negro problem," he insisted. "The problem is whether the American people have honesty enough, loyalty enough, honor enough, patriotism enough to live up to their own Constitution."[67] Clearly, taking the Supreme Court as a measure, they did not.

### BUT I KEPT ON

Despite setbacks such as *Plessy* and *Giles*, blacks continued pushing forward on all fronts. Some stressed the need for ongoing political and judicial efforts. Others focused on education and self-reliance. Still others attacked Jim Crow through the press, publicizing violent atrocities as widely as they could. These men and women sometimes argued over approach, but what united them was the realization that black self-agency was essential to progress. Ida B. Wells was tireless in her efforts to combat lynching with her speeches and writings. W. E. B. Du Bois was instrumental in founding the National Association for the Advancement of Colored People (NAACP), which fought Jim Crow through the courts for decades. Booker T. Washington was a leading advocate of vocational and agricultural education, establishing east Alabama's Tuskeegee Institute to serve as an example.[68]

---

[66] *Boston Guardian*, May 2, 1903; "The Alabama Decision," *Colored American Magazine* 6 (July 1903): 539.

[67] *Chicago Tribune*, August 26, 1893.

[68] See Wells, *Crusade for Justice*; Paula Giddings, *Ida: A Sword among Lions: Ida B. Wells and the Campaign against Lynching* (New York: HarperCollins, 2008); W. E. B. Du Bois, *The Autobiography of W. E. B. Du Bois: A Soliloquy on Viewing My Life from the Last Decade of Its First Century* (New York: International Publishers, 1968); David Levering Lewis, *W. E. B. Du Bois, 1868–1919: Biography of a Race* (New York: Henry Holt, 1993); David Levering Lewis, *W. E. B. Du Bois, 1919–1963: The Fight for Equality and the American Century* (New York: Henry Holt, 2000); Booker T. Washington, *Up from Slavery: An Autobiography* (Garden City, N.Y.: Doubleday and Co., 1901); Robert J. Norrell, *Up from History: The Life of Booker T. Washington* (Cambridge: Belknap Press of Harvard University Press, 2009). See also R. Volney Riser, *Defying Disfranchisement: Black Voting Rights Activism in the Jim Crow South, 1890–1908* (Baton Rouge: Louisiana State University Press, 2010).

A major difficulty with Washington's approach was that agricultural education did little good without land to work. Continued ownership of the South's prime farm land was a key element in planters' ability to regain and maintain control. At the war's end, many slaves had been promised forty acres and a mule. It would have been little enough compensation for people who had labored to enrich others all their lives with no pay for themselves. But the promise was a hollow one. Mississippi freedman Isaac Stier recalled that "the Yankees . . . made big promises, but they was poor reliance. . . . They promised us a mule and forty acres of land. Us aint seen no mule yet." Louis Hill of Missouri insisted that the government should have "compelled slave-holders to give slaves a little trac[t] of land," pointing out that "the slave had made what the white man had."[69]

The forty-acre promise originated with General William T. Sherman's Special Field Orders Number 15, issued in Savannah on January 16, 1865, reserving tidewater areas between Hilton Head, South Carolina, and Jacksonville, Florida, for black settlement. Planters had largely abandoned the region in the war's early years, leaving it in the hands of former slaves. In May, upholding Lincoln's earlier amnesty decree, President Andrew Johnson's own Amnesty Proclamation restored those lands to the planters.[70] A committee representing freedmen on South Carolina's Edisto Island wrote the president that they had learned of his decision "with deep sorrow and Painful hearts."

Here is w[h]ere we have toiled nearly all Our lives as slaves and were treated like dumb Driven cattle, This is our home, we have made These lands what they are. we were the only true and Loyal people that were found in posession of these Lands. . . . are not our rights as A free people and good citizens of these United States To be considered before the rights of those who were Found in rebellion against this good and just Government. . . . if government Does not make some provision by which we as Freedmen can obtain A Homestead, we have Not bettered our condition. . . . and now after What has been done will the good and just government take from us all this right and make us Subject to the will of those who have cheated and Oppressed us for many years God Forbid! . . . without some provision is Made our future is sad to look upon.[71]

[69] Isaac Stier, *Mississippi Narratives*, 147; Louis Hill, *Missouri Narratives*, 189. See also Patsy Hyde, *Tennessee Narratives*, 35; John Crawford, *Texas Narratives*, part 1, 258; John Davenport, *South Carolina Narratives*, part 1, 243; Hilliard Yellerday, *North Carolina Narratives*, part 2, 436.

[70] Special Field Orders No. 15, Headquarters, Military Division of the Mississippi, January 16, 1865, in Berlin et al., *Lower South*, 338–40; *Statutes at Large*, 13: 737–39, 758–60.

[71] Henry Bram et al. to the President of these United States, October 28, 1865, in Hahn et al., *Land and Labor*, 442–44.

Decades after the war, former slave Jacob Thomas remarked that he "always thought a lot of Lincoln" for having so much faith in black folk as to think that they "could live on nothin' at all."[72]

Planters were backed in their repossession efforts not only by the presidency but also by northern elites who came to their defense whenever anyone raised the prospect of carving up plantations and redistributing land. It mattered little that planters had made war on the Union. Nor did it matter that without the aid of blacks, the Union might not have survived. Blacks were of no more use in that respect to their former allies. "As the war for the Union recedes into the misty shadows of the past," wrote Frederick Douglass, "and the Negro is no longer needed to assault forts and stop rebel bullets, he is in some sense, of less importance. Peace with the old master class has been war to the Negro."[73]

Northern financiers and industrialists helped prosecute that war with their fierce opposition to land redistribution. Such a thing would not only upset business relations with their planter partners but would also set a dangerous precedent. An editorial in the *New York Times* summed up northern elite fears. "Is it not manifest that the same philosophy which seeks to recompense the Southern laborer by confiscating a portion of employer's property, will also seek to recompense the Northern laborer in a similar manner?"[74] A threat to men of wealth anywhere was a threat to men of wealth everywhere. The government they controlled would protect their property rights.[75]

Men of little wealth, black or white, enjoyed no such protection. Holding land became increasingly difficult for poor whites as well throughout the late nineteenth century. Many Confederate soldiers lost their farms to wealthier neighbors during the war as their families bartered away land for food.[76] Others lost land after the war, driven into poverty by exorbitant interest rates. With few skills other than farming and no land of their own to farm, most blacks and many whites became locked in sharecropping and tenancy.

---

[72] Jacob Thomas, *North Carolina Narratives*, part 2, 351.

[73] *Address by Hon. Frederick Douglass, delivered in the Congregational Church, Washington, D.C., April 16, 1883*, in Foner, *Life and Writings of Frederick Douglass*, 4: 355.

[74] *New York Times*, July 9, 1867.

[75] The economic impetus for waning commitment to Reconstruction in the North is explored in Heather Cox Richardson, *The Death of Reconstruction: Race, Labor, and Politics in the Post-Civil War North, 1865–1901* (Cambridge: Harvard University Press, 2001).

[76] For a discussion of the South's food shortage and its impact see Williams, *Bitterly Divided: The South's Inner Civil War*, 61–107. See also Andrew F. Smith, *Starving the South: How the North Won the Civil War* (New York: St. Martin's, 2011).

Ironically, planters as a class lost little with Confederate defeat. They retained the labor of blacks and added many thousands of whites to their work force. Nor did they lose much in terms of wealth. Wealth in the South had long been tied to land ownership, and that remained true in the postwar era. Historian Robert McKenzie points out that land ownership actually became more concentrated during the 1860s. In western Tennessee, for example, the top 5 percent of white land owners increased their share of real and personal property by nearly one-fourth. By 1870, Tennessee's agricultural elites controlled up to half the state's farm land "while the bottom half of farm households were still virtually landless." In Alabama, Dallas County's wealthiest 10 percent of landowners held 57 percent of the real estate. In Marengo County, they owned 63 percent by 1870, an 8 percent increase from ten years earlier. Professor Gavin Wright reinforces the point in *The Political Economy of the Cotton South*, noting that "despite the decline in average farm size reported in the 1870 census, there was no basic change in the concentration of land ownership. Antebellum holdings were not really broken up in favor of either blacks or white nonslaveholders, and most of the new small farms were tenancies of one kind or another."[77]

Although usually associated with the post–Civil War era, tenant farming and sharecropping were not new at all. In the late 1850s, roughly one in four white southern farmers worked land owned by someone else. In parts of the Old South, landless tenants made up nearly half the rural white population. But tenancy did see a phenomenal growth after the war. By the early twentieth century, two-thirds of farmers, black and white, in vast swaths of the Deep South were tenants. In Alabama's Barbour County alone, the tenancy rate was more than 75 percent.[78]

---

[77] Robert Tracy McKenzie, *One South or Many?: Plantation Belt and Upcountry in Civil War-Era Tennessee* (Cambridge: Cambridge University Press, 1994), 98, 100; Roger L. Ransom and Richard Sutch, *One Kind of Freedom: The Economic Consequences of Emancipation* (Cambridge: Cambridge University Press, 2001), 78; Gavin Wright, *The Political Economy of the Cotton South: Households, Markets, and Wealth in the Nineteenth Century* (New York: W. W. Norton, 1978), 160–64. For excellent studies making many of the same points regarding survival of the planter class see Roger Wallace Shugg, "Survival of the Plantation System in Louisiana," *Journal of Southern History* 3 (1937): 311–25; Jonathan M. Wiener, "Planter Persistence and Social Change: Alabama, 1850–1870," *Journal of Interdisciplinary History* 7 (1976): 235–60; Lee W. Formwalt, "Planter Persistence in Southwest Georgia, 1850–1870," *Journal of Southwest Georgia History* 2 (1984): 40–58. See also Lewis Nicholas Wynne, *The Continuity of Cotton: Planter Politics in Georgia, 1865–1892* (Macon, Ga.: Mercer University Press, 1986); Roger W. Shugg, *Origins of Class Struggle in Louisiana* (Baton Rouge: Louisiana State University Press, 1939).

[78] Christopher C. Meyers and David Williams, *Georgia: A Brief History* (Macon, Ga.: Mercer University Press, 2012), 146; Louis Vandiver Loveman, *Historical Atlas of*

Old or new, tenant farming was for many a kind of slavery. Farmers worked for a share of the crop and borrowed against expected earnings. With local landholders and merchants (who were often the same people) keeping the books, tenants' annual incomes almost never covered their previous year's debt. They were tied to the land until they could pay off what they owed, which was nearly impossible under a system of revolving, ever-increasing indebtedness. Once caught in the cycle of debt, tenants were usually tied to the land and trapped for life unless, as in slavery times, they managed to slip away.

"We all light in and work like old horses, thinking now we making money and going to get some of it." That was how Ann Evans remembered her postwar expectations. "But we never did get a cent. We never did get out of debt." It was not from lack of trying, and she knew where the fault lay. "We always get through with fine big crops and owed the white man more than we did when we started the crop, and got to stay to pay the debt. It was awful. All over was like that." With no land of their own coming out of slavery, most blacks had little choice but to endure debt slavery. Roberta Mason recalled that "there was nothing else we could do but stay on with some of the white folks 'cause we had nothing to farm with and nothing to eat and wear." It was the only way they had "to keep from perishing."[79]

Some blacks did manage to purchase land, although usually marginal land that no one else wanted. In Georgia, within ten years of the Civil War's end, blacks held 338,769 acres. By 1900, that figure had reached more than a million acres. In the interior North Carolina counties of Halifax, Warren, and Granville, between 20 and 29 percent of black farmers owned all or part of the lands they worked. Yet even for these farmers, it was tough to make ends meet. Much like their landless neighbors, small landowners were subject to a kind of debt slavery under the oppressive crop lien system. Because they could get credit nowhere else, farmers were forced to put up their next year's crop as collateral with local merchants in exchange for seed, tools, and other supplies. But interest rates were so high, ranging as high as 50 to 100 percent, that small farmers often ended up deeper in debt than they had been the year before. One North Carolina farmer complained that "we are obliged to buy on time and pay 50 or more percent." Said another, "We are sometimes forced to pay one and a half to two bushels of corn in fall for one borrowed in summer."

*Alabama, 1519–1900* (Gadsden, Ala.: Loveman, 1976), 58. See also Jeremy Atack, "Tenants and Yeomen in the Nineteenth Century," *Agricultural History* 62 (1988): 6, 21.

[79] Ann Ulrich Evans, *Missouri Narratives*, 117; Roberta Mason, *North Carolina Narratives*, part 2, 104.

Frequently unable to keep up with debt payments under such oppressive rates, farmers often had their land dispossessed and were forced into tenancy. As embittered freedman Morris Sheppard put it, "I lost my land trying to live honest and pay my debts."[80]

A major problem was that creditors usually required cotton planting as a condition of the crop lien contract, ensuring overproduction and low income.[81] Yet even under such circumstances, surviving records show that blacks made repeated attempts to pay down balances. Sometimes they paid off part of their accounts before "settling-up" time at harvest season. These accounts also show another side of black folk's economy, one that gave them a degree of independence even under tenancy and debt slavery.

Sharecropping and crop lien were imposed systems that blacks had to endure for access to tools, seed, housing, and credit. But they also developed a parallel system, almost a shadow economy, upon which they depended for much more. At nights, on Sundays, and during off-seasons – almost any time that they were not in the fields – they chopped wood, raised chickens and hogs, gathered eggs, picked berries, baked pies, hunted and fished, made butter, and produced garden crops. They bartered or sold much of it for whatever they could get. They worked seasonally and part-time in turpentining and railroading. They hired themselves out as day laborers, carpenters, cooks, maids, midwives, nurses, and teachers.[82] Their work never ended. In the post–Civil War years, black folk demonstrated a far greater work ethic than any former slaveholder who had lived, and continued to live, off the labor of others.

Blacks used some of their hard-earned funds to pay down debt. Knowing, however, that no matter how much they paid, creditors could simply hike prices and interest rates to keep them in debt, they held back what little they could to support community churches and schools and to pay for their children's education when possible. Urban blacks did much the same. Decades of hard work and dogged frugality gave rise to a class of

---

[80] Cimbala, *Under the Guardianship of the Nation*, 221–22; Holt, *Making Freedom Pay*, 133; *First Annual Report of the Bureau of Labor Statistics of the State of North Carolina for the Year 1887* (Raleigh: Joseph Daniels, State Printer, 1887), 129; Morris Sheppard, *Oklahoma Narratives*, 292.

[81] See Roger L. Ransom and Richard Sutch, "The 'Lock-In' Mechanism and Overproduction of Cotton in the Postbellum South," *Agricultural History* 49 (1975): 405–25.

[82] Postwar black economies are perhaps most fully explored in Ransom and Sutch, *One Kind of Freedom*, and Holt, *Making Freedom Pay*. For an overview of primarily tenant economies see Mark D. Hersey, "'Their Plows Singing Beneath the Sandy Loam': African American Agriculture in the Late-Nineteenth-Century South," in Haggard, *African Americans in the Nineteenth Century*, 133–47.

black professionals – doctors, dentists, journalists, lawyers, educators, and ministers – that served black communities and institutions all over the country. Many became the public voice of black folk, continually pushing the nation toward its promise of freedom.

Such people stood on the shoulders of men like Duncan Winslow – former slave, Union veteran, wounded survivor of the Ft. Pillow Massacre – who worked out his life as a farmer in Illinois and never learned to sign his name. But his grandsons Rollins and Henry, although they went to segregated schools in the 1920s and were denied access to the local public library, grew up with a chest full of books and encouragement to read. Both eventually earned graduate degrees. Rollins entered the ministry. Henry went into teaching. For their opportunities, they always credited their grandfather Duncan "and the blood offering he yielded to the end that generations of his progeny might have access to the blessings of learning and liberty."[83]

Later generations also owed much to women like Mattie Curtis of North Carolina. Born in slavery, she recalled at age ninety-eight that "freedom ain't give us nothin' but pickled horse meat and dirty crackers, and not half enough of that." Despite her initial excitement at slavery's downfall, what the whites called emancipation was a bitter disappointment to Mattie. Well into her twenties at war's end, a Union officer had "come to our place and told us that the land was goin' to be cut up and divided among the slaves, they would also have a mule and a house apiece." She "always had craved a home" and land on which to make a living, "but the slaves ain't got none of it that I ever hear about." Although she had worked for others all her life with little but misery in return, now she would have to start from nothing.

She was able to buy a tract of fifteen throw-away acres on credit. It was heavily wooded, not much use for farming at first, so "I cut down the big trees that was all over these fields and I mauled out the wood and sold it, then I plowed up the fields and planted them." She did "a heap of work at night too, all of my sewin' and such." The small garden plot near her house "never got no work 'cept at night."

The first cotton bale she ever sold, the first she could call her own, was an especially gratifying memory. "I was some proud of that bale of cotton, and after I had it ginned I set out with it on my steer cart for Raleigh." She did not know where the cotton market was and did not dare ask whites because they "hated" blacks, especially those "what was making something."

---

[83] Henry Winslow to brother Rollins Winslow, August 28, 1986. Photocopy of letter in author's collection, courtesy of Rollins's son, Leonard L. Winslow.

I thought that I could find the place by myself, but I rid all day and had to take my cotton home with me that night 'cause I can't find no place to sell it at. But that night I think it over and the next day I goes and asks a policeman about the market. Lo and behold child, I found it on Blount Street, and I had pass by it several times the day before.

Mattie and her husband Josh had nineteen children, some of them "borned in the field." Fifteen died before they were grown. Josh died too, said Mattie, "but I kept on."[84]

Like so many others, simple survival was for Mattie the most enduring form of resistance. It was a matter of never giving up, making what they could of an incomplete freedom. They kept freeing themselves by degrees and teaching their children to do the same, just as they had done all their lives.

[84] Mattie Curtis, *North Carolina Narratives*, part 1, 217–22

# Index